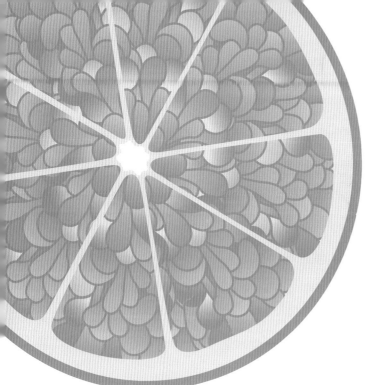

American English File

Student Book 2

Clive Oxenden
Christina Latham-Koenig
Paul Seligson

OXFORD
UNIVERSITY PRESS

Paul Seligson and Clive Oxenden are the
original co-authors of *English File 1* (pub. 1996)
and *English File 2* (pub. 1997).

Contents

		Grammar	Vocabulary	Pronunciation

Look out for Study Link

This shows you where to find extra material for more practice and review.

1
A

G word order in questions
V common verb phrases, classroom language
P vowel sounds, the alphabet

> What do you do? Where do you live?

Who's who?

1 INTRODUCING YOURSELF

a Introduce yourself to all the other students. Try to remember their names.

> Hello. I'm ___ .

> Hi. I'm ___ .
> Nice to meet you.

b Can you remember? Does anybody in the class have…?

- a very long name
- a very short name
- a name that's difficult to spell

- an unusual name
- the same name as a famous person from your country

- a very traditional name
- the same name as another student

2 GETTING TO KNOW EACH OTHER

a Complete the groups of questions 1–5 below with a verb.

b **1.1** Listen and repeat the **FREE TIME** questions. Copy the <u>rhythm</u>.

c In pairs, ask and answer the questions.
Can you find two things you have in common?

> We live in the city and we do yoga.

1 HOME AND FAMILY
Where ____ you from?
Where do you ____?
Do you ____ any brothers and sisters?

2 JOB / STUDIES
What do you ____?

Where do you ____?   What school / university do you ____ to?

Do you ____ your job?   What year ____ you in?

Do you ____ any foreign languages? Which?

3 FREE TIME
What kind of music do you ____ to?
Do you ____ a musical instrument? Which?
Do you ____ TV? What programs?
Do you ____ any sports? Which ones?
What books or magazines do you ____?

4 THE FUTURE
Where are you going to ____ after the class?
What are you going to ____ this weekend?

5 THE PAST
Where ____ you born?
Where did you ____ English before?
What did you ____ last summer?

3 GRAMMAR word order in questions

a Can you remember the questions? Reorder the words.

1 from are you where?
2 watch you do TV?
3 to music you what kind of listen do?
4 English where you before did study?
5 are do what you weekend going this to?

b ○ **p.126 Grammar Bank 1A.** Read the rules and do the exercises.

4 LISTENING & SPEAKING

a 〔 1.2 〕 Listen and choose **a** or **b**.

Days of the week	
1 What day of the week is the test?	
a Tuesday	**b Thursday**
2 What day is it today?	
a Sunday	**b Monday**

Telling the time	
3 What time is it?	
a 8:35	**b 9:25**
4 What time does the class start?	
a 9:45	**b 10:15**

The date	
5 When was the woman born?	
a August 21st	**b August 23rd**
6 What day does he want tickets for?	
a June 5th	**b July 5th**

Numbers	
7 What number is the house?	
a 117	**b 170**
8 How much are the flowers?	
a $15	**b $50**

b In pairs, ask and answer the questions.

What day is it today?
  What days do you have your English class?
What time does the class start and finish?
  What time is it now?
    When's your birthday?
    What's today's date?
What's the number of your house or apartment?

5 CLASSROOM LANGUAGE

a Complete the teacher's and student's phrases.

Please _____ _____ your cell phone.

Sorry, could you _____ that, please?

b ○ **p.144 Vocabulary Bank** *Classroom language.*

6 PRONUNCIATION vowel sounds, the alphabet

a How do you pronounce the letters of the alphabet below? Use the sound pictures to help you.

eɪ	A H _ K
i	B C D E _ P T V Z
ɛ	F L M N S _
aɪ	I _
oʊ	_
u	Q U _
ɑr	

b Complete the alphabet chart with these letters.

W G Y R J X O

c Practice saying the letters of the alphabet.

d In pairs, play *What does it mean?* Think of six words that you can spell and pronounce. Then test another pair.

What does "awful" mean? — Very bad.

How do you spell it? — A-W-F-U-L.

G simple present
V family, personality adjectives
P third person and plural -*s*

He likes movies.
He doesn't smoke.

Who knows you better?

1 VOCABULARY family, personality adjectives

a Can you remember these words?
  Do the puzzle in pairs.

  1 The opposite of *thin* or *slim* is …
  2 Your brother's wife is your …
  3 Your sister's daughter is your …
  4 Your mother's brother is your …
  5 Your aunt's children are your …
  6 *Light* hair is the opposite of … hair.
  7 The opposite of *short* is …
  8 Your brothers, sisters, cousins, etc. are your …

b What's the " mystery word " ?

c ➡ **p.145 Vocabulary Bank** *Adjectives*. Do part 1.

2 READING

a Who do you think knows you better, your family or your friends? Why?

b Read the introduction to the article.

  1 Who is Richard?
  2 Who is Danny?
  3 What do Richard's mother and Danny try to do?
  4 What does Richard have to do?

c Now read what Richard says. Mark the sentences T (true) or F (false). Correct the false ones.

  1 He sometimes travels for his job. *T*
  2 He's friendly and outgoing.
  3 He likes music and parties.
  4 He prefers women who are shorter than he is.
  5 He likes women who talk a lot.
  6 He doesn't talk to his family about women.
  7 His mother doesn't think he's good at choosing girlfriends.

d Guess the meaning of the highlighted words or phrases.

Who knows you better, your family or your friends?

In our weekly "test," single people who are looking for a partner ask their mother and their best friend to help. The mother chooses one partner and the best friend chooses another. The test is to see who can choose the best partner!

This week's single man is Richard Taylor, a 26-year-old musician from Vancouver, Canada. His mother, Meg, chooses one woman, and his best friend, Danny, chooses another. Then Richard goes on a date with each woman. Which woman does he prefer? Who knows him better, his mother or his best friend? Who chooses the right woman for him?

Richard Taylor with his mother, Meg, and his friend Danny

❝ I usually work in Canada, but sometimes I work abroad, too. When I'm not working, I like going to the movies and eating in nice restaurants. I don't like sports very much, and I don't exercise, but at least I don't smoke.

I think I'm open and friendly – I get along well with most people – but I can be kind of shy, too. For example, I don't like going to parties. I prefer to meet friends individually or in small groups.

I like intelligent, funny women who make me laugh, and ideally who love music. Physically, I prefer women with dark hair who are not taller than me. And I like women who are good listeners.

I'm sure that my friend Danny knows me better than my family because we often talk about girlfriends and the problems we have. I don't usually talk to my family about that kind of thing. My mom always says that I look for the wrong kind of woman, but that's what mothers always say! ❞

3 GRAMMAR   simple present

a Complete the questions about Richard.

Where _does he live_____ ?
In Vancouver, Canada.
1 What _____ do?
He's a musician.
2 Where _____ ?
In Canada and abroad.
3 _____ smoke?
No, he doesn't.
4 _____ exercise much?
No, he doesn't.
5 What kind of women _____ ?
Intelligent and funny ones.
6 _____ to his mother about girls?
No, he doesn't.

b ⮕ **p.126 Grammar Bank 1B.** Read the rules and do the exercises.

c Cover the text. In pairs, try to remember five things about Richard.

He lives in Vancouver.

d Look at the photos of Claire and Rosa.

HIS FRIEND'S CHOICE
Claire

HIS MOTHER'S CHOICE
Rosa

⮕ **Communication** *Claire and Rosa A p.108 B p.112.*
Who do you think is more Richard's type? Why?

4 LISTENING

a Listen to Richard talking about what happened when he met Claire and Rosa. Does he like them? What are the problems?

1.3 Claire   **1.4** Rosa

b Now listen again and write any adjectives or expressions that Richard uses to describe Claire and Rosa.

Claire *Very friendly*   **Rosa** *Very attractive*

c Who knows Richard better, his mother or Danny? Are you surprised?

5 PRONUNCIATION   -s endings

a **1.5** Listen and repeat.

	He works abroad.
/s/	She likes good food.
	She laughs a lot.
	He plays the piano.
/z/	She lives in Mexico.
	He enjoys comedies.
	She exercises every day.
/ɪz/	He relaxes at night.
	She dresses very well.

b How do you say the *he* / *she* / *it* form of these verbs?

choose   cook   go   know   stop   teach

c How do you say the plural of these nouns?

book   friend   language   niece   parent   party

d **1.6** Listen and repeat the verbs and nouns.

6 SPEAKING

a Work in pairs, **A** and **B**. Think of a person you know well, a family member or a friend, who is single. You are going to tell your partner about him / her. Look at the chart below and prepare what you are going to say.

- **NAME?**
- **AGE?**
- **JOB/STUDIES?**
- **LIVES IN?**
- **PHYSICAL APPEARANCE?**
- **PERSONALITY?**
- **SMOKES?**
- **LIKES?**
- **DOESN'T LIKE?**

b **A** describe your person to **B**.
B listen and ask for more information. Do you know anybody who would be a good partner for this person? Then change roles.

1 C

G present continuous
V the body, prepositions of place
P vowel sounds

The woman on the right is wearing a hat.

At the Moulin Rouge

1 VOCABULARY   the body

Portrait of Dora Maar **(1937) Pablo Picasso**

a Look at this painting. Do you like it? Why (not)?

b Label the woman's face with words from the box.

| ear | eyes | hair | lips | mouth | neck | nose |

c ⬤ **p.146 Vocabulary Bank** *The body*.

d In pairs, how many words can you remember in two minutes?

2 PRONUNCIATION   vowel sounds

a Look at the sound pictures. What are the words and sounds?

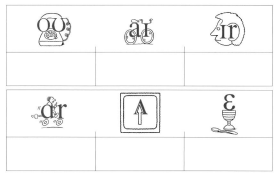

b **1.7** Put the words in the correct columns. Listen and check.

| arms | bite | ears | eyes | head | hear | heart |
| nose | shoulders | smell | stomach | touch | | |

c ⬤ **p.157 Sound Bank.** Look at the typical spellings for these sounds.

3 GRAMMAR   present continuous

a Look at the painting *At the Moulin Rouge*. In pairs, ask and answer the questions.

1 What clothes are the people wearing?
2 What are the people at the table doing?
3 What are the two women in the back doing?
4 What are the two men in the back doing?
5 Describe the woman on the right. What do you think she's doing?
6 One of the people in the painting is the artist, Toulouse-Lautrec. Which person do you think he is?

I think the artist is the tall man who is sitting between the two women.

b Underline the correct form of the verb.

1 In the picture the men **wear** / **are wearing** hats.
2 In some countries women often **wear** / **are wearing** hats to weddings.
3 Karina usually **sits** / **is sitting** at the front of the class.
4 Today she **sits** / **is sitting** at the back.

c ⬤ **p.126 Grammar Bank 1C.** Read the rules and do the exercises.

4 LISTENING

a **1.8** Listen to a guide in an art gallery talking about *At the Moulin Rouge*. Answer the questions.

1 What was the Moulin Rouge famous for?
2 Who did Toulouse-Lautrec include in his paintings and posters?
3 Which person is Toulouse-Lautrec?
4 Why do some people think he liked painting the dancers?

b Listen again. Write the numbers of the people next to their names.

Toulouse-Lautrec ☐
His cousin Gabriel ☐
His friend, a photographer ☐
Jane Avril, a dancer ☐
La Macarona, a dancer ☐
La Goulue, a singer ☐

At the Moulin Rouge (1892/5) Henri Marie Raymond de Toulouse-Lautrec

5 SPEAKING

a Match the prepositions with the pictures.

behind	between	in	in front of	in the middle	next to
on	on the left	on the right	across from	under	

1_____

2_____

3_____

4_____

5_____

6_____

7_____

8_____

9_____

10_____

11_____

b ⊃ **Communication** *Describe and draw A p.108 B p.112.* Describe your picture for your partner to draw.

c In small groups, ask and answer the questions.

1 Do you paint or draw? What kinds of things?
2 Do you have a favorite painter? Who?
3 Do you have a favorite painting? What? Can you describe it?
4 What pictures or posters do you have on the wall in your bedroom or living room?

d Look again at the paintings in this lesson (here and on pages 108 and 112). Which one would you choose to have in your house or apartment?

6 1.9 **SONG** ♪ *Ain't got no – I got life*

G defining relative clauses (*a person who…, a thing that…*)
V expressions for paraphrasing: *like, for example,* etc.
P pronunciation in a dictionary

> A dentist is a person who takes care of your teeth.

The Devil's Dictionary

1 READING

a Look at the dictionary definition. What do you think the missing word is?

> _____ is a person who puts metal in your mouth and takes coins out of your pocket.

b Read the text once. Where is the definition from?

A *different* kind of dictionary

AMBROSE BIERCE was a 19th-century American author and journalist. His most popular book is probably the *Devil's Dictionary*, written between 1881 and 1887. Bierce's dictionary does not contain normal definitions – his definitions are funny and cynical. For example, in a normal dictionary, the definition of *dentist* is "a kind of doctor who takes care of people's teeth." But in the *Devil's Dictionary*, the definition of *dentist* is "a person who puts metal in your mouth and takes coins out of your pocket." Today on the Internet you can find many websites with more modern versions of the *Devil's Dictionary*.

c Read the text again and answer the questions.

1 Who was Ambrose Bierce?
2 What is the normal definition of *dentist*?
3 Where can you find modern versions of the *Devil's Dictionary*?

d In pairs, think of *normal* definitions for these words or phrases.

a bank   a boring person   the brain   a movie star   a friend   a secret

e Now match the words / phrases in **d** to these *cynical* definitions.

1 _____ is a person who works all her life to become famous and then wears sunglasses so people don't recognize her.

2 _____ is something that you only tell one person.

3 _____ is somebody who talks about himself when you want to talk about yourself.

4 _____ is somebody who dislikes the same people as you.

5 _____ is a place where you can borrow money only if you can show that you don't need it.

6 _____ is something that starts working when you get up in the morning and stops working when you get to work or school.

2 GRAMMAR   defining relative clauses

a Read the definitions in **1e** again. When do we use *who*, *that*, and *where*?

b ◐ **p.126 Grammar Bank 1D.** Read the rules and do the exercises.

c Tell a partner about *three* of the things below. Say why.

- a person who is very important to you
- a famous person who you like a lot
- something that you couldn't live without
- a thing that you often lose
- a place where you'd like to go for a special evening
- a place where you were very happy when you were a child

3 LISTENING

a **1.10** Listen to the introduction to a TV game show, *What's the word?* How do you play the game?

b **1.11** Now listen to the show. Write down the six answers.

1 _____   4 _____
2 _____   5 _____
3 _____   6 _____

c **1.12** Listen and check your answers.

4 VOCABULARY paraphrasing

a What's the best thing to do if you're talking to someone in English and you don't know a word that you need?
   a Panic and stop talking.
   b Try to mime the word.
   c Try to explain what you mean using other words you know.

b **1.13** Complete the **useful expressions** with these words. Then listen and check.

example	how	kind	like	opposite	person
place	similar	somebody	thing		

Useful expressions
explaining a word that you don't know

1 It's _____ who works in a restaurant.

2 It's the _____ who takes the food from the kitchen to the tables.

3 It's a _____ where you go when you want to buy something.

4 It's a _____ that you use to talk.

5 It's a _____ of machine.

6 It's the _____ of *fat*.

7 It's _____ *thin*, but it means "thin and attractive."

8 It's _____ to *worried*.

9 It's _____ you feel when you have a lot of things to do.

10 For _____, you do this with the TV.

c Complete the definitions for these words.
   1 **a tourist**   *It's somebody…*
   2 **a gym**   *It's a place…*
   3 **a key**   *It's a thing…*
   4 **worried**   *It's how you feel…*
   5 **laugh**   *You do this …*

5 SPEAKING

a **1.14** Listen to the definitions and complete the crossword.

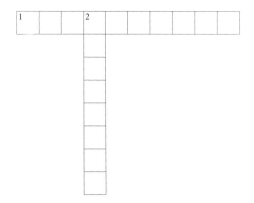

b   **Communication** *Crossword A p.108 B p.112*. Give each other definitions to complete the missing words in the crossword.

6 PRONUNCIATION using a dictionary

a Look at the two dictionary extracts. How do you pronounce the words?

> **busy** /ˈbɪzi/ adj   having a lot of work or tasks to do
> **guitar** /ɡɪˈtɑr/ n   a musical instrument with strings

> This mark (ˈ) shows stress. The stressed syllable is the one after the stress mark.

b Look carefully at the pronunciation of the words below. Practice saying them correctly.

laugh /læf/   **eyes** /aɪz/   **example** /ɪɡˈzæmpl/
keys /kiz/   **kind** /kaɪnd/   **eighteen** /eɪˈtin/

> The **Sound Bank** on pages 156–159 can help you use your dictionary better.

THE STORY SO FAR

1.15 Listen to the story of Mark and Allie. Answer the questions.

1 Where are Mark and Allie from?
2 What company do they work for?
3 Where did they meet?
4 What did they do?
5 Did they get along well?
6 What's Mark doing now?

AT IMMIGRATION

a **1.16** Cover the dialogue and listen. How long is Allie going to stay in the United States?

YOU HEAR	YOU SAY
Good evening, _ma'am_.	Good evening.
_____ are you arriving from?	From London.
_____ the purpose of your visit?	Business. I'm here for a conference.
_____ long are you staying in the US?	A week.
_____ are you staying?	In San Francisco. At the Pacific View Hotel.
_____ you know anybody here?	Yes, Mark Ryder.
_____ he family or a friend?	He's a colleague – and a friend.
_____ you have his phone number?	Yes, his mobile is 405-655-7182.
_____ this your first visit to the US?	Yes, it is.
Enjoy your stay in San Francisco.	Thank you.

b Listen again. Complete the **YOU HEAR** phrases.

c **1.17** Listen and repeat the **YOU SAY** phrases. <u>C</u>opy the <u>rhy</u>thm.

d In pairs, role-play the conversation.
A (book open) you're the immigration officer, B (book closed) you're Allie. Change roles.

SOCIAL ENGLISH Allie arrives

a **1.18** Listen. Answer the questions.

1 How long was Allie's flight?
2 Why couldn't she sleep?
3 What time is it…?
  a in San Francisco b in London
4 Where is Mark going to take her?
5 Where is Mark's car?

🇺🇸 US English	🇬🇧 UK English
parking lot	_car park_
cell phone	_mobile_

b Complete the **USEFUL PHRASES**. Listen again and check.

c **1.19** Listen and repeat the phrases. How do you say them in your language?

USEFUL PHRASES

M You look g_____!
M How was the f_____?
M You must be really t_____.
M I'm so p_____ you came!
A It's great to see you a_____.

Study Link MultiROM

a Read the e-mail. The computer has found ten mistakes.
They are either grammar, punctuation, or spelling. Can you correct them?

From: Alessandra [alessandra@andes.com.ar]
To: Daniel [dani2199@yoohoo.com]
Subject: Hi from Argentina

Hi Daniel,

My name's Alessandra. It's an italian name because my grandmother was from Italy, but I'm Argentinian. I live in Mendoza, a big city in the west of the country. I live with my parents and my two brothers. I have 19 years old, and I'm in college. I'm studing computer science. I'm in my first year, and I really like it.

I'm going to tell you about myself. As you can see from the foto, I have long, light brown hair and greens eyes. I wear glasses, but I want to get contact lenses soon.

I think I'm a positive person. I'm pretty outgoing and frendly. My mother says I'm very talkative – I think she mean that I talk too much!

In my free time I love reading and going to the movies. But I dont have much free time becuase I have classes every day, and a lot of work to do even on weekends. I also go to English classes on friday afternoon.

Please write soon and tell me about you and your life.

Best wishes,

Alessandra

b Read the e-mail again from the beginning. Then cover it and answer the questions from memory.

1 Where is Alessandra from?
2 Why does she have an Italian name?
3 Where does she live?
4 Who does she live with?
5 What does she do?
6 What color are her eyes?
7 Is she shy?
8 What does she like to do in her free time?
9 When does she go to English classes?

WRITE a similar e-mail about you. Write four paragraphs.

Paragraph 1 name, nationality, age, family, work / study
Paragraph 2 physical appearance
Paragraph 3 personality
Paragraph 4 hobbies and interests

CHECK the e-mail for mistakes
(grammar , punctuation , and spelling).

ⓘ
Do you know these "e-mail" verbs?
open   reply
close   send
save   print
delete

GRAMMAR

Circle the correct answer, a, b, or c.

What's _____ name?

a yours   (b) your   c you

1 **A** What _____?
    B I'm a student.
    a you do
    b do you do
    c do you work

2 Where _____ from?
    a your parents are
    b is your parents
    c are your parents

3 _____ David like sports?
    a Does
    b Is
    c Do

4 Liz _____ at an elementary school.
    a teach
    b teachs
    c teaches

5 Sonia _____ a job.
    a hasn't
    b doesn't have
    c don't have

6 _____ a picture in your bedroom?
    a Is there
    b Is it
    c There is

7 The girl in the painting _____ a blue dress.
    a wears
    b wearing
    c is wearing

8 You don't need an umbrella. It _____.
    a isn't raining
    b doesn't rain
    c not raining

9 She's the woman _____ works in the office.
    a what
    b which
    c who

10 I need a workbook _____ has all the answers.
    a what
    b that
    c who

10

VOCABULARY

a classroom language

Complete the sentences with one word.

Sit _down_ and open your books.

1 _____ do you say *coche* in English?
2 What does *abroad* _____?
3 Go _____ page 78, please.
4 See you _____ Monday!
5 _____ a good weekend.

b word groups

Underline the word that is different.

third	seventh	<u>eighteen</u>	twentieth
1 uncle	grandfather	niece	husband
2 shy	tall	dark	slim
3 stingy	unfriendly	lazy	generous
4 arms	ears	eyes	fingers
5 mouth	blond	head	nose

c definitions

Read the definitions. Write the word.

It's the place where you sleep. _____ _bed_ _____

1 It's the opposite of *lazy*. _____
2 It's a place where you can buy stamps. _____
3 It's a person who plays a musical instrument. _____
4 It's a verb. You do it when you're thirsty. _____
5 It's a kind of food, for example, macaroni. _____

15

PRONUNCIATION

a Underline the letter or word with a different sound.

1	🐑	B	E	J	T
2	🪚	abroad	walk	along	don't
3	🐦	person	word	third	heart
4	🪑	chair	parents	hear	wear
5	🚲	give	shy	quiet	eyes

b Underline the stressed syllable.

infor<u>ma</u>tion

relax   university   exercise   stomach   example

10

What can you do?

REVIEW & CHECK

CAN YOU UNDERSTAND THIS TEXT?

a Read the article and match the headings with paragraphs A–D.

Space invaders ☐
Small children ☐
Conversation makers ☐
Nervous fliers ☐

b Put a check (✓) next to the things the writer says.

1 You can't sleep if there are children next to you.
2 Children eat all your food.
3 Some people want to talk all through the flight.
4 "Space invaders" have long arms and legs.
5 Nervous fliers have a drink every five minutes.

c What do the highlighted words mean? Circle a or b.

1 a letting (toys) fall from your hand
  b putting (toys) somewhere
2 a say hello to
  b know and understand
3 a goes into the air
  b touches the ground
4 a try to do something
  b give the impression of doing something
5 a space
  b seat

Not next to me, please!

When you're traveling by plane or train, there are some passengers you just don't want to have next to you...

A _____
Perhaps you normally like them, but when you are sitting next to them on a plane, it's a different thing. They usually spend the whole flight moving around and [1] dropping their toys on the floor, and when they're drinking their orange juice it ends up on your clothes. Then they decide they want to play with you, so you can't have the little nap that you were planning.

B _____
You [2] recognize this type as soon as you sit down. They immediately start talking about the plane, or the weather, or they ask you a personal question. It's very difficult not to talk to these people, and you'll probably have to continue talking until the plane [3] lands .

C _____
These are the people with pale faces who sit down and immediately ask for a drink. Every five minutes they call a flight attendant to ask if there are any problems with the plane. They also tell you about air disasters (which you are not interested in!). The best thing to do is to [4] pretend to sleep.

D _____
These people are not necessarily very big, but they have a terrible habit of taking up all their space, and some of your space, too. They usually sit so that you can't move, with their arms and legs in your space. They also have a lot of hand luggage, which takes up all the [5] room in the overhead compartment.

CAN YOU UNDERSTAND THESE PEOPLE?

a **1.20** Listen to five short conversations. Circle the correct answer: a, b, or c.

1 Her party is on _____.
  a Wednesday the 6th   b Saturday the 9th   c Friday the 8th
2 How old is his mother?
  a 59   b 50   c 60
3 Mr. Wong has a problem in _____.
  a his left leg   b his right knee   c his left knee
4 John doesn't like the painting of _____.
  a the woman   b the boy   c the guitar
5 The woman wants to buy _____.
  a a computer   b a digital camera   c a USB cable

b **1.21** Listen to a woman showing her friend some photos. Complete the sentences with a name.

Martin   Alice   Bill   Serena   Gary

1 _____ is in college.
2 _____ doesn't live in the United States.
3 _____ wears glasses.
4 _____ doesn't like sports.
5 _____ isn't very hardworking.

CAN YOU SAY THIS IN ENGLISH?

a Can you...? Yes (✓)

☐ give personal information about yourself
☐ talk about a person in your family
☐ describe a picture you have in your home
☐ give definitions for these words

journalist   hospital   guidebook   airplane

b Complete the questions with *is*, *are*, *do*, or *does*.

1 What kind of books _____ you read?
2 _____ there an art gallery in your town? Where?
3 What _____ your friends usually do on weekends?
4 _____ your town have a local festival? When?
5 What do you think your parents _____ doing right now?

c Ask your partner the questions in **b**. Ask for more information.

15

2 A

G simple past: regular and irregular verbs
V vacations
P -ed endings, irregular verbs

When did you go there?
I went when I was 17.

Right place, wrong time

1 VOCABULARY vacations

a In one minute, write down five things you like doing when you're on vacation.

b ● **p.147 Vocabulary Bank** *Vacations*.

The Travel Magazine

In the **right** place… but at the **wrong** time!

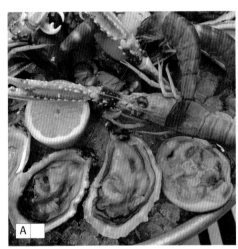

A   B   C

Last week we asked you to tell us about a vacation when the destination was perfect but, for some reason, the time wasn't right… Here are some of your replies.

**1 Tim, 20, student
from San Antonio, Texas**

When I was a teenager, I went on vacation with my parents to the Gulf Coast in Texas. My parents rented a fabulous house on the beach, and the weather was great. But I was 17, and I didn't want to be on vacation with my mom and dad and my little brother. I wanted to be with my friends. We went to the beach every day and sunbathed, and we went to a fantastic seafood restaurant for my birthday. But I was miserable and hated every minute of it. I didn't smile once in two weeks. What really made me furious was that my parents let my older sister, who was 19, go to Mexico with her friends.

**2 Gabriela, 28, marketing manager
from Rome, Italy**

I'm from Rome, and the summer here is really hot. So last year my husband and I decided to go to Sweden, to escape from the heat. We booked a 10-day vacation in Stockholm, where the temperature in the summer is normally about 20 degrees centigrade. But when we got to Stockholm, there was a heat wave, and it was 35°C every day. It was awful because there was no air-conditioning anywhere. We couldn't sleep at night – it was boiling in the hotel, and in the stores and museums, too. We didn't want to go shopping or go sightseeing or do anything. We were too hot. We just sat in cafes and argued all day. We didn't need to go to Sweden to do that!

**3 Kelly, 26, TV journalist
from Ottawa, Canada**

Three years ago I broke up with my boyfriend, and I decided to go on vacation by myself to the Seychelles. My travel agent told me that it was a wonderful place. But he didn't tell me it was also a very popular place for people on their honeymoon. Everywhere I looked, I saw couples holding hands and looking romantically into each other's eyes! The travel agent also said it was always sunny there – but the weather was terrible – it was cloudy and windy. To pass the time, I decided to take a diving course (one of my lifetime ambitions). But it was a complete disaster because the first time I went under the water, I had a panic attack. I couldn't escape from the island, so I spent an incredibly boring (and expensive) two weeks in "paradise."

2 READING

a Read the three letters to **The Travel Magazine** and match them with the photos.

b Complete the sentences with **Tim**, **Gabriela**, or Kelly.

1 _____ wanted to go somewhere warm and sunny.
2 _____ wanted to go somewhere cool.
3 _____ had great food.
4 _____ wanted to forget somebody.
5 _____ had trouble sleeping.
6 _____ wanted to go on vacation with different people.

c Find four adjectives in the article that mean *very good* and two that mean *very bad*. Underline the stressed syllable.

fabulous (text 1)

3 GRAMMAR   simple past: regular and irregular verbs

a What is the simple past of these verbs? Are they regular or irregular? Check your answers with text 1.

be _____   go _____   rent _____
want _____   sunbathe _____   make _____   let _____

b Now underline the other + simple past verbs in texts 2 and 3. What are the base forms?

c Underline two negative simple past verbs in the magazine article. How do you make negatives and questions in the simple past…?
• with normal verbs
• with *was / were*
• with *could*

d ⭕ **p.128 Grammar Bank 2A.** Read the rules and do the exercises.

4 PRONUNCIATION   *-ed* endings, irregular verbs

> ⚠ Remember! There are three possible pronunciations of regular *-ed* verbs.

a 🔊 **2.1** Listen and repeat the sentences. When do you pronounce the *e* in *-ed*?

👕 /t/	🐕 /d/	/ɪd/
We booked a vacation. We walked to the hotel.	We sunbathed. We argued all day.	They rented a house. I decided to go to Hawaii.

b How do you pronounce the simple past of these verbs?

ask   hate   need   smile   stay   talk

c 🔊 **2.2** Listen and check.

d Circle the irregular verb with the different vowel sound.
1 bought   saw   told   caught
2 put   spoke   took   could
3 paid   said   made   came

Ibiza

5 LISTENING

a 🔊 **2.3** Listen to the story about Bill's uncle and aunt. Why was the vacation a disaster?
1 Because the weather was awful.
2 Because the place was very noisy.
3 Because they argued a lot.

b Listen again. Correct the wrong information.
1 Bill went to Ibiza.
  His aunt and uncle went to Ibiza.
2 They're about sixty.
3 They wanted an exciting vacation.
4 They usually spend their vacation abroad.
5 They knew it was "the party island."
6 They first went there in the 1950s.
7 They booked the vacation at a travel agency.
8 The hotel was in a quiet part of town.
9 They're going to go abroad again next year.

6 SPEAKING

a Think about your answers to these questions.

Your last vacation

Where / go? When?

Who / go with?

How / get there?

Where / stay?

How long / be / there?

/ have good weather?

What / do during the day?

What / do at night?

/ have a good time?

/ have any problems?

b Work in pairs.
Ask a partner about his / her vacation.
Listen and ask for more information.

c Change roles.

2 B

G past continuous
V prepositions of time and place: *at, in, on*
P /ə/ and /ər/

A moment in time

> What was happening when he took the photo?

1 GRAMMAR past continuous

a Look at the photos. Where are they? What do you think is happening?

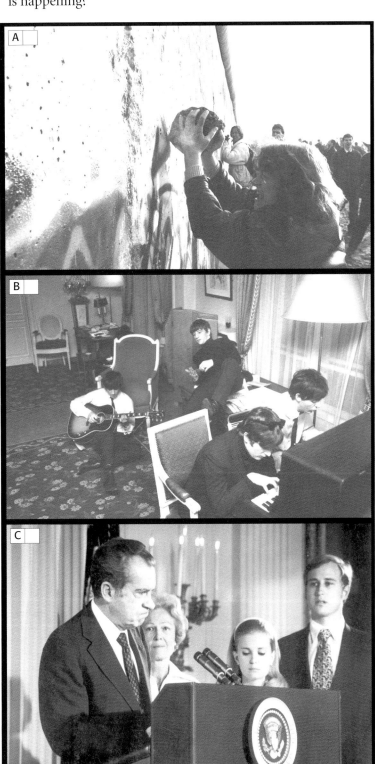

b Read the text and match paragraphs 1–3 with the photographs.

HARRY BENSON spent 50 years taking dramatic and memorable photographs for international newspapers and magazines. Here he talks about three of his best-known pictures.

1 I took this picture on August 9th, 1974. He was saying good-bye to his cabinet and the White House staff after the "Watergate" scandal. His family was standing around him. You can see from their faces what they were feeling.

2 In 1989, I was working on a story in London, when suddenly I heard the news that the Russians were planning to make Berlin an open city. So I got on a plane. When I arrived in Berlin, many people, young and old, were attacking the wall with stones. The woman in the photo was shouting, "I hate it, I hate it."

3 When I took this photo, we were in a hotel room in Paris in 1964. John and Paul were at the piano, and at first nothing much was happening, but suddenly they became completely focused. First the melody came, and then the words. *"Baby's good to me you know, she's happy as can be you know...."* They were composing their song *I Feel Fine*.

c Read the texts again. Cover them and try to remember. What was happening when he took the photos?

When he took the photo in Berlin, people were attacking the wall, and a woman was shouting.

d Look at the highlighted verbs in paragraph 1. What tense are they? What's the difference?

e ○ **p.128 Grammar Bank 2B.** Read the rules and do the exercises.

2 READING & LISTENING

a Look at the photo on the right. What can you see? Where are the people? What are they doing?

b Read what the photographer says and check your answers to **a**. What happened to the photo? What happened 30 years later?

c **2.4** Now listen to Marinette and Henri talking about their photo. Are they still in love?

d Listen again and mark the sentences T (true) or F (false).

1 They always knew that their photo was famous.
2 Marinette saw the book with their photo in a bookstore.
3 When the photographer took the photo, they were laughing.
4 Marinette wanted Henri to stand near her.
5 They didn't know that the photographer was taking their photo.
6 Henri was trying to kiss Marinette.
7 Henri thinks they were arguing about their wedding.
8 They got married a year after the photo.
9 Marinette and Henri work together every day.
10 She says that she and Henri are very similar.

3 VOCABULARY *at, in, on*

a Complete the sentences with *at*, *in*, or *on*.

1 President Nixon left the White House _____ August 9th, 1974.
2 The Beatles were _____ a hotel room _____ Paris _____ 1964.
3 Willy Ronis took the photo _____ the balcony _____ March 1957.
4 The young couple went up to the balcony _____ 3:00 in the afternoon.
5 Henri and Marinette see each other every day, _____ home and _____ work.

b ⭗ **p.148 Vocabulary Bank** *Prepositions*. Do part 1.

4 PRONUNCIATION /ə/ and /ər/

> ⚠ /ə/ is the most common sound in English.

a **2.5** Listen and repeat the sound words and sounds.

b **2.6** Listen to these words and underline the stressed syllable.

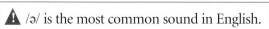

about   exhibition   photographer   together   balcony   October

c Listen again and repeat the words. Practice making the /ə/ and /ər/ sounds.

d **2.7** Listen and repeat the dialogue. Copy the rhythm.

A Where were you at six o'clock in the evening?
B I was at work.
A What were you doing?
B I was having a meeting with the boss.

e In pairs, take turns answering the questions about yesterday.

Where were you at…?   What were you doing?
6:00 p.m.   6:30 a.m.   3:00 p.m.   11:00 a.m.   lunchtime   10:00 p.m.

Willy Ronis talks about his most famous photo

"It was March 1957, and I was taking photographs in Paris. One afternoon I went up the Bastille, and I saw two lovers on a balcony. They were standing very near each other. They were talking. I took just one photo and they didn't hear me. I called it *Lovers at the Bastille*. Luckily for me this photo became very popular in France. Soon posters and postcards with my picture of the two lovers were everywhere. But I never knew who the two young people were. They never contacted me."

"Thirty years later I had an exhibition of my photos in Paris. I was talking to some friends when suddenly a man came up to me and said, 'I know your two lovers. They live near here. I can take you there if you want.' I immediately decided to go and meet them. This was their story."

5 SPEAKING

a ⭗ **Communication** *Famous photos* *A p.109 B p.113*. Tell your partner about a famous photo.

b Talk to a partner. Ask more questions if you can.

Do you have a photo you really like? *Who took it? What was happening at the time?*
Do you have any photos in your bedroom or living room?
Do you like taking photos?
Who is good at taking photos in your family?
Do you like being in photos?

2C
G questions with and without auxiliaries
V question words, pop music
P /w/ and /h/

Who wrote that song?

Fifty years of pop music

Quiz

1 VOCABULARY & SPEAKING

a In pairs or groups, answer the questions.

1 What music / song / album do you like listening to...?
   when you're happy   when you're in a car
   when you're sad   when you're studying
   when you're at a party   when you're in love

2 Which is your favorite decade for pop music? (the 1980s, 1990s, etc.)

3 Who are your favorite bands / singers of all time?

4 What was the last CD you bought?

b Complete the quiz questions with a question word.

How   How many   Where   What   How long
Which (x2)   Why   Who (x2)   Whose   When

c In pairs, answer the questions.

2 GRAMMAR   questions with and without auxiliaries

a Cover the quiz and from memory complete the questions.

1 How long _____ the Beatles _____ together?

2 Who _____ *Hips Don't Lie?*

b Answer these questions.

1 How is question 1 different from question 2?

2 What is the subject of the verb in question 1?

3 What is the subject of the verb in question 2?

c ⭗ **p.128 Grammar Bank 2C.** Read the rules and do the exercises.

1	_____ did Freddie Mercury, the lead singer of Queen, die?	**a** 1981 **b** 1991 **c** 2001
2	_____ did the Eagles stay in their 1976 song?	**a** Heartbreak Hotel **b** Hotel California **c** Hilton Hotel
3	_____ did the Beatles stay together?	**a** For eight years **b** For thirteen years **c** For seventeen years
4	_____ husband is the movie director Guy Ritchie?	**a** Dido's **b** Barbra Streisand's **c** Madonna's
5	_____ happened to Mick Jagger in 2004?	**a** He left the Rolling Stones. **b** He became Sir Mick Jagger. **c** He divorced Jerry Hall.
6	_____ song did the Beach Boys sing?	**a** California Dreamin' **b** Good Vibrations **c** Like a Rolling Stone
7	_____ sang *Hips Don't Lie*?	**a** Britney Spears **b** Shakira **c** Beyoncé
8	_____ did Nirvana stop playing in 1994?	**a** Because they argued. **b** Because Kurt Cobain left. **c** Because Kurt Cobain died.
9	_____ band included Phil Collins and Peter Gabriel?	**a** Dire Straits **b** Genesis **c** Pink Floyd
10	_____ Spice Girls were there?	**a** Four **b** Five **c** Six
11	_____ did Elvis Presley die?	**a** In a plane crash **b** He shot himself. **c** An accidental drug overdose
12	_____ did Chris Martin, lead singer of Coldplay, marry in 2003?	**a** Gwyneth Paltrow **b** Kate Winslet **c** Drew Barrymore

3 PRONUNCIATION /w/ and /h/

a Look at the two sound pictures.
What are the words and sounds?

b Write the words in the correct column.

how   what   when   where   which   who   whose   why

c **2.8** Listen and check. Practice saying the words.

d ➲ **p.159 Sound Bank.** Look at the typical spellings for these sounds.

e **2.9** Listen and write the questions. Say the questions. Copy the rhythm.

4 SPEAKING

➲ **Communication** *Music quiz A p.109 B p.113.*
First write the questions. Then ask your partner the questions.

5 READING

a Read the article once and mark the sentences T (true) or F (false).

1 *Imagine* was a hit three times.
2 Yoko Ono helped write *Imagine.*
3 Ono wrote poems for John Lennon.
4 Lennon never said that Yoko helped him with the song.
5 *Imagine* was written in two places.
6 John Lennon opened the new Liverpool Airport.

b Read the article again. Number the sentences in the order that things happened.

A John Lennon read Ono's poems. ☐
B John Lennon wrote *Imagine.* ☐
C Yoko Ono helped her little brother. ☐ 1
D John Lennon spoke about the song in an interview. ☐
E Liverpool Airport was renamed John Lennon Airport. ☐
F Yoko Ono spoke about the song on a TV program. ☐
G The song became a hit again after Lennon died. ☐
H The song became popular again after September 11, 2001. ☐

6   2.10   SONG ♪ *Imagine*

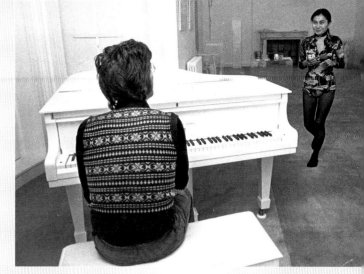

Who wrote *Imagine?*

Imagine, John Lennon's most famous song, was recently voted "Britain's favorite song of all time." It is an idealistic song about peace and the hope for a better world. "Imagine all the people living life in peace." The song was a big hit in 1971, and again in 1980 after Lennon was murdered in New York. It became a hit for a third time after the terrorist attacks of September 11, 2001.

But who really wrote the song? Until recently the answer to this question was always John Lennon. But on a TV program this week, Lennon's wife, Yoko Ono, spoke for the first time about how she, in fact, helped write the song.

Ono said that the idea and inspiration for *Imagine* came from some of her poems that John Lennon was reading at that time. The poems began with the word *imagine*: "Imagine a raindrop, Imagine a goldfish." Ono said, "When I was a child in Japan during the Second World War, my brother and I were terribly hungry. I imagined delicious menus for him, and he began to smile. If you think something is impossible, you can imagine it and make it happen."

In an interview just before he died, Lennon admitted that Yoko deserved credit for *Imagine*. He said, "A lot of it – the lyrics and the concept – came from her, from her book of poems, imagine this, imagine that." Lennon said that he was "too macho" to share the credit with her at the time.

Ono said that part of the song was written when they were flying across the Atlantic, and the rest was written on the piano in their bedroom at their home in England. Ono said, "The song speaks about John's dream for the world. It was something he really wanted to say." *Imagine* became a popular song for peace activists everywhere.

In March 2002 the airport in his home town of Liverpool was renamed John Lennon Airport. A sign above the main entrance has a line from *Imagine*: "Above us only sky."

21

2
D

G *so, because, but, although*
V verb phrases
P the letter *a*

One October evening

She was going very fast because she was in a hurry.

1 READING

A ☐ The next day Jamie called Hannah and invited her to dinner. He took her to a very romantic restaurant, and they talked all evening. After that Jamie and Hannah saw each other every day. Every evening when Hannah finished work, they met at 5:30 in a coffee shop on Bridge Street. They were madly in love.

B ☐ Suddenly, a man ran across the street. He was wearing a dark coat, so Hannah didn't see him until it was too late. Although she tried to stop, she hit the man. Hannah panicked. She didn't stop, and she drove to the coffee shop as fast as she could. But when she arrived, Jamie wasn't there. She called him, but his cell phone was turned off, so she waited for ten minutes and then went home.

C 1 **Hannah met Jamie last summer.** It was Hannah's twenty-first birthday, and she and her friends went to a club. They wanted to dance, but they didn't like the music, so Hannah went to speak to the DJ. "This music is awful," she said. "Could you play something else?" The DJ looked at her and said, "Don't worry, I have the perfect song for you."

D ☐ Two hours later a police car arrived at Hannah's house. A policewoman knocked at the door. "Good evening, ma'am," she said. "Are you Hannah Davis? I'd like to speak to you. Can I come in?"

E ☐ One evening in October, Hannah was at work. As usual she was going to meet Jamie at 5:30. It was dark and it was raining. She looked at her watch. It was 5:20! She was going to be late! She ran to her car right away and got in. At 5:25 she was driving along Bridge Street. She was going very fast because she was in a hurry.

F ☐ Two minutes later he said, "The next song is by Coldplay. It's called *Yellow*, and it's for a beautiful girl who's dancing over there." Hannah knew that the song was for her because she was wearing a yellow dress. When Hannah and her friends left the club, the DJ was waiting at the door. "Hi, I'm Jamie," he said to Hannah. "Can I see you again?" So Hannah gave him her phone number.

a 2.11 Read the story and order the paragraphs 1–6. Listen and check.

b Read the story again and answer the questions.
1. When did Hannah meet Jamie?
2. Why did Hannah go and speak to Jamie in the club?
3. Why did Jamie play *Yellow*?
4. What happened when Hannah left the club?
5. Where did they go on their first date?
6. Where did they go every evening?
7. What was the weather like that evening in October?
8. Why was Hannah driving fast?
9. Why didn't she see the man?
10. What did she do after the accident?
11. Was Jamie at the coffee shop?
12. What happened two hours later?

2 GRAMMAR *so, because, but, although*

a Complete these sentences from the story with *so*, *because*, *but*, or *although*. Use each word once.
1. She was going very fast _____ she was in a hurry.
2. _____ she tried to stop, she hit the man.
3. They wanted to dance, _____ they didn't like the music.
4. He was wearing a dark coat, _____ Hannah didn't see him.

b ⊃ p.128 **Grammar Bank 2D.** Read the rules and do the exercises.

3 VOCABULARY verb phrases

a Make verb phrases with a verb from circle **1** and a phrase from circle **2**.

invite somebody to dinner

b Cover circle **1**. Try to remember the verb for each phrase.

1

invite

meet

take

knock

play

run   be

wait

try

2

in a hurry

across the street

on the door

a song/CD

somebody to dinner

in a coffee shop

somebody to a restaurant

to stop

for somebody

4 PRONUNCIATION the letter *a*

> Hannah met Jamie last summer.
>
> ⚠ The letter *a* has different pronunciations.

a 2.12 Listen and repeat the sound words in the chart.

b 2.13 Put these words in the right columns. Listen and check.

across	again	all	along	although
arrive	away	awful	dance	later
madly	panic	play	rain	ran
romantic	saw	take	talk	wait

æ	eɪ	ɔ	
madly	later	saw	along
panic	take	talk	across

5 SPEAKING

1   2   3   4   5   6

a Read the story of Hannah and Jamie in **1** again.

b In pairs, use the pictures 1–6 to retell the story.

6 LISTENING

> ⚠ Remember! When people speak fast, they link words together.

a 2.14 That evening a policewoman went to Hannah's house. Listen to six extracts from their conversation. What are the missing words?

1 A policewoman _____ _____ the door.
2 Can _____ _____ _____?
3 Well, I'm afraid I have _____ _____ news for you.
4 It was a _____ _____ _____ _____ car.
5 The police _____ _____ _____ her.
6 Did you know your _____ _____ is broken?

b 2.15 Now listen to the whole conversation. **When the teacher pauses the recording,** answer the questions.

1 What do you think the policewoman is going to say?
2 What do you think the bad news is?
3 Do you think Jamie is OK?
4 Who do you think was driving the car?
5 Why do you think the policewoman wants to see Hannah's car?

c Now close your books and listen again. Can you follow the story?

CHECKING IN

2.16 Listen to Allie checking in. Answer the questions.

1 Does the receptionist call Allie "Ms. Gray" or "Mrs. Gray"?
2 How many nights is Allie staying?
3 What's her room number?
4 What time is breakfast?
5 Which floor is the Pavilion Restaurant on?

	US English	*elevator*
	UK English	*lift*

CALLING RECEPTION

a **2.17** Cover the dialogues and listen. Who does Allie call? Why?

YOU HEAR	YOU SAY
Hello, reception.	Hello. This is room 419.
How can I help you?	I have a problem with the air-conditioning. It isn't working, and it's very hot in my room.
I'm sorry, ma'am. I'll _____ someone up to look at it right now.	Thank you.
_____ service. Can I help you?	Hello. This is room 419. Can I have a tuna sandwich, please?
Whole wheat or _____ bread?	Whole wheat, please.
_____ or without mayo?	Without.
With _____ _____ or salad?	Salad, please.
_____ to drink?	Yes, a Diet Coke.™
With _____ and lemon?	Just ice.
It'll be there in five minutes, ma'am.	Thank you.

b Listen again. Complete the **YOU HEAR** phrases.

c **2.18** Listen and repeat the **YOU SAY** phrases. Copy the <u>rhythm</u>.

d In pairs, role-play the dialogues. **A** (book open) you're the receptionist / room service, **B** (book closed) you're Allie. Change roles.

SOCIAL ENGLISH   coffee before the conference

a **2.19** Listen and mark the sentences T (true) or F (false).

1 Mark is going to take Allie to dinner tonight.
2 The cocktail party is on Thursday.
3 Allie wants to see the bay and the Golden Gate Bridge.
4 Brad is from the San Francisco office.
5 Brad offers to take Allie sightseeing.

b Complete the **USEFUL PHRASES**. Listen again and check.

c **2.20** Listen and repeat the phrases. How do you say them in your language?

USEFUL PHRASES
M Did you s_____ well?
A How are t_____?   M They're fine.
A What are the p_____ for the week?
M Allie, t_____ is Brad Martin.
M It's t_____ to go.

Study Link MultiROM

Every week we ask readers to send in a favorite photo with a short description of why the photo is important to them. This week's winner is Dominic, a graphic designer from Chicago.

1 One of my favorite photos is of a man cooking fish.

2 I took the photo ¹ _in_ the summer of 1999 when I was ² _____ vacation in Africa.

3 We were ³ _____ Zanzibar, and we were sailing around the islands. We caught some fish and then landed ⁴ _____ one of the islands. Our guide made a fire and cooked the fish.

4 Richie, the guide, was a wonderful person, and he became a good friend. He was also a fantastic cook. I can't remember exactly what kind of fish he was cooking in the photo, but it tasted delicious!

5 I keep this photo ⁵ _____ the wall in my studio. ⁶ _____ a freezing cold day in Chicago, I just have to look ⁷ _____ it. Then memories of a wonderful adventure come back, and I can imagine that I'm ⁸ _____ sunny Africa again.

a Match the questions with paragraphs 1–5.

What was happening when you took the photo? ☐
Where do you keep it? Why do you like it? ☐
What's your favorite photo? ☐
Who took it? When? Where? ☐
Tell me more about who or what is in the photo. ☐

ⓘ You can keep a photo…

in	an album.
	your wallet.
	your bedroom.
on	the wall.
	a table.
by	your bed.

b Complete the text with *at*, *in*, or *on*.

WRITE about your favorite photo. Answer the questions in **a** in the right order.

CHECK your description for mistakes (grammar , punctuation , and spelling). Attach a copy of the photo if you can.

GRAMMAR

Circle the correct answer, a, b, or c.

What's _____ name?

a yours (b) your c you

1 Where _____ on vacation last year?
  a you went
  b did you go
  c you did go

2 He didn't _____ to go to the movies with us.
  a wanted
  b wants
  c want

3 We _____ to San Francisco last summer.
  a flown
  b fly
  c flew

4 When I took the photo, you _____ looking at me.
  a weren't
  b wasn't
  c didn't

5 What _____ doing when you called him?
  a he was
  b was he
  c were he

6 Who _____ that song?
  a did write
  b wrote
  c did wrote

7 When _____?
  a he died
  b died he
  c did he die

8 She was driving fast _____ she was late.
  a although
  b because
  c so

9 _____ the music was awful, we danced all night.
  a But
  b Although
  c So

10 It was dark, _____ she didn't see him.
  a but
  b so
  c because

10

VOCABULARY

a travel verbs

Complete the phrases with a verb.

_____go_____ shopping

1 _____ photos
2 _____ for a walk
3 _____ at a hotel
4 _____ two days in Rio / 1,000 yen
5 _____ a good time

b prepositions

Complete the sentences with *at*, *in*, or *on*.

I'm sitting _____in_____ a taxi.

1 We met _____ a party.
2 The two lovers were talking _____ a balcony.
3 We were sitting _____ the garden.
4 There was a photo _____ the wall.
5 I was waiting _____ the bus stop.

c question words

Complete the questions with a question word.

_____Who_____ was the Beatles' drummer?

1 _____ did the Beatles make their first record?
2 _____ wrote their songs?
3 _____ albums did they sell?
4 _____ happened to them in the end?
5 _____ of their songs do you like best?

15

PRONUNCIATION

a Underline the word with a different sound

1		wore	forgot	story	airport
2		took	could	found	put
3		shop	choose	exhibition	musician
4		whose	how	who	when
5		job	argue	jealous	manager

b Underline the stressed syllable.

information

incredible horrible photographer suddenly although

10

CAN YOU UNDERSTAND THIS TEXT?

Mountain climbers rescued by text message

Two British climbers were rescued yesterday after sending an SOS text message to a friend in London.

Rachel de Kelsey, 32, and a friend, Jeremy Colenso, 33, who are both experienced climbers, were on a mountain-climbing vacation last week in Switzerland. But on Saturday night, when they were 3,000 meters up in the mountains, there was a terrible storm. The wind was incredibly strong, and the snow was two meters deep. They couldn't move, so they had to spend the night on the mountain. Rachel had her cell phone with her, so she sent a text message to five friends in the UK, asking for help.

About four hours later, one of her friends, Avery Cunliffe in London, replied with a text message. Avery said, "I don't usually have my cell phone in the bedroom. At about 4 A.M. I woke up and saw Rachel's message. I found the number of the police in Switzerland and called them. They contacted the mountain rescue team."

But the weather was so bad that the helicopter couldn't get to the two climbers. The rescue team sent a text message to Rachel and Jeremy telling them that they had to spend a second night on the mountain. The message said: "So sorry Rachel. We tried. Wind too strong. Have to wait till morning. Take care. Be strong." Rachel said, "I thought we were going to die. It was freezing, −15°C, and really windy on the mountain. We spent the night talking and planning a vacation in the sun!"

The next morning the storm passed, and the helicopter arrived to take them off the mountain. Avery said, "When I heard that Rachel and Jeremy were safe, I was dancing around my apartment." Rachel said that she and Jeremy were now looking forward to a hot bath and a good meal. But first they were going to buy the rescue team a gift!

Adapted from a newspaper

a Read the article and mark the sentences T (true), F (false), or DS (doesn't say).
1 Rachel and Jeremy were climbing for the first time.
2 They couldn't go down the mountain because of bad weather.
3 Avery was sleeping when Rachel's message came.
4 Avery called the mountain rescue team in Switzerland.
5 Rachel's other four friends didn't reply.
6 The helicopter couldn't rescue them immediately.
7 Rachel and Jeremy spent three nights on the mountain.
8 They wanted to buy Avery a gift.

b Underline and learn six new words or expressions from the article. Use your dictionary to check the meaning and pronunciation.

CAN YOU UNDERSTAND THESE PEOPLE?

a **2.21** Listen and circle the correct answer: a, b, or c.
1 Where did the woman go on vacation this year?
a Peru   b Mexico   c Hawaii
2 What was the weather like in Toronto?
a It snowed.   b It was hot.   c It was sunny.
3 Where did the photographer take the photo of the actor?
a On the stairs   b In the hotel lobby   c On the street
4 What was the model doing when he took the photo?
a Talking   b Reading   c Walking on the runway
5 What year did the pop group make their last album?
a 2003   b 2004   c 2005

b **2.22** Listen to the story and mark the sentences T (true) or F (false).
1 She was driving to work.
2 It was raining.
3 She saw a man in the middle of the road asking her to stop.
4 The two men drove away in her car.
5 She called the police on her cell phone.

CAN YOU SAY THIS IN ENGLISH?

a Can you...? Yes (✓)
☐ talk about your last vacation
☐ talk about your favorite photo
☐ talk about your favorite singer or group

b Complete the questions with *was, were, do, did,* or –.
1 What kind of books _____ you read?
2 Where _____ you at 9:00 this morning?
3 What _____ happening when you got home last night?
4 What _____ you doing on September 11, 2001?
5 How many people _____ came to class today?

c Ask your partner the questions in b. Ask for more information.

3
A

G *going to*, present continuous (future arrangements)
V *look (for, through*, etc.)
P sentence stress

When are you going?
When are you coming back?

Where are you going?

1 READING

a When was the last time you went to an airport? Were you meeting someone or going somewhere?

b Read the magazine article. Complete it with these questions.

A		*Do you know anybody here?*
B		*Are you going to stay for long?*
C	1	*Is this your first visit?*
D		*What are you planning to do?*
E		*When are you leaving?*
F		*Does he know you're coming?*
G		*How are you going to get there?*
H		*How long are you going to stay?*
I		*Where are you staying in New York?*

c Read the article again and write **M** (Marina), **J** (Jonathan), or **K** (Koji).

1 _K_ is going to stay at a hotel.
2 ___ is going to stay at a friend's house.
3 ___ is going to visit a family member.
4 ___ is going to the theater tomorrow.
5 ___ is only going to be in the US
for four weeks.
6 ___ is going to work.

2 GRAMMAR *going to*, present continuous

a In pairs, cover the text. Can you remember three of Marina's plans? Can you remember three of Jonathan's plans?

Marina is going to work.

b Look at the interview with Maki and Koji. Highlight six present continuous sentences. Do they refer to the *present* or the *future*?

c 🡆 **p.130 Grammar Bank 3A.** Read the rules and do the exercises.

✈ Airport Stories

John F. Kennedy Airport in New York City is a busy international airport. Every day thousands of travelers arrive at JFK Airport from many different countries. Every one of them has a different story to tell. We spent an afternoon in the arrivals area at JFK last week talking to travelers arriving from abroad. We asked them: Why are you here?

🡆 LOOKING FOR A JOB
Marina, 23, from Porto Alegre, Brazil

Why are you here?

I'm going to look for a job. Maybe as an au pair, taking care of children. And I want to improve my English too, so I can get a better job when I go back home. I hope I can find some work quickly. I'm going to look through the newspaper ads today.

1 Is this your first visit?

Yes, it is. I'm really looking forward to living here, but I'm a little nervous, too.

2 _____

Six months or a year. It depends how things go.

3 _____

Yes, I have a friend who's working here in a restaurant. I'm going to stay with her for a few weeks until I can find my own apartment.

🡆 A FAMILY REUNION
Jonathan, 35, just arrived from Melbourne, Australia

Why are you here?

I'm going to see my dad in Connecticut. It's his seventieth birthday tomorrow.

4 _____

No. It's going to be a big surprise for him. And it's going to be very emotional, too. I moved to Australia in 1998, and the last time I saw my dad was five years ago. It's too expensive to visit very often, and my father can't fly – he had a heart operation last year.

5 _____

By train. The whole family is waiting at my parents' house. We're going to have a big party there tomorrow night.

6 _____

Yes, for a month. It's too far to come for a short time – and I want to see all my old friends here as well as my family.

ON THEIR HONEYMOON
Maki, 25, and Koji, 27, from Nagasaki, Japan

Why are you here?

We're on our honeymoon. We got married last Saturday.
Congratulations!

7 _____

We're staying at the Kitano Hotel. We're just here for a few days.

8 _____

Everything is organized for us. Tomorrow we're taking a bus tour of the city, and in the evening we're seeing a Broadway show. Then on Tuesday we're going to a baseball game at Yankee Stadium, and on Wednesday we're flying to Boston.

9 _____

On Friday. We're going to Toronto next, and then to Montreal...

3 LISTENING

a **3.1** Listen to Marina talking six months later. Mark the sentences T (true) or F (false).

1 She's working in a Mexican restaurant.
2 It was easy to find a job.
3 She isn't living with her friend now.
4 She isn't going to English classes.
5 She doesn't know if she's going to go back to Brazil.
6 She's leaving the restaurant next month.
7 Her boyfriend is a waiter.
8 Her family is very happy that she's getting married.

b Listen again for more details. Correct the false sentences.

4 VOCABULARY *look (for, through, etc.)*

a Look at Marina's interview on page 28 again. Find and <u>underline</u> three expressions with *look*. Match them to their dictionary definitions.

1 _____ try to find something
2 _____ wait with pleasure for something that is going to happen
3 _____ read something quickly

b Complete the sentences with *for*, *forward to*, or *through*.

1 I always look _____ my notes before a test.
2 She's going to Peru next month. She's really looking _____ it.
3 I can't find my keys. Can you help me look _____ them?
4 I'm not looking _____ the final exam – it's going to be very difficult.
5 Our house is a little too small. We're looking _____ a new one.
6 As soon as he gets home, he looks _____ the mail.

c Tell your partner...

• something you are looking forward to
• something you often have to look for in the morning
• something that you usually look through

5 PRONUNCIATION sentence stress

a <u>Underline</u> the words that are important for communication in these questions (the stressed words).

1 Where are you going?   4 Where are you staying?
2 When are you leaving?   5 When are you coming back?
3 How are you getting there?

b **3.2** Listen and check. Listen again and repeat. <u>Copy</u> the rhythm.

6 SPEAKING

a Write down three plans or arrangements that you have for this week. Work in pairs. A tell B your plans. B listen and ask for more information. Then change roles.

> I'm going to the movies on Friday night.

> What are you going to see?

b ◑ **Communication** *Where are you going on vacation? p.116.* Find a travel companion for an exotic vacation.

3 B
G *will / won't* (predictions)
V opposite verbs
P contractions (*will / won't*), /ɑ/ and /oʊ/

> I'm taking my driving test today.
> You'll fail.

The pessimist's phrase book

YOU	THE PESSIMIST
1 We're having a picnic in the park.	*It'll rain.*
2 I'm taking my driving test tomorrow.	*You won't pass.*
3 We're meeting Ana and Daniel at 7:00.	
4 I'm taking my first skiing lesson today.	
5 My brother has a new girlfriend.	
6 I lent Tony some money yesterday.	
7 I'm going to watch a movie in English.	
8 We're going to drive into the city.	
9 My team is playing tonight.	
10 I'm catching the 7:30 train.	

1 GRAMMAR *will / won't* for predictions

a Look at the picture. Who is the optimist? Who is the pessimist? Which are you?

b Read the **YOU** phrases. Find the **THE PESSIMIST'S** responses in the box below and write them in the phrase book.

He won't pay you back.	You'll miss it.	You won't understand a word.
~~You won't pass.~~	They'll be late.	It won't last.
They'll lose.	~~It'll rain.~~	You'll break your leg.
You won't find a parking space.		

c **3.3** Listen and check. Repeat the responses.

d Practice in pairs.
A (book open) read the **YOU** phrases.
B (book closed) say **THE PESSIMIST** phrase.
Then change roles.

e Look at **THE PESSIMIST** phrases and answer the questions.
1 Do the sentences refer to the present or the future?
2 What are the full words in the contractions **'ll** and **won't**?

f ⏵ **p.130 Grammar Bank 3B.** Read the rules and do the exercises.

2 VOCABULARY opposite verbs

a What's the opposite of the verbs in **A**? Use a verb from **B**.

b ⏵ **p.149 Vocabulary Bank** *Verbs.* Do part 1.

A
pass
win
lose
lend

B
fail
borrow
find
lose

3 PRONUNCIATION contractions (*will*/*won't*), /ɑ/ and /oʊ/

a **3.4** Listen and repeat the contractions. <u>C</u>opy the <u>r</u>hythm.

I'll	I'll be late	I'll be late for work.
You'll	You'll break	You'll break your leg.
She'll	She'll miss	She'll miss the train.
It'll	It'll rain	It'll rain tomorrow.
They'll	They'll lose	They'll lose the game.

b **3.5** Listen. Can you hear the difference?

	want	I want to pass.		won't	I won't pass.

c **3.6** Listen and write down the six sentences.

4 LISTENING

a **3.7** Listen to the introduction to a radio program. Why is positive thinking good for you?

b Try to guess the missing words in these tips.

	Tip
Caller 1	Live in the _____, not in the _____.
Caller 2	Think _____ thoughts, not negative ones.
Caller 3	Don't spend a lot of time reading the _____ or watching the _____ on TV.
Caller 4	Every week make a list of all the _____ _____ that happened to you.
Caller 5	Try to use _____ _____ when you speak to other people.

c **3.8** Listen and check.

d Listen again. Write down any extra information you hear.

e Which tips do you think are useful?

5 SPEAKING

a In pairs, match the positive phrases with the situations.
Make a positive prediction, *I'm sure you'll…, I'm sure it'll…*, etc.

Your friend says…	You say…	
1 I have an important exam tomorrow.	*Good luck!*	*I'm sure you'll pass.*
2 I'm getting married next month.		
3 I'm a little depressed today.		
4 I'm going to Peru next month.		
5 I can't go out tonight. I don't have any money.		

b Ask and answer with a partner. Use a phrase from the box and say why.

Are you a positive thinker?
Do you think…

- you'll go somewhere exciting for your next vacation?
- you'll pass your next test?
- you'll get a good (or better) job?
- you'll do something fun this weekend?
- you'll get an interesting e-mail from someone tonight?
- you'll get to the end of this book?

I <u>h</u>ope <u>s</u>o. (I <u>h</u>ope <u>n</u>ot.)
I <u>th</u>ink <u>s</u>o.
I don't <u>th</u>ink <u>s</u>o.
<u>M</u>aybe. / <u>P</u>ossibly.
<u>P</u>robably.
<u>D</u>efinitely.

3 C

G will / won't (promises, offers, decisions)
V verb + *back*
P word stress: two-syllable words

It's a secret.
OK, I won't tell anyone.

I'll always love you

1 READING

a Look at the six promises below. What do you think they have in common?

I won't tell anyone.	**I'll write.**
I'll always love you.	**I'll pay you back tomorrow.**
I'll come back tomorrow.	**This won't hurt.**

b Read the article once and write the correct promise in the blanks 1–6.

c Read the text again. Find words that match the definitions. <u>Underline</u> the stressed syllable.

1 _____ (n) a person who repairs water pipes, toilets, etc.

2 _____ (n) studies to find more information about something

3 _____ (n) putting medicine under the skin with a needle

4 _____ (v) give something to somebody in return for something else

5 _____ (adv) every time

6 _____ (adj) something that lasts forever

2 PRONUNCIATION   word stress: two-syllable words

 Most two-syllable words are stressed on the first syllable, e.g., *father*. When words are stressed on the second syllable, e.g., *although*, <u>under</u>line the stress and learn them.

a Look at these two-syllable words from the text. Which **four** are stressed on the second syllable?

secret	worry	exist
always	forget	dentist
borrow	complete	money
promise	e-mail	doctor
builder	before	stingy

b **3.9** Listen and check. Practice saying the words.

Promises, promises

We make them and we break them because some promises are very hard to keep. Here are the top six most common broken promises ...

1 _____

You always hear this from builders, plumbers, and electricians. But the truth is very different. They won't come back until next week (or later). And you will probably need to call them five times first.

2 _____

We love hearing secrets and we happily make this promise. And at the time we really mean it. "Don't worry," we say, "your secret is safe with me." But of course it isn't. Research shows that everybody will always tell one other person the secret. Very soon the whole world will know!

3 _____

A favorite phrase of doctors, dentists, and nurses. They usually say it just before they give you a shot. But the phrase is not complete. The full phrase is: "This won't hurt me (but it will probably hurt you a lot)."

4 _____

You make a new friend on vacation or on a long flight, you exchange e-mail addresses, and you make this promise. Six months later you find a name and e-mail address on a card or an old piece of paper. "Uh-oh!" you think — but then you remember that they didn't write to you, either!

5 _____

In *Hamlet*, Shakespeare told us never to borrow or lend money. He was right. When we lend people money, they always make this promise, but then they forget. If we then ask for the money back, they think we are stingy. If we don't ask, we never get the money back.

6 _____

Whitney Houston sang a song about this. Every day, all over the world, thousands of people make the same promise to each other. We know eternal love exists, but is this promise the most difficult one to keep of them all?

3 GRAMMAR will / won't for promises, offers, and decisions

a Look at the cartoons. What do you think the people are saying?

A ☐ B ☐ C ☐ D ☐

E ☐

Meat or fish?

F ☐

b Complete sentences 1–6 with a verb from below. Then match the sentences with the cartoons (A–F).

have	help	love	open	pay	take

1 I'll ____ the steak, please.
2 I'll ____ you back tomorrow.
3 I'll ____ you!
4 I'll always ____ you.
5 I'll ____ the window.
6 Yes, it's very nice. I'll ____ it.

c Look at the sentences again. In which two are people…?

making a promise   _2_ and ____
making a decision   ____ and ____
offering to do something   ____ and ____

d ➲ **p.130 Grammar Bank 3C.** Read the rules and do the exercises.

4 VOCABULARY verb + back

a Look at the sentences. What's the difference between *go* and *go back*?

I'm **going** to Mexico.   I'm **going back** to Mexico.

b Complete the dialogues with a phrase from the box.

call back	come back	give it back	pay me back	take it back

1
A I love that shirt you gave me for my birthday, but it's a little small.
B Don't worry. I'll _____ to the store and exchange it.

2
A Can I speak to Mr. Park, please?
B I'm sorry. He's not here right now.
A OK. I'll _____ later.

3
A Excuse me. Could I talk to you for a moment?
B I'm really busy right now. Could you _____ in five minutes?

4
A That's my pen you're using!
B No, it's not. It's mine.
A No, it's mine. _____!

5
A Can you lend me $50?
B It depends. When can you _____?
A Tomorrow. I'll go to the bank first thing in the morning.

c ◉ **3.10** Listen and check. In pairs, practice the dialogues.

5 SPEAKING

➲ **Communication** *I'll game p.117.* Follow your teacher's instructions to play.

6 ◉ 3.11 SONG ♫ *White Flag*

G review of tenses: present, past, and future
V verbs + prepositions
P sentence stress

I dreamed about a road.
That means you're going to travel.

I was only dreaming

1 READING & LISTENING

a In pairs, say if you think these statements are true or false.

1 We can only remember a dream if we wake up in the middle of it.
2 We always appear in our dreams.
3 People often have the same dream many times.
4 Psychoanalysts use dreams to help their patients.
5 Dreams can predict the future.

b **3.12** You're going to listen to a psychoanalyst talking to a patient about his dreams. Cover the dialogue and listen. Number the pictures 1–6 in the correct order.

Dr. Muller	So, _tell_ me, what did you dream about?
Patient	I was at a party. There were a lot of people.
Dr. Muller	What ＿＿ they ＿＿?
Patient	They were ＿＿ and ＿＿.
Dr. Muller	Were _you_ drinking?
Patient	Yes, I ＿＿ ＿＿ champagne.
Dr. Muller	And then what ＿＿?
Patient	Then, suddenly I ＿＿ in a garden. There ＿＿ a lot of flowers…
Dr. Muller	Flowers, yes… what kind of flowers?
Patient	I ＿＿ really see – it was dark. And I ＿＿ hear music – somebody ＿＿ ＿＿ the violin.
Dr. Muller	The violin? Go on.
Patient	And then I ＿＿ an owl, a big owl in a tree…
Dr. Muller	How ＿＿ you ＿＿? Were you frightened?
Patient	No, not frightened really, no, but I ＿＿ I felt very cold. Especially my feet – they were freezing. And then I ＿＿ ＿＿.
Dr. Muller	Your feet? Hmm, very interesting, very interesting indeed…
Patient	So what ＿＿ it ＿＿, doctor?

c Now uncover the dialogue. Listen again and fill in the blanks with a word or phrase.

d What do you think the patient's dream means? Match the things in his dream with interpretations 1–6.

Understanding your dreams

You dream ...		This means ...
that you are at a party.	☐	1 the person you love doesn't love you.
that you are drinking champagne.	☐	2 you are going to be very busy.
about flowers.	☐	3 you'll be successful.
that somebody is playing the violin.	☐	4 you're feeling positive about the future.
about an owl.	☐	5 you want some romance in your life. You are looking for a new partner.
that you have cold feet.	☐	6 you need to ask an older person for help.

e **3.13** Now listen to Dr. Muller interpreting the patient's dream. Check your answers to **d**.

f Listen again. Look at the pictures again and remember what Dr. Muller said about each thing. Compare with your partner.

> The party means he's going to meet people.

2 GRAMMAR review of tenses

a Look at the chart. Write the sentences below the chart in the correct place in the **Example** column.

Tense	Example	Use
simple present	*You work in an office.*	D
present continuous		
simple past		
past continuous		
going to + base form		
will / *won't* + base form		

I was drinking champagne.
You'll have a meeting with your boss.
I saw an owl.
You're going to meet a lot of people.
~~You work in an office.~~
I'm meeting her tonight.

b Now complete the **Use** column with uses A–F.

A Future plans and predictions.
B Finished actions in the past.
C Things happening now, or plans for a fixed time/place.
D ~~Things that happen always or usually.~~
E Future predictions, decisions, offers, and promises.
F Actions that were in progress at a past time.

c ➲ **p.130 Grammar Bank 3D.** Read the rules and do the exercises.

3 PRONUNCIATION sentence stress

a **3.14** Listen to sentences 1–6 and <u>underline</u> the stressed (information) words.

1 You'll have a <u>meeting</u> with your <u>boss</u>.
2 Somebody was playing the violin.
3 You're going to meet a lot of people.
4 How did you feel?
5 I'm meeting her tonight.
6 She doesn't love me.

b Listen and repeat the sentences. <u>Copy</u> the <u>rhythm</u>.

4 SPEAKING

➲ **Communication** *Dreams A p.110 B p.114.*
Role-play interpreting your partner's dream.

5 VOCABULARY verbs + prepositions

Complete the questions with a preposition from the box.

| about (x3)   for   of   to (x3)   with (x2) |

1 What did you **dream** _____ last night?
2 What radio station do you usually **listen** _____?
3 What do you **talk** _____ with your friends?
4 Did you **wait** _____ a bus or a train today?
5 Who do you usually **agree** _____ in your family?
6 Are you going to **write** _____ anybody tonight?
7 What do you **think** _____ this book?
8 What are you **thinking** _____ now?
9 Do you **argue** _____ people a lot?
10 Who was the first person you **spoke** _____ this morning?

ORDERING A MEAL

3.15 Listen to Allie and Mark at the restaurant. Answer the questions.

1 What do they order for appetizers?
2 What does Allie order for her main course?
3 What kind of potatoes do they order?
4 How does Mark want his steak – rare, medium, or well-done?
5 What are they going to drink?

Menu

Appetizers | **Main courses**

Appetizers	Main courses
Tomato and mozzarella salad	Fried chicken
Mushroom soup	T-bone steak
Grilled shrimp	Grilled salmon

All main courses served with a baked potato or fries.

PROBLEMS WITH A MEAL

a   **3.16**   Cover the dialogue and listen. What three problems do they have?

YOU HEAR	YOU SAY
Chicken for you, ma'am, and the steak for you, sir.	I'm sorry, but I asked for a baked potato, not fries.
No problem. _____ _____ _____.	
	Excuse me.
Yes, sir?	I asked for my steak rare, and this is well-done.
I'm very sorry. _____ _____ _____ back to the kitchen.	
	Could we have the check, please?
Yes, sir.	
Your check.	Thanks. Excuse me. I think there's a mistake in the check. We only had two glasses of wine, not a bottle.
Yes, you're right. I'm very sorry. It's not my day today! _____ _____ _____ a new check.	Thank you.

	US English	*fries*	*check*
	UK English	*chips*	*bill*

b Listen again. Complete the YOU HEAR phrases.

c   **3.17**   Listen and repeat the YOU SAY phrases. Copy the rhythm.

d In pairs, role-play the dialogue. A (book open) you're the waiter, B (book closed) you're Mark and Allie. Change roles.

SOCIAL ENGLISH   after dinner

a   **3.18**   Listen to Mark and Allie. Mark the sentences T (true) or F (false).

1 Jennifer is Mark's ex-wife.
2 Mark was married for three years.
3 His wife left him for another man.
4 Allie met her previous boyfriend at work.
5 After dinner they're going to go dancing.

b Complete the USEFUL PHRASES. Listen again and check.

c   **3.19**   Listen and repeat the phrases. How do you say them in your language?

USEFUL PHRASES

A   That was a l_____ dinner.
M   I'm g_____ you enjoyed it.
A   Can I ask you s_____?
M   We could have a _____ cup of coffee.

1 221 Baker Street

2 _____

3 _____

4 _____ ,

Thank you for your letter. We're very happy that you're coming to stay with us in August, and we're sure you'll have a good time.

What time are you arriving at the airport? You can get a train to the city from there. Do you have a cell phone? Then you can call us when you're on the train, and we'll meet you at the station.

Could you also tell me a few more things about yourself? Is there anything you can't eat or drink? Do you want a single room, or do you prefer to share a room? Are you going to go back to Seoul right after the course ends? If not, how many more days are you going to stay with us?

5 _____ .

6 _____ ,

Jane Sanders

7 _____ I'm sending you a photo of the family so you'll recognize us at the station!

a Chan-ho is a Korean student who's going to study English in San Francisco. He's going to stay with a family. Read the letter from Mrs. Sanders and complete it with expressions from the box.

San Francisco, CA 94111   Best wishes   ~~221 Baker Street~~   P.S.
Dear Chan-ho   April 14, 2007   Looking forward to hearing from you

b Read the letter again and answer the questions.

1 When is Chan-ho going to the United States?
2 How is he going to get there?
3 How many questions does Mrs. Sanders ask him?
4 Does *Looking forward to hearing from you* mean…?
   a I hope you will write soon.
   b I'm going to write again soon.
5 Why does Mrs. Sanders send Chan-ho a photo?

c What differences are there between an informal letter and an e-mail?

Imagine you are going to stay with Mrs. Sanders. Answer her letter using your own information. Remember to include your address and the date.

WRITE three paragraphs:

Paragraph 1   Thank her for her letter.
Paragraph 2   Say when you are arriving, etc.
Paragraph 3   Answer her other questions.

End the letter with *Best wishes* and your name.

CHECK your letter for mistakes (grammar , punctuation , and spelling).

3 What do you remember?

GRAMMAR

Circle the correct answer, a, b, or c.

What's _____ name?
a yours   (b) your   c you

1 We _____ live with John's parents.
  a 're going
  b 're going to
  c go to
2 What time _____?
  a you are leaving
  b are you leaving
  c are you leave
3 I'm sure _____ lose the game.
  a they
  b they'll
  c they going to
4 It's very late. They probably _____ come now.
  a won't to
  b won't
  c don't
5 I _____ pass the test.
  a don't think she'll
  b not think she will
  c don't think she won't
6 It's very hot in here. I _____ open the window.
  a go to
  b 'll
  c don't
7 A I don't have a car.
  B Don't worry. _____ take you.
  a We
  b We are
  c We'll
8 I _____ about my grandmother.
  a dream often
  b often am dreaming
  c often dream
9 I _____ in the park when I saw an enormous dog.
  a walked
  b was walking
  c 'm walking
10 Where _____ go next summer?
  a are you going to
  b you will
  c are you | **10**

VOCABULARY

a prepositions

Complete the sentences with the correct preposition.

Where do you come ___from___?

1 Last night I dreamed _____ being alone on a desert island.
2 I looked _____ you everywhere. Where were you?
3 I'm looking _____ to the weekend.
4 I waited _____ the bus for half an hour.
5 I often argue _____ my dad about politics.

b verbs + *back*

Match the phrases.

"I'm going tomorrow."   "When are you coming back?"

1 "Could you lend me $50?"   [ ] A "Yes, I'll give it back tomorrow."
2 "I'm sorry, she's not at home." [ ] B "No. Go away and don't come back."
3 "Do you have my book?"   [ ] C "OK, I'll call back later."
4 "My new phone doesn't work."   [ ] D "If you can pay me back before Friday."
5 "Don't you want to see me again?"[ ] E "Take it back to the store."

c opposite verbs

Write the opposite verb phrase.

push the door   ___pull the door___
1 lose a game   _____
2 remember to pay   _____
3 buy a car   _____
4 learn Spanish   _____
5 get a letter   _____ | **15**

PRONUNCIATION

a <u>Underline</u> the word with a different sound.

1		love	come	home	month
2		lose	too	good	do
3		lot	won't	box	doctor
4		go	know	don't	down
5		borrow	tonight	open	probably

b <u>Underline</u> the stressed syllable.

in<u>for</u>mation

pessimist   prediction   remember   important   interesting | **10**

38

CAN YOU UNDERSTAND THIS TEXT?

2020 woman the hunter, man the househusband

A new report on life in 2020 was published yesterday. This report predicts big changes, not just in technology but also changes in the way we live. These are some of the predictions for work and family life.

Family life

☐ One in five fathers will be househusbands, while the mothers go out to work.

☐ People will live near other people who have the same interests, for example, in golf villages.

☐ There will often be three generations living in the same house, e.g., grandparents, parents, and children.

☐ People will live until their mid-eighties, but women will still live slightly longer than men.

Work and study

☐ One in five school classes will be online via the Internet. Students will also often have video classes with a "superteacher" from another city or country.

☐ Most workers will have short-term contracts. They will have to learn to do lots of different jobs because they will change jobs frequently.

☐ Most people will work a twenty-five hour week. This will usually mean working five hours a day, although some people may work three eight-hour days and have four days off.

Adapted from a newspaper

a Read the article about 2020. Put a check (✓) next to the predictions that you think would be a good thing.

b Read the article again. Mark the sentences T (true), F (false), or DS (doesn't say).

According to this report, in 2020…

1 20% of fathers will stay home and take care of the children.
2 People will live near other people who like the same things.
3 Grandparents will take care of their grandchildren.
4 Men and women will live until they are 80.
5 "Superteachers" will sometimes travel to give classes.
6 Many people will work in the same job all their lives.
7 Everybody will work five hours a day.

c Underline and learn six new words or expressions from the article. Use your dictionary to check the meaning and pronunciation.

CAN YOU UNDERSTAND THESE PEOPLE?

a **3.20** Listen to five short conversations. Circle a, b, or c.

1 On Saturday the woman is going to _____.
   a stay home   b go swimming
   c play volleyball
2 Who do they think will win the World Cup?
   a Mexico   b Brazil   c Italy
3 This weekend the weather is going to be _____.
   a wet and cold   b sunny but cold
   c warm and sunny
4 The woman is going to buy _____.
   a the red sweater   b the blue sweater
   c the black sweater
5 Last night the student _____.
   a had a bad dream   b had a good dream
   c didn't dream

b **3.21** Listen and complete the flight details.

Supertravel

Flight from Miami to [1]_____

Departure	Tuesday May 6th
Return	[2]_____
Flight times	Outbound: leaves 6:30, arrives [3]_____
	Return: leaves [4]_____, arrives 11:30
Passenger's name	Henry [5]_____

CAN YOU SAY THIS IN ENGLISH?

a In English, can you…? Yes (✓)

☐ talk about your plans for tonight
☐ talk about your plans for next year
☐ make three future predictions about your town
☐ make three promises about your English

b Reorder the words to make questions.

1 doing weekend this what you are ?
2 English year you next going study to are ?
3 think do who will election next you win the ?
4 rain think tomorrow will you do it ?
5 you dreams how your remember do often ?

c Ask your partner the questions in **b**. Ask for more information.

4 A

G present perfect (experience) + *ever* and *never*; present perfect or simple past?
V clothes
P vowel sounds

Have you ever been to that store?
What did you buy?

From rags to riches

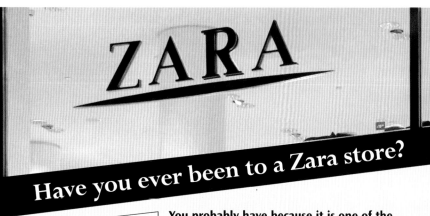

Have you ever been to a Zara store?

You probably have because it is one of the fastest-growing chains in the world. The person behind Zara is Amancio Ortega. He is the richest man in Spain, but very few people know his face. There are only two official photographs of him, and he rarely gives interviews. Although he is a multimillionaire businessman, he doesn't look like one. He doesn't like wearing suits or ties and prefers to wear jeans and a shirt.

When he was young, he worked as a salesperson in a clothing store, but he always dreamed of having his own business. In 1963 he started a small company that made women's pajamas. In 1975, at the age of 40, he opened his first clothing store in La Coruña, a city in northwest Spain, and named it Zara. Now you can find Zara stores all over the world, from New York to Moscow to Singapore. So why is Zara so successful?

The main reason is that Zara reacts extremely quickly to the latest designer fashions and produces clothes that are fashionable but inexpensive. Zara can make a new line of clothes in three weeks. Other companies normally take about nine months. The clothes also change from week to week, so customers keep coming back to see what's new. Zara produces 20,000 new designs a year, and none of them stay in stores for more than a month.

So if you've seen a new jacket or skirt that you like in a Zara store, hurry up and buy it because it won't be there for long.

1 READING & VOCABULARY

a What is the most popular place to buy clothes in your town? Do you buy your clothes there? If not, where?

b Read the text about Zara. Then cover it and answer the questions below from memory.

1 Who is Amancio Ortega?
2 What is unusual about him?
3 What was his first job?
4 When did he open the first Zara store?
5 Where are there Zara stores now?
6 What are the secrets of Zara's success?

c Read the text again and underline any words that are connected with clothes.

d ⬥ **p.150 Vocabulary Bank** *Clothes*.

2 PRONUNCIATION vowel sounds

a **4.1** Put two clothes words in each column. Listen and check. Practice saying the words.

| belt cap clothes coat jacket shirt |
| shoes skirt socks suit sweater top |

b Ask and answer with a partner.

What did you wear yesterday?
What are you going to wear tonight?
What were the last clothes you bought?
What's the first thing you take off when you get home?
Do you always try on clothes before you buy them?
How often do you wear a suit?

3 LISTENING

4.2 Listen to three people being interviewed about Zara. Complete the chart with their information.

	Woman 1	Woman 2	Man	Your partner
1 Have you ever been to a Zara store?				
2 When did you last go there?				
3 Where?				
4 What did you buy?				
5 Are you happy with it?				

4 GRAMMAR present perfect or simple past?

a Interview your partner about Zara (or another store in your area) and write his / her answers in the chart.

b Look at questions 1 and 2 above.
What tense are they?
Which question refers to a specific time in the past?
Which question is about some time in your life?

c ⭕ **p.132 Grammar Bank 4A.** Read the rules and do the exercises.

5 SPEAKING

a Complete the questions with the past participle of the verb.

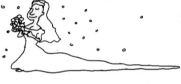

1 Have you ever _worn_ (wear) something only once?
What? When / wear it?

2 Have you ever _____ (be) to a fashion show?
Where? / enjoy it?

3 Have you ever _____ (dance) in very uncomfortable shoes?
Where? What / happen?

4 Have you ever _____ (wear) a costume?
When? What / wear?

5 Have you ever _____ (meet) someone who was wearing exactly the same clothes as you? When? How / you feel?

6 Have you ever _____ (buy) something and never worn it?
What? Why / not wear it?

7 Have you ever _____ (ruin) clothes in the washing machine?
What? What / happen?

8 Have you ever _____ (have) an argument with your family about clothes? What about?

b Interview a partner with the questions. If he / she answers, "Yes, I have," ask follow-up questions in the simple past.

Have you ever worn something only once? Yes I have. A suit.

When did you wear it? To a job interview.

6 **4.3** SONG ♪ *True Blue*

G present perfect + *yet* and *already*
V verb phrases
P /h/, /y/, /dʒ/

> Have you cleaned up your room yet?
> Yes. I did it this morning.

Family conflicts

1 VOCABULARY verb phrases

a Read the magazine article and complete it with these verbs.

changes	cleaned	cleans up
does (x2)	leaves	makes	take

Parents of teenagers tell us what drives them crazy.

Here are some of the top "hates."

1 He never *makes* his bed. If I make it, I find strange things in it like dirty socks, CDs without their cases…

2 He never _____ his room – it's always a mess. The floor is covered with empty soda cans, more dirty socks…

3 She_____ wet towels on the bathroom floor and doesn't pick them up.

4 She walks around the house eating food without a plate, usually just after I've _____ the floor. Then she says "I'm sorry" with a sweet smile.

5 He has breakfast, lunch, and dinner at home, but he never _____ the dishes.

6 When she comes into the living room, she always _____ the channel on the TV – usually when I'm watching my favorite program.

7 We bought a dog for him because he promised to _____ it for a walk every day. Guess who always does it?

8 She always _____ her homework at the last minute – usually late on Sunday night. This means she needs the Internet, just when her sister is "chatting" online with her friends.

b Cover the text. Can you remember the eight bad habits?

c In pairs, say which of these things are a problem in your home and why. What else is a problem?

housework	food
the TV / computer	the bathroom
pets (e.g., a dog)	homework

2 GRAMMAR present perfect + *yet* and *already*

a **4.4** Listen and number the pictures 1–4.

b Listen again and complete the dialogues with a past participle.

1 A Have you _____ yet?
B No, not yet.
A Well, hurry up! I'm going to be late for work.

2 A You left a towel on the floor.
B I haven't _____ a chance to clean up my room yet.
A Well, don't forget to pick it up.

3 A When are you going to do your homework?
B I've already _____ it.
A Really? When?
B I did it on the bus this afternoon.

4 A I've already _____ you to get a plate for that sandwich. I just cleaned the floor, you know.
B OK. Oops – sorry. Too late.

c Look at the conversations and <u>underline</u> *yet* and *already*. What tense is the verb with them? What do you think they mean?

d ⟳ **p.132 Grammar Bank 4B.** Read the rules and do the exercises.

3 PRONUNCIATION & SPEAKING /h/, /y/, /dʒ/

a **4.5** Listen and repeat. Practice saying the sentences.

	He hasn't helped with the housework today.
	Have you used your new computer yet?
	Jim has joined a judo class.

b ⬥ **Communication** *Has he done it yet? p.116.*

4 READING

a Answer the questions in pairs.

1 At what age do young people usually leave home in your country?

2 What do you think is the right age for a young person to leave home? Why?

b Read the paragraphs and put them in order. Number them 1–5.

c Now read the whole article in the correct order. Choose the best summary, A, B, or C.

A Mr. and Mrs. Serrano argued with their children. The children decided to leave home.

B Mr. and Mrs. Serrano argued a lot. Their children were unhappy, so they left home.

C Mr. and Mrs. Serrano argued with their children a lot. They told their children to leave home.

d In pairs, <u>underline</u> any words or phrases you don't know. Try to guess their meaning. Then check with the teacher or with your dictionary. Choose five to learn.

e Do you think Mr. and Mrs. Serrano were right or wrong? Why? Do you think the story will have a happy ending?

f **4.6** Listen and check.

Problems with your teenage children?
Why not throw them out?

A What did the Serranos' boys do? In fact, they didn't go very far from home. The oldest boy, David, went to live with his girlfriend and just started a job in her father's construction company. The youngest son has rented an apartment near the family home. (His mother paid the first month's rent only.)

B So Maria and Mariano asked their sons to leave the family home. But the two boys didn't want to go. Then, Mr. and Mrs. Serrano made an unusual decision – they went to court.

C Do you have rude and moody teenage children living in your home? Have you ever secretly wanted to throw them out? A Spanish couple, Mr. and Mrs. Serrano from Zaragoza in Spain, have done exactly that.

D Maria and her husband, Mariano, lived with their two sons, David, 20, and Mariano, 18. "The situation was impossible," said Maria. "We were always arguing, our children were treating our house like a hotel, and they weren't contributing anything. Also they weren't studying or looking for work. They were complaining all the time and insulting us. They didn't respect us. I love my children, but in the end it was ruining our lives."

E Normally, under Spanish law, parents do not have the right to make their children leave home. But in this case the judge decided that the situation in the Serrano family was "intolerable." He gave Mr. and Mrs. Serrano the right to tell their children to go.

Elizabeth Nash, *The Independent*, October 18, 1999

G comparatives, *as…as, less… than…*
V time expressions: *spend time, waste time*, etc.
P sentence stress

> We work harder, and we have less free time.

Faster, faster!

1 GRAMMAR comparatives, *as… as, less… than…*

a Read the introduction to the article *We're living faster…* Is it optimistic or pessimistic? Why?

b Read it again and cross out the wrong word.
According to James Gleick, today we…
1 work **longer** / **shorter** hours.
2 have **more** / **less** free time.
3 talk **faster** / **more slowly**.
4 are **more relaxed** / **less relaxed**.
5 will probably have **longer** / **shorter** lives than our parents.

c Complete the sentences with *as* or *than*. Then check with the text.
1 We sleep less ____ previous generations.
2 If we don't slow down, we won't live ____ long ____ our parents.

d ⮕ **p.132 Grammar Bank 4C.** Read the rules and do the exercises.

2 PRONUNCIATION sentence stress

> ⚠ Remember! Unstressed words like *a*, *and, as,* and *than* have the sound /ə/, and *-er* is pronounced /ər/.

4.7 Listen and repeat the sentences. Copy the rhythm.
1 I'm busier than a year ago.
2 Life is more stressful than in the past.
3 We work harder than before.
4 We walk and talk faster.
5 I'm not as relaxed as I was.
6 We won't live as long as our parents.

3 READING & VOCABULARY

a You're going to read about some ways in which our lives are faster. Work in pairs. A read 1–3, B read 4–6.

b A tell B about paragraphs 1–3, B tell A about paragraphs 4–6. Use the pictures to help you. Are any of these things true in your country?

c Now read paragraphs 1–6. In pairs, look at the highlighted expressions with the word *time* and guess their meaning.

WE'RE LIVING FASTER,

NOT LONG AGO people believed that in the future we would work less, have more free time, and be more relaxed. But sadly this has not happened. Today we work harder, work longer hours, and are more stressed than ten years ago. We walk faster, talk faster, and sleep less than previous generations. And although we are obsessed with machines that save us time, we have less free time than our parents and grandparents had. But what is this doing to our health?
In his book *Faster: the acceleration of just about everything*, American journalist James Gleick says that people who live in cities are suffering from "hurry sickness" – we are always trying to do more things in less time. As a result, our lives are more stressful. He says that if we don't slow down, we won't live as long as our parents. For most people, faster doesn't mean better.

4 LISTENING & SPEAKING

a **4.8** Look at the questionnaire. Listen to four people answering question 1. Which activity (working, studying, etc.) are they talking about?

1 _____

2 _____

3 _____

4 _____

b Listen again. Why do they spend more (or less) time on these things?

c In pairs, interview each other using the questionnaire.

ARE YOU LIVING FASTER...?

1 Compared to two years ago, do you spend more or less time on these things? Say why.

working or studying	sitting in traffic	cooking
talking on the phone	seeing friends	eating
working on a computer	shopping	sleeping

2 Do you have more or less free time than a year ago? Why? What <u>don't</u> you have enough time for?

3 How do you get to work / school? How long does it take you? Is this longer than a year ago?

4 Do you usually arrive on time...? Why (not)?
for work/school   for your English class   to meet your friends

5 Which machines save you time? Do they make your life simpler or more complicated?

6 Do you waste a lot of time every day? Doing what?

BUT ARE WE LIVING BETTER?

1 No time for the news

Newspaper articles today are shorter and the headlines are bigger. Most people don't have enough time to read the articles; they only read the headlines! On TV and the radio, announcers speak more quickly than ten years ago.

2 No time for stories

In the US there is a book called *One-Minute Bedtime Stories* for children. These are shorter versions of traditional stories, specially written for "busy parents" who want to save time!

3 No time to listen

Some answering machines now have "quick playback" buttons so that we can replay people's messages faster — we can't waste time listening to people speaking at normal speed!

4 No time to relax

Even when we relax, we do everything more quickly. Ten years ago when people went to art galleries, they spent ten seconds looking at each picture. Today they spend just three seconds!

5 No time for slow sports

In the US, baseball is not as popular as before because it moves slowly, and games take a long time. Nowadays many people prefer faster and more dynamic sports like basketball.

6 ...but more time in our cars

The only thing that is slower than before is the way we drive. Our cars are faster, but the traffic is worse, so we drive more slowly. We spend more time sitting in our cars, feeling stressed because we are worried that we won't arrive on time. Experts predict that in ten years the average speed on the road in cities will be 17 km/hour.

4D

G superlatives (+ *ever* + present perfect)
V opposite adjectives
P word stress

It's the most beautiful city I've ever been to.

The world's friendliest city

1 READING & LISTENING

a Read the introduction to the article. In pairs, answer the questions.
1 What are the three tests?
2 Do you think they are good ones?
3 Which city do you think will be the friendliest / most unfriendly?

Big cities often have a reputation for being rude, unfriendly places for tourists. Journalist Tim Moore went to four cities, London, Rome, Paris, and New York, to find out if this is true. He went dressed as a foreign tourist and used three tests to see which city had the friendliest and most polite inhabitants. The three tests were:

1 The photo test

Tim asked people on the street to take his photo (not just one photo, but several – with his hat, without his hat, etc.). Did he find someone to do it?

2 The shopping test

Tim bought something in a store and gave the salesperson too much money. Did the person give back the extra money?

3 The accident test

Tim pretended to fall down on the street. Did anybody come and help him?

Adapted from a newspaper

	New York	Paris	Rome
The photo test	I asked an office worker who was eating his sandwiches to take my photo. "Of course I'll take your picture. Again? Sure! Again? No problem. Have a nice day!"	I asked some gardeners to take my photo in front of the Eiffel Tower. They couldn't stop laughing when they saw my hat.	I asked a very chic woman in sunglasses. She took a photo of me with my hat on, then without my hat. Then with my sunglasses. Then she asked me to take a photo of her!
The shopping test	I bought an *I love New York* T-shirt and drinks from two different people. I gave them too much money, but they both gave me the extra money back.	I bought some fruit in a grocery store and gave the man a lot of coins. He carefully took the exact amount.	I bought a newspaper at a newstand near the train station. It was three euros. I gave the man four, and he didn't give me any change.
The accident test	I fell down in Central Park. I didn't have to wait more than thirty seconds. "Oh, no!" a man said. "Is this your camera? I think it's broken."	I fell down on the Champs Elysées. A minute passed before someone said, "Are you OK?" And he was Scottish!	When I fell down, about eight people immediately hurried to help me.

b Read about what happened in New York, Paris, and Rome. Answer the questions with **NY**, **P**, or **R**.
1 Which city do you think was the friendliest in the photo test? ____
2 In which city did he take a photo, too? ____
3 In the shopping test, where didn't he get the right change? ____
4 Where did he buy a souvenir? ____
5 In the accident test, where did he wait longest for help? ____
6 In which city were people most helpful? ____

c **4.9** Now listen to Tim Moore talking about what happened in London. Answer the questions.

London

The photo test	1	Who did he ask first?
	2	What did the man say?
	3	Who did he ask next? What happened?
The shopping test	4	What did he buy? Where?
	5	How much was it?
	6	Did he get the right change?
The accident test	7	Where did he do the accident test?
	8	Did anyone help him?
	9	What did the man say?

2 GRAMMAR superlatives (+ *ever* + present perfect)

a Cross out the wrong form in these questions.

1 Which city was **the friendlier / the friendliest** of the four?
2 Which city was **the more unfriendly / the most unfriendly**?
3 What's the friendliest place you've ever **been to / be to**?

b Ask and answer the questions with a partner.

c ○ **p.132 Grammar Bank 4D.** Read the rules and do the exercises.

3 VOCABULARY opposite adjectives

a What are the opposites of these adjectives?

friendly   rude   noisy   boring

b ○ **p.145 Vocabulary Bank** *Adjectives.* Do part 2.

c In pairs, choose five questions and ask a partner.

What's ...
the _____ (unfriendly)
the _____ (beautiful)
the _____ (ugly)
the _____ (expensive)
the _____ (polluted)   **place you've ever been to?**
the _____ (exciting)
the _____ (dangerous)
the _____ (noisy)

4 PRONUNCIATION word stress

a Underline the stressed syllable in the adjectives below.

1 It's the most **polluted** city I've ever been to.
2 He's the most **impatient** person I've ever met.
3 This is the most **comfortable** hotel I've ever stayed at.
4 It's the most **interesting** book I've ever read.
5 They're the most **expensive** shoes I've ever bought.
6 It's the most **beautiful** place I've ever seen.

b **4.10** Listen and check. What other words are stressed?

c Listen and repeat the sentences. Copy the rhythm.

5 SPEAKING

a ○ **Communication** *The best and the worst A p.110 B p.114.* Read your instructions and write the names of people, places, etc. in the ovals.

b Ask and answer questions about the things you and your partner wrote in the ovals. Ask for more information.

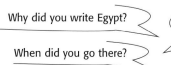

Why did you write Egypt?
Because it's the hottest place I've ever been to.
When did you go there?

DIRECTIONS

4.11 Listen to Allie talking to the hotel receptionist. Order the directions 1–5.

It's the third street on the left. ☐
Go straight ahead, down Sutter Street. ☐
Go out of the hotel and turn left. ☐
Union Square will be right in front of you. ☐
Turn left at Stockton. ☐

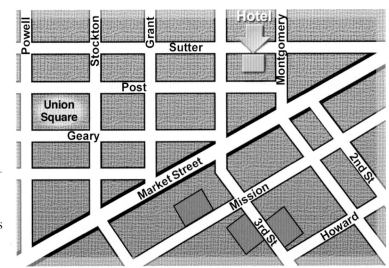

ASKING FOR INFORMATION

a **4.12** Cover the dialogue and listen. Where does Allie want to go? How is she going to get there? Mark the route from Union Square on the map.

⌐YOU SAY	YOU HEAR
Can you recommend a good museum?	Well, SFMOMA is fantastic.
Sorry? Where did you say?	SFMOMA. The San Francisco _____ of Modern Art.
Where is it?	On _____ Street.
How far is it from Union Square?	Not far. It's just a _____ of blocks.
Can I walk from there?	Sure. It'll _____ you ten minutes.
Can you show me on the map?	Yes, Union Square is here, and the museum is here. From Union Square you go down Geary to the _____ and turn right. That's Third Street. Go down Third and you'll see SFMOMA on the _____.
What time does it open?	It opens at _____.
Thanks very much.	Have a good day. I'm sure you'll _____ the museum!

b Complete the **YOU HEAR** phrases. Listen and check.

c **4.13** Listen and repeat the **YOU SAY** phrases. Copy the rhythm.

d In pairs, role-play the dialogue. **A** (book open) you're the receptionist, **B** (book closed) you're Allie. Change roles.

SOCIAL ENGLISH looking for Union Square

a **4.14** Listen and circle **a** or **b**.

1 Allie and the man... **a** have met before. **b** haven't met before.
2 Mark is... **a** meeting Allie later. **b** in a meeting.
3 Del Monico's is... **a** a coffee shop. **b** a restaurant.
4 Brad wants to... **a** go shopping with Allie. **b** take Allie to Union Square.
5 Brad loves... **a** Allie's conversation. **b** Allie's pronunciation.

b Complete the **USEFUL PHRASES**, Listen again and check.

c **4.15** Listen and repeat the phrases. How do you say them in your language?

USEFUL PHRASES

B Don't I k_____ you?
A I don't t_____ so.
B What are you d_____ here?
A I'm l_____ for (Union Square).
A That's really k_____ of you.
A Are you s_____?

a Read the text and match the questions with paragraphs 1–5.

What is it famous for? ☐

What is the weather like? ☐

What is the best thing about it? Do you like living there? ☐

Describe your hometown. ☐

Where do you live? Where is it? How big is it? ☐

b Complete the text with these words.

air city festival lifestyle parks
population shopping streets tourist weather

c Find one grammar mistake in each highlighted phrase. Correct it.

The place where I live

1 I live in Guadalajara, which is the largest ¹ _city_ in the state of Jalisco in Mexico. It's ² _____ is over three million people, making it the second bigger city in Mexico.

biggest

2 Guadalajara is a beautiful place, and it's great for walking around. There are lots of tree-lined ³ _____, and the city is full of monuments, ⁴ _____, and fountains. There is many reminders of the city's rich history, with fabulous colonial architecture everywhere you look.

3 The ⁵ _____ here is ideal – both summer and winter arc mild and pleasant. During the summer months, it often rain in the afternoons . Afterwards, the ⁶ _____ is much cleaner.

4 Guadalajara is known for many things, especially mariachi bands, who originated here . Every September Guadalajara holds its famous mariachi ⁷ _____ , attracting musicians from all over the world. One of the biggest ⁸ _____ attractions is the Mercado Libertad, the largest covered market in Mexico. Some people calls it a ⁹ _____ paradise.

5 But I think the best things about Guadalajara are the people and the ¹⁰ _____ . It's a major business center, yet the pace seems to remain calm and leisurely. The people have a real sense of history, and that's why I like live here so much.

WRITE a description of the place where you live.
Write five paragraphs. Answer the questions in **a** in the correct order.

CHECK your description for mistakes (grammar , punctuation , and spelling).
Attach a photo if you can.

GRAMMAR

Circle the correct answer, a, b, or c.

What's _____ name?

a yours (b) your c you

1 _____ ever been to a Zara store?
   a Do you
   b Have you
   c Did you

2 I've never _____ him in a suit and tie.
   a seen
   b see
   c saw

3 **A** Would you like a coffee?
   B No, thanks. _____ four cups today.
   a I've had already
   b I've already had
   c I already have had

4 You haven't done the dishes _____.
   a already
   b never
   c yet

5 I've _____ seen that movie twice.
   a already
   b ever
   c yet

6 The traffic is _____ than it was an hour ago.
   a badder
   b worse
   c more bad

7 Radio announcers speak more _____ than before.
   a quickly
   b quick
   c quicker

8 TV game shows aren't as _____ they once were.
   a popular than
   b popular that
   c popular as

9 What's the _____ city you've ever seen?
   a most beautiful
   b more beautiful
   c beautifulest

10 This is the _____ city in the world.
   a most noisiest
   b noisiest
   c noisier

`10`

VOCABULARY

a verb phrases

Complete the phrases.

_____make_____ your bed

| do | pick up | take out | clean up | waste |

1 _____ your room
2 _____ things on the floor
3 _____ the garbage
4 _____ the dishes
5 _____ time

b clothes

Complete the sentences.

That's a very nice j_acket_.

1 Levi's are famous for their j_____.
2 Business people usually have to wear a s_____ to work.
3 I always t_____ on clothes before I buy them.
4 Take o_____ your coat. It's very hot in here.
5 Put on your p_____ and go to bed.

c adjectives

Write the opposite adjective.

big   _____small_____

1 rude   _____
2 noisy   _____
3 possible   _____
4 dangerous   _____
5 patient   _____

`15`

PRONUNCIATION

a Underline the word with a different sound.

1	 ər	shirt	work	shorts	skirt
2	 aʊ	bought	blouse	towel	mouth
3	 ɛ	friendly	pretty	men	many
4	 eɪ	make	complain	great	fast
5	 y	yet	yellow	already	your

b Underline the stressed syllable.

informa<u>tion</u>

| pajamas | already | nearly | busier | friendliest |

`10`

CAN YOU UNDERSTAND THIS TEXT?

N 1952, Audrey Hepburn was in Rome, making the movie *Roman Holiday*. She was **engaged** to marry James Hanson, a London "playboy," and she asked a famous Italian designer, Zoe Fontana, to make her a dress for the **wedding** .

Signora Fontana said, "Audrey was 23. She was so young and so beautiful then. She tried the dress on many times. It was in white lace, with a lot of tiny buttons down the back, and she wanted to wear flowers on her head."

But two weeks before the wedding, Audrey Hepburn decided not to get married. She called Zoe Fontana and said, "I've canceled the wedding. But I want another girl to wear my **wedding dress** , perhaps a poor girl who could never pay for a dress like this one. Find a beautiful young woman and give the dress to her."

Signora Fontana found a poor 20-year-old girl in Latina, a town near Rome. She was exactly the same size as Hepburn and the dress fit her perfectly. Her name was Amabile Altobello.

Signora Altobello said, "I wanted to get married, but my **fiancé** and I didn't have enough money for a wedding. When Audrey Hepburn gave me the dress, it was like a dream come true. Everybody in the town was very excited, and they also gave us furniture, and even arranged a **honeymoon** for us in Paris."

Today Signora Altobello is over 75 years old, but she still has the dress. "We are still poor and we have had a hard life, but we have three daughters and five grandchildren. We have had a happy **marriage** , so the dress brought me luck."

Adapted from a newspaper

a Read the article and mark the sentences T (true), F (false), or DS (doesn't say).

1 Audrey Hepburn was going to marry a playboy.
2 She wanted to get married in Rome.
3 Her wedding dress was white with flowers on it.
4 Before the wedding, she fell in love with another man.
5 She asked Zoe Fontana to give the dress to a friend.
6 Amabile Altobello was the same age as Audrey Hepburn.
7 The people of Latina also gave her things for her house.
8 Amabile Altobello and her husband are still married.

b Guess the meaning of the highlighted words.

CAN YOU UNDERSTAND THESE PEOPLE?

a **4.16** Listen and circle the correct answer, a, b, or c.

1 He thought the fashion show was _____ .
   a exciting   b interesting   c boring
2 The woman bought _____ .
   a a shirt   b a skirt   c some shoes
3 The floor is _____ .
   a wet   b dry   c dirty
4 What time does he finish work?
   a 7:00   b 8:00   c 9:00
5 The most beautiful place he's been to is _____ .
   a the Amazon rainforest   b Phuket   c the Grand Canyon

b **4.17** Listen to an interview with a model. Mark the sentences T (true) or F (false).

1 She often wears clothes she doesn't like.
2 She broke her leg during a fashion show.
3 She has never been to Africa.
4 She went to Argentina two years ago.
5 She would like to go to India again.

CAN YOU SAY THIS IN ENGLISH?

a Can you...? Yes (✓)

☐ say what clothes you wore yesterday
☐ say what housework you / other people in your family do
☐ say if you have more or less free time than last year, and why

b Make five questions with the present perfect and a superlative.

What / good book / ever / read?
What's the best book you've ever read?

1 What / hot place / ever / be to?
2 What / bad movie / ever / see?
3 Who / generous person / ever / meet?
4 What / good restaurant / ever / be to?
5 What / long trip / taken?

c Ask your partner the questions in **b**.

5A

G uses of the infinitive
V verbs + infinitive
P word stress

> I want to go to the party.

Are you a party animal?

How to survive at a party...
(when you don't know anybody!)

Has this ever happened to you? You arrive at a party or wedding reception where you don't know anybody. Everybody there seems to know each other. What can you do? Here are five simple tips.

- Don't stand in the corner. You need [1] ___to be___ positive. Find somebody you think you would like [2] _____ and go and introduce yourself.

- Try [3] _____ impersonal questions like "I love your bag. Where did you get it?" That will help [4] _____ a conversation.

- Try [5] _____ the conversation. When you are nervous, it's very easy [6] _____ about yourself all the time. Nobody wants [7] _____ to your life story when they've only just met you.

- Smile, smile, smile. Use your body language [8] _____ a positive, friendly impression. That way people will want [9] _____ to you.

- If you want [10] _____ from a really boring person, say that you are going to the bar [11] _____ another drink or that you need [12] _____ to the restroom. Don't come back!

1 SPEAKING

Interview a partner with the questionnaire. Ask for more information. Is your partner a "party animal"?

Do you like going to parties? Why (not)?
Do you like giving parties? Why (not)?

When was the last time you went to a party or celebration? (for example, a wedding, a birthday party, etc.)

Whose party was it?

Did you have a good time?

What did you wear?

What kind of music did they play?

Did you dance?

Did you meet anybody new?

What did you have to eat and drink?

Did you stay until the end?

2 GRAMMAR uses of the infinitive

a Read the article about parties. Complete the five rules with an infinitive.

to ask	to~~ be~~	not to dominate	to escape	to get
to give	to go	to listen	to meet	to start	to talk (x2)

b Read the article again and then cover it. Can you remember the tips?

c Match the examples A–C from the text with rules 1–3 below.

> A It's very easy **to talk** about yourself all the time.
> B Say that you're going to the bar **to get** another drink.
> C Try **to ask** impersonal questions.

Use the infinitive...
1 after some verbs (e.g., *want*, *try*, etc.) ☐
2 after adjectives ☐
3 to say why you do something. ☐

d ➡ **p.134 Grammar Bank 5A.** Read the rules and do the exercises.

3 READING & LISTENING

a Read this article about the right things to say to different people at parties. In pairs, guess how to complete the **Don't say** phrases.

What to say
(and what not to say)
to people at parties

If you're talking to a doctor…
Don't say: I have a _____ . Could you _____ ?
Say: You look tired. Would you like a drink?

If you're talking to a teacher…
Don't say: You're so lucky! You have _____ .
Say: I'm sure it's very difficult to motivate teenagers.

If you're talking to a travel agent…
Don't say: Can you recommend _____ ?
Say: What's the most interesting place you've ever been to?

If you're talking to a hairdresser…
Don't say: What do you think of _____ ? Is it too _____ ?
Say: What do you think will be the new style this year?

If you're talking to a psychiatrist…
Don't say: Are you _____ ?
Say: Do you work with children or adults?

b 🔊 **5.1** Now listen to some people at a party who say the wrong things. Complete the *Don't say* phrases. Did you guess any of them?

c Listen to the people at the party again. Complete the conversations with an infinitive.

Conversation 1	I want _____ _____ him a "Happy Birthday."
Conversation 2	Maybe you would like _____ _____ my class sometime.
Conversation 3	I'd like _____ _____ somewhere hot.
Conversation 4	You're just the person I want _____ _____ to.
Conversation 5	I need _____ _____ to the restroom.

4 VOCABULARY   verbs + infinitive

a ⭕ **p.154 Vocabulary Bank** *Verb forms* (Verb + infinitive). Look at some other verbs followed by the infinitive. Highlight any that you didn't know.

b ⭕ **Communication** *Guess the infinitive A p.110 B p.114.*

5 PRONUNCIATION & SPEAKING   word stress

> ⚠️ Two- and three-syllable nouns and adjectives usually have the stress on the first syllable. With verbs, the stress is often on the second syllable. Always <u>un</u>derline the stress in new words.

a In pairs <u>un</u>derline the stressed syllable in these words.

dangerous	decide	difficult	forget	important
interesting	possible	pretend	promise	remember

b 🔊 **5.2** Listen and check. Practice saying the words.

c Choose five questions and ask a partner.

Do you find it **difficult to remember** people's names?

Do you think it's **important to learn** to cook?

What's the most **interesting place to visit** in your town?

Have you ever **forgotten to turn off** your cell phone in a movie theater or a concert hall?

Do you think it's **possible to learn** a foreign language without going to the country?

Is there any part of your town where it's **dangerous to go** at night?

Do you always **remember to send** your friends a birthday card?

When was the last time you **promised not to come** home late?

Have you ever **pretended to be** sick (when you weren't)?

Have you **decided to go** anywhere next summer?

5
B

G uses of the *-ing* form of verbs
V verbs followed by *-ing*
P /ŋ/

I love waking up on a sunny morning.

What makes you feel good?

We asked readers from all over the world to tell us what makes them feel good.

- Eating outside. I enjoy sitting in street cafes or having meals in the yard, even when the weather's not perfect — which it often isn't.

- Being with people I like (and not being with people I don't like).

- Sitting on a plane when it takes off. You can't control what's going to happen for the next 2–3 hours, so you can really relax.

- Waking up on a sunny morning during my vacation when I know I have a whole day ahead to do whatever I feel like doing.

- Getting out of the city. It doesn't matter where to: to the beach, or to the country, or to the forest. Being in the middle of nature makes me feel alive.

- Watching heavy rain storms through the window from a comfortable, warm room with a fire, and knowing I don't need to go out.

- Talking to intelligent people: good conversation is one of life's great pleasures.

- Having time for myself. Unfortunately, it doesn't happen very often.

- Reading books or magazines in English — I'm Colombian, and I still find it hard to believe that I can enjoy reading without using a dictionary in a language that once was a complete mystery.

- Cleaning my closets. It stops me from thinking about my problems.

1 READING

a Read the article once. How many people mention…?
1 the weather
2 vacation and traveling
3 housework
4 nature
5 other people

b Read the article again and put a check (✓) next to the *three* things you agree with most. Then put an (✗) next to any you don't agree with. Compare with a partner. Say why.

c <u>Underline</u> five new words or phrases you want to learn from the text.

2 GRAMMAR uses of the *-ing* form of verbs

> A **Being** with people I like (makes me feel good).
> B I enjoy **sitting** in cafes…
> C I can enjoy reading without **using** a dictionary.

a Match sentences A–C with rules 1–3 below.
Use the *-ing* form…
1 after some verbs (e.g., *enjoy, feel like*, etc.) ☐
2 when we use a verb as a noun (e.g., as the subject of a sentence) ☐
3 when we use a verb after a preposition ☐

b Look at the **highlighted** verbs. Can you remember the spelling rules for making the *-ing* form?

c ➲ **p.134 Grammar Bank 5B.** Read the rules and do the exercises.

d Now write about two things that make *you* feel good (that are not in the article). Compare with a partner.

3 PRONUNCIATION /ŋ/

a **5.3** Listen and repeat the sound picture and the words.

ŋ	thing	bring	wrong	language
	sitting	watching	thanks	think

b ⟹ **p.159 Sound Bank.** Look at the typical spellings for this sound.

> ⚠ When we add *-ing* /ŋ/ to a verb, the pronunciation of the original verb doesn't change.
> *do* /du/ → *doing* /ˈduɪŋ/
> *forget* → *forgetting*

c **5.4** Listen and say the *-ing* form of the verbs you hear.

4 VOCABULARY & SPEAKING

a ⟹ **p.154 Vocabulary Bank** *Verb forms* (Verb + *-ing*). Look at other verbs that are followed by the *-ing* form.

b Work in pairs. Choose five things to talk about from the list below.

a job you **don't mind** doing in the house
a sport you **enjoy** watching
something you **feel like** doing tonight
something you **practice** doing regularly
something you **haven't finished** doing today
something you **spend** a lot of time doing
somebody you **dream of** meeting
something you **dislike** doing alone
a country you are **interested in** visiting
something you are **thinking of** doing this weekend
something you have recently **stopped** doing
something you are not very **good at** doing

c A tell B about the five things. Say why. B ask for more information. Then change roles.

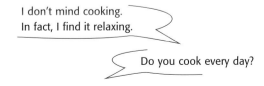

I don't mind cooking.
In fact, I find it relaxing.

Do you cook every day?

5 LISTENING

a Ask and answer these questions in pairs.

Do you ever sing…?
in the shower
in the car
at karaoke bars
while you're listening to a CD
in a choir /ˈkwaɪər/ or a band

b In pairs, say if you think sentences 1–7 are T (true) or F (false).
1 Singing is good for your health.
2 To sing well you need to learn to breathe correctly.
3 People who sing are fatter than people who don't.
4 Not everybody can learn to sing.
5 You need to know how to read music to be able to sing well.
6 If you make a surprised face, you can sing high notes better.
7 It takes a long time to learn to sing better.

c **5.5** Now listen to an interview with the director of a singing school and a student who took a course there. Were you right?

d Listen again. Choose the right answer.

1 When you are learning to sing, you need to _____ correctly.
  a stand   **b** dress   **c** eat
2 Singing well is 95% _____.
  a repeating   **b** listening   **c** breathing
3 Jenny's course lasted _____.
  a one day   **b** one week   **c** one month
4 Jenny has always _____.
  a been good at singing   **b** been in a band   **c** liked singing
5 In the morning the students learned to _____.
  a breathe and sing   **b** listen and breathe   **c** listen and sing
6 At the end of the afternoon, they could sing _____.
  a perfectly   **b** much better   **c** a little better

G *have to, don't have to, must, must not, can't*
V modifiers: *a little (bit), extremely, fairly, really,* etc.
P sentence stress

> You have to come to all the classes.
> You don't have to take a test.

How much can you learn in a month?

1 GRAMMAR *have to, don't have to, must, must not, can't*

a Look at these signs. Have you seen any like these in your school?

A
SILENCE
Exam
in progress

B
Tonight's movie:
Pirates of the Caribbean
Admission free

C
Course fees
to be paid
in advance

D

E
No food or beverages

F
Extra pronunciation class
5:00 P.M.

b Match the signs with the rules.

1 You **have to** pay before you start. ☐
2 You **don't have to** come if you don't want to. ☐
3 You **must not** eat or drink in here. ☐
4 You **must** turn off your cell phone. ☐
5 You **can't** talk near here. ☐
6 You **don't have to** pay to see this. ☐

c Look at the highlighted expressions and answer the questions.

1 Which two phrases mean...?   *You have to*
It is a rule. There's an obligation to do this.   _____

2 Which phrase means...?   _____
It isn't obligatory. It isn't necessary.

3 Which two phrases mean...?   _____
It isn't permitted. It is against the rules.   _____

d ➲ **p.134 Grammar Bank 5C.** Read the rules and do the exercises.

2 PRONUNCIATION sentence stress

a 🔊 **5.6** Listen and write the five sentences.

b Listen again and repeat the sentences. Copy the rhythm.

c Make true sentences about the rules in the school where you are studying English. Use *We have to, We don't have to,* or *We can't.*

1 _____ come to class on time.
2 _____ turn off our cell phones.
3 _____ eat or drink in the classroom.
4 _____ come to class on Saturday.
5 _____ bring a dictionary to class.
6 _____ take a final exam.
7 _____ smoke in the building.
8 _____ do homework after each class.
9 _____ take a test every week.

3 READING & LISTENING

a Do you think people from your country are good at learning languages? Why (not)?

b Read about Anna, an American journalist who took an intensive Portuguese course. Then cover the article and answer the questions.

1 Why did Anna choose to learn Portuguese?
2 Where did she take the course?
3 What did she think was the most difficult thing about Portuguese?
4 Where is she going to take the "tests"?
5 What five things does she have to do?
6 What are the rules?

Anna in São Paulo

How much can you learn in a month?

I work for a magazine, which was doing an article about Americans learning foreign languages. As an experiment, they asked me to learn a completely new language for one month. Then I had to go to the country and take some "tests" to see if I could "survive" in different situations. I decided to study Portuguese because I've always been fascinated by Brazilian culture and really wanted to travel there.

I took a one-month intensive course at a language school in Atlanta. At first, Portuguese sounded like Russian to my ear. Luckily, I found that some words were similar to English, such as *computador* (computer) and *música* (music). However, the pronunciation turned out to be extremely difficult for me. Some of the sounds are hard to imitate because we don't use them in English. Also, the spelling is tricky until you get used to it. For example, the letter *r* at the beginning of a word often sounds like an *h* in English, and the letter *o* at the end sounds like *ooh*. So *Rio* sounds almost like "hee-ooh." Wow!

My course finished yesterday, and I'm traveling to Brazil next week for my tests. A local guide named Fabiana will go with me and will give me a score of 1–10.

These are the tests and the rules:

Tests

You have to…
1 get a taxi.
2 order a drink in a cafe.
3 ask for directions (and follow them).
4 call and ask to speak to someone.
5 ask somebody what time it is.

Rules

– you can't use a dictionary or phrasebook.
– you can't speak English at any time.
– you must not use your hands or mime.

---

c **5.7** Which test do you think will be the easiest for Anna? Which will be the most difficult? Listen to Anna taking the tests in São Paulo and check your answers.

d Listen again. Mark the sentences T (true) or F (false). Correct the false ones.
1 The taxi driver couldn't speak English.
2 Anna understood the waitress's question.
3 She ordered a small coffee.
4 Anna asked for directions to a bank.
5 She couldn't understand what the woman on the street said.
6 Anna couldn't understand everything the woman on the phone said.
7 Anna thought telling the time in Portuguese was very easy.
8 She didn't find out what time it was.
9 Fabiana gave her eight out of ten for her Portuguese.

4 SPEAKING

a How well could you do Anna's five tests in English? How much do you think you can learn in a month?

b Talk to a partner.

Have you ever…

spoken in English on the phone? Who to? What about?
seen a movie in English? Which? How much did you understand?
spoken to a tourist in English? When? Why?
read an English book or magazine? Which one(s)?
asked for directions in a foreign city? Where? What happened?
learned another foreign language? How well can you speak it?

5 VOCABULARY   modifiers

The pronunciation was **extremely** difficult.
I felt **a little** stupid when the taxi driver spoke perfect English.

---

a Complete the chart with the words in the box.

| a little (bit)   extremely   ~~not very~~   fairly   really   ~~very~~ |

Portuguese is ___ very ___ difficult.

not very

b Complete the sentences with one of the words, so they are true for you. Compare with a partner.
1 I'm _____ good at learning languages.
2 I'm _____ motivated to improve my English.
3 English pronunciation is _____ difficult.
4 English grammar is _____ tricky.
5 I'm _____ worried about the next English test.
6 English is _____ useful for my work / studies.

5
D

G expressing movement
V prepositions of movement, sports
P prepositions

The name of the game

The ball went over the net.

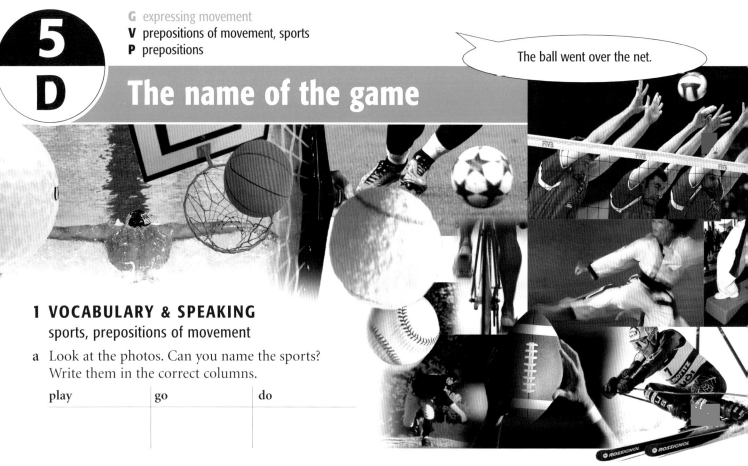

1 VOCABULARY & SPEAKING
sports, prepositions of movement

a Look at the photos. Can you name the sports?
Write them in the correct columns.

play	go	do

b **5.8** Listen and check.

c In pairs, say…

Which of the sports in **a** are usually team sports?
How many **players** are there?
In which sports do you…the ball?
a **hit** b **throw** c **kick** d **shoot**

d Ask and answer with a partner.

Do you play any sports? Which one(s)?
Which sports do you enjoy watching?
Which sports do you hate watching?
Are you (or is anyone in your family) a fan of a sports team?
  Which one?
Do you (or they) watch their games? Where?

e Where did the ball go? Complete with a preposition.

across	along	down	into	over

The ball went _over_ the wall, _____ the street, _____
the steps, _____ the street, and _____ the river.

f ➡ **p.148 Vocabulary Bank** *Prepositions.* Do part 2.

2 GRAMMAR expressing movement

The rules of the game

1 You play this sport outside with one, two, or more
players. You have to hit the ball into a small hole. You
must not hit the ball into the water.

2 You can play this sport outside or inside with two or four
players. You have to hit the ball over a net and the
ball must not go out of bounds.

3 You usually do this sport outside (but it can be inside).
You have to go around a track many times and be the first
one to go past the finish line. Sometimes you have to
go around a country, for example, France.

4 You play this sport outside with two teams. You have to pass
the ball to other players with your foot and try to kick the ball
into the goal. You can't touch the ball with your hands.

5 You play this sport on a field with two teams. You have
to throw the ball to other players and carry the ball into
the end zone to score a touchdown. You also kick the ball
through two high posts to get points.

a Match the rules to the sports in **1**. What are the sports?

b **5.9** Listen and check.

c Look at the sports rules again and the highlighted
words. How do you express movement in English?

d ➡ **p.134 Grammar Bank 5D.** Read the rules and
do the exercises.

3 PRONUNCIATION prepositions

a Match the prepositions with the phonetics. How do you pronounce the words?

across	along	around	into
over	through	toward	

1 /ˈɪntə/ _____
2 /ˈoʊvər/ _____
3 /əˈraʊnd/ _____
4 /tɔrd/ _____
5 /əˈkrɔs/ _____
6 /θru/ _____
7 /əˈlɔŋ/ _____

b **5.10** Listen and check. <u>Und</u>erline the stressed syllable, and practice saying the prepositions.

c ➤ **Communication** *Cross country p.117.* Tell your partner where the runner went.

4 READING & SPEAKING

a How long does a normal soccer match last? How many minutes are added after each half?

b Read the article and complete it with a word from below.

champions	fans	goal	match	field
players	referee	scored	stadium	team

c Read the text again. Number the sentences 1–6.

A Manchester United scored their first goal. ☐
B The Bayern Munich fans started celebrating. ☐
C The 90 minutes finished, and the referee added three minutes. ☐
D Bayern Munich scored a goal. 1
E Manchester United scored their second goal. ☐
F The UEFA president left his seat to go to present the cup. ☐

d What is the most exciting sporting event you've ever seen? Prepare your answers to these questions.

1 What sport was it?
2 When and where was it?
3 Who was taking part?
4 Were you there or did you see it on TV?
5 What happened?

e Ask and answer the questions with a partner.

5 **5.11** SONG ♫ *We are the champions*

Your most exciting sporting moments...
This week, Duc from Vietnam writes:

The most exciting soccer [1] _match_ I have ever seen was the 1999 Champions' League Final between Manchester United and Bayern Munich in the Nou Camp [2] _____ in Barcelona.

After 90 minutes Manchester United was losing 1–0. The Bayern Munich [3] _____ in the stadium were already celebrating their [4] _____'s victory. The Manchester United fans in the stadium and millions around the world were watching in despair.

There were now just three minutes of added time. Twenty seconds passed and United got a corner. The atmosphere in the stadium was incredibly intense. All the Manchester United [5] _____ (including their goalkeeper) were in the Bayern Munich penalty area. David Beckham took the corner and Teddy Sheringham [6] _____. It was 1–1!

The Manchester United fans were ecstatic. There was only about one minute left now, but United attacked again and scored another [7] _____. Now it was 2–1! Thirty seconds later we heard the [8] _____ blow his whistle. The match was over. The United players were the [9] _____! Many of the Bayern fans and players were crying. They had lost the match in less than three minutes.

The next day I read that the UEFA president missed both Manchester United's goals. He was going down to the [10] _____ to give the cup to the German team when United scored their first goal, and he was going back up to his seat when they scored their second! He missed the most exciting and unforgettable three minutes of soccer I have ever seen.

BUYING CLOTHES

5.12 Listen to Allie shopping. Answer the questions.

1 What does Allie want to buy?
2 What size is she?
3 Does she try it on?
4 How much does Allie think it costs?
5 How does she pay?

TAKING SOMETHING BACK

a **5.13** Cover the dialogue and listen. What's the problem with Allie's sweater? Does she exchange it or ask for her money back?

YOU HEAR	YOU SAY
Can I help you?	Yes, I bought this sweater about half an hour ago.
Yes, I remember. Is there a _____?	Yes, I've decided it's too big for me.
What _____ is it?	Medium.
So you need a _____. I don't see one here.	Do you have any more?
I'll go and check. Just a _____.	
I'm sorry but we don't have _____ one in black.	Oh dear.
We can order one for you. It'll only take a few _____.	No, I'm leaving on Saturday.
Would you like to exchange it for _____ else?	Not really. Could I have a refund?
No problem. Do you _____ the receipt?	Yes, here you are.

b Listen again. Complete the **YOU HEAR** phrases.

c **5.14** Listen and repeat the **YOU SAY** phrases. Copy the <u>rhythm</u>.

d In pairs, role-play the dialogue. **A** (book open) you're the salesperson, **B** (book closed) you're Allie. Change roles.

SOCIAL ENGLISH the conference cocktail party

a **5.15** Listen and complete with *Mark*, *Allie*, or *Brad*.

1 _Allie_ tells _____ about the shopping and museum.
2 _____ comes to say hello to _____ and _____.
3 _____ is surprised that _____ and _____ met this morning.
4 _____ asks _____ if she wants a drink.
5 _____ is annoyed, but he goes to get the drinks.

b Complete the USEFUL PHRASES. Listen again and check.

c **5.16** Listen and repeat the phrases. How do you say them in your language?

USEFUL PHRASES

M What did you t_____ of it?
A Never m_____.
A What a l_____ evening!
A I got l_____.
M What would you like to d_____?
B What a good i_____.

Study Link MultiROM

a Read the e-mail to a language school. Check (✓) the questions that Hugo wants the school to answer.

☐ How much do the courses cost?
☐ When do the courses start and finish?
☐ How many students are there in a class?
☐ Are there business English classes?
☐ Where can students stay?
☐ Where are the teachers from?

b Look at the highlighted expressions. How would they be different in an informal e-mail (or letter)?

Formal e-mail	Informal e-mail
Dear Sir / Madam,	_____
I am writing	_____
I would like	_____
I look forward to hearing from you	_____
Sincerely,	_____

From: Hugo Lopez [hlop31@medell.net]

To: The Language Center of California [info@califlang.com]
Subject: Information about courses

Dear Sir / Madam,

I am writing to ask for information about your language courses. I am especially interested in an intensive course of two or three weeks. I am 31 and I work in the library at the National University of Colombia at Medellin. I can read English fairly well, but I need to improve my listening and speaking. The book I am currently studying is at a pre-intermediate level.

I have looked at your website, but there is no information about intensive courses next summer. Could you please send me information about dates and prices? I would also like some information about accommodation. If possible, I would like to stay with a family. My wife is going to visit me for a weekend when I am at the school. Could she stay with me in the same family?

I look forward to hearing from you.

Sincerely,

Hugo Lopez

---

c Read the advertisements and choose a course. Think of two or three questions you would like to ask.

Thai Cooking Classes in Chiang Mai

Learn to cook Thai food in northern Thailand. One week sessions, from April to October. Your accommodation in Chiang Mai is included. Beginners welcome. E-mail us for more information at thaicook@blueelephant.com

Tennis lessons in Canada

One- or two-week sessions in different parts of the country. Professional tennis coaches. All levels, beginners to advanced. Small groups or private lessons. For more information e-mail us at info@cantennis.com

---

WRITE a formal e-mail asking for information. Write two paragraphs.

Paragraph 1 Explain why you are writing and give some personal information.

Paragraph 2 Ask your questions, and ask them to send you information.

CHECK your e-mail for mistakes (grammar , punctuation , and spelling).

GRAMMAR

Circle the correct answer, a, b, or c.

What's _____ name?

a yours   (b) your   c you

1 We want _____ a party next month.
   a have
   b to have
   c having

2 It's often difficult _____ new friends.
   a to make
   b make
   c for make

3 I don't have anything _____ to the wedding.
   a for to wear
   b for wear
   c to wear

4 _____ early on a sunny morning makes me feel good.
   a Waking up
   b Wake up
   c To waking up

5 My brother doesn't enjoy _____ by plane.
   a travel
   b to travel
   c traveling

6 I'm tired of _____ TV. Let's do something different.
   a to watch
   b watching
   c watch

7 I like Saturdays because I _____ work.
   a must not
   b don't have to
   c haven't to

8 She can't come to the movies because she _____ to study.
   a must
   b have
   c has

9 You _____ drive a car without a license.
   a can't
   b must not to
   c don't must

10 The golf ball _____ the hill and into the river.
   a down
   b downed
   c went down

	10

VOCABULARY

a verb phrases

Complete the sentences.

   I don't _enjoy_ going to parties.

decide dream of forget hate hope learn like need start try

1 **A** Which movie would you _____ to see?   **B** I don't care. You choose.
2 Don't _____ to buy some milk at the supermarket.
3 I _____ finding the perfect job someday.
4 Your hair's very long. You _____ to go to the hairdresser.
5 What did you _____? Are you coming or not?
6 I'd like to _____ to play chess. Can you teach me?
7 I always travel by train or car because I _____ flying.
8 I _____ to see you soon.
9 _____ to read in English as much as you can.
10 Don't _____ running until you hear "Go."

b prepositions of movement

Complete the sentences with a preposition.

   In the 100-meter race the athletes have to run _along_ a track.
1 In golf you have to hit the ball _____ the hole.
2 In tennis you have to hit the ball _____ the net.
3 In soccer you have to pass the ball _____ the other players on your team.
4 In auto racing you have to drive _____ a track.
5 In basketball you have to throw the ball _____ the net.

c sports verbs

Complete the sentences with *play*, *do*, and *go* in the correct form.

1 We _____ baseball every Saturday.
2 I _____ skiing last year.
3 He _____ judo twice a week.
4 She often _____ cycling after work.
5 They love _____ aerobics.

	20

PRONUNCIATION

a Underline the word with a different sound

1	ɪ	hit	mind	kick	finish
2	aɪ	promise	like	decide	tired
3	eɪ	hate	have	game	race
4	aʊ	out	around	down	throw
5	ū	through	must	doing	two

b Underline the stressed syllable.

information

promise decide forget enjoy practice

	10

CAN YOU UNDERSTAND THIS TEXT?

a Read the article. Is Alexandra Kosteniuk…?

1 beautiful but not very good at chess

2 not very beautiful but good at chess

3 beautiful and good at chess

b Read the article again and mark
the sentences T (true), F (false),
or DS (doesn't say).

1 The International Chess Federation
wants chess to have a more modern image.

2 Alexandra never wears glasses.

3 Alexandra's father taught her to play chess.

4 She became a grandmaster after playing
chess for five years.

5 She thinks that chess should be more
popular.

6 If you have Internet access, you can play
chess with Alexandra.

7 Nigel Short has an attractive personality.

The new face of chess

Alexandra Kosteniuk is changing the world of chess. The International Chess Federation has asked her to be the new face of the game, which traditionally has had an image of middle-aged men wearing glasses.

Alexandra started playing chess when she was five. She learned to play from her father and became a grandmaster when she was only 14. Experts say that her game is one of the most exciting they have seen for a long time.

"Chess is not as popular as it should be, and I think I could help it," Kosteniuk said last week. "It is an honor for me to be described as the face of the game." She has her own website with pictures, poems, and the opportunity to play chess against her.

Making the game faster is another part of the campaign to make chess more popular. There are now strict time limits for making moves. Games that once lasted for hours can now take place in five minutes. The longest international tournament games, which sometimes took days, now last only four to seven hours.

Grandmaster Nigel Short says, "There are a lot of attractive women in chess, but Alexandra Kosteniuk has made a very big impression. She is obviously very talented. Any sport needs attractive personalities, and I have no problem with marketing the game through her."

Adapted from a newspaper

CAN YOU UNDERSTAND THESE PEOPLE?

a **5.17** Listen to five short conversations. Circle a, b, or c.

1 Anna _____ to go to the party.
   a wants   b doesn't want   c isn't sure if she wants

2 The concert was _____.
   a awful   b pretty good   c very good

3 Claudia is _____ late for class.
   a never   b hardly ever   c often

4 The woman speaks _____ very well.
   a Spanish   b Italian   c Portuguese

5 Henri kicked the ball _____.
   a into the goal   b over the top of the goal   c to the left of the goal

b **5.18** Listen and complete the form for the sports center.

Sport: ¹ _____	Day: ² _____
Time: from ³ _____	to ⁴ _____
Name: ⁵ _____	Cost: ⁶ _____

CAN YOU SAY THIS IN ENGLISH?

a Can you…? Yes (✓)

☐ talk about the last party you went to

☐ talk about what makes you feel good and why

☐ say what you have to do to learn a language

☐ describe the rules for a sport you know

b Complete the questions with a verb
in the *-ing* form or infinitive.

1 Where do you want _____ for your
next vacation?

2 Have you ever tried to learn _____?
What happened?

3 Do you enjoy _____? Why (not)?

4 Do you have to _____ at work / school?

5 What sport would you like _____?

c Ask your partner the questions in **b**.
Ask for more information.

G *if* + present, *will* + base form (first conditional)
V confusing verbs
P vowels

If you change lines, the other one will move faster.

If something bad can happen, it will

1 GRAMMAR *if* + present, *will* + base form

a Read the beginning of the story. Why do you think the Italian doesn't want to lend his newspaper to the American?

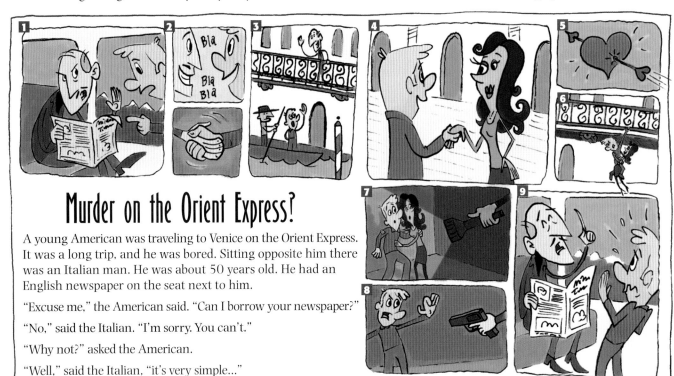

Murder on the Orient Express?

A young American was traveling to Venice on the Orient Express. It was a long trip, and he was bored. Sitting opposite him there was an Italian man. He was about 50 years old. He had an English newspaper on the seat next to him.

"Excuse me," the American said. "Can I borrow your newspaper?"

"No," said the Italian. "I'm sorry. You can't."

"Why not?" asked the American.

"Well," said the Italian, "it's very simple..."

b Look at the pictures. Number the rest of the story 1–9.

☐ "If you meet Nicoletta, you'll fall in love with her."
☐ "If we start talking, we'll become friends."
☐ "If I invite you to my house, you'll meet my beautiful daughter, Nicoletta."
☐ "So that's why I won't lend you my newspaper."
☐ "If I find you, I'll kill you."
☐ "If you fall in love with her, you'll run away together."
☐ "If we become friends, I'll invite you to my house in Venice."
1 "If I lend you my newspaper, we'll start talking."
☐ "If you run away, I'll find you."

c 6.1 Listen and check. Then cover sentences 1–9 and look at the pictures. Try to remember the sentences.

d Look at the sentences again. What tense is the verb after *if*? What tense is the other verb?

e ➲ **p.136 Grammar Bank 6A.** Read the rules and do the exercises.

2 VOCABULARY confusing verbs

a What's the difference between *know* and *meet*, and *borrow* and *lend*? Underline the right verb.

1 You'll **know** / **meet** my beautiful daughter, Nicoletta.
2 Do you **know** / **meet** my sister's boyfriend?
3 Can I **borrow** / **lend** your newspaper?
4 If I **borrow** / **lend** you my newspaper, we'll start talking.

b ➲ **p.149 Vocabulary Bank** *Verbs*. Do part 2.

3 READING

a If you are in a supermarket and you change lines, what will happen?

b Read the first paragraph of the article *Murphy's Law*. Who was Murphy? What exactly is his law?

c Read the rest of the article. Can you guess how the examples 1–8 of Murphy's Law finish?

Murphy's Law

If you change lines in a supermarket, what will happen? The line that you were in before will move more quickly. You know what will happen because there's a law of life that says, "if something bad can happen, it will happen." It's called Murphy's Law, and it took its name from Captain Edward Murphy, an American airplane engineer in the 1940s. He was investigating why planes crashed, and not surprisingly, he got a reputation for always thinking of the worst thing that can happen in every situation…

At home

1 If you wash your car,… ☐
2 If you look for something you lost,… ☐

Social life

3 If you wear something white,… ☐
4 If someone near you is smoking,… ☐

Shopping

5 If you find something that you really like in a store,… ☐
6 If you take something that doesn't work back to a store,… ☐

Transportation

7 If you stop waiting for a bus and start walking,… ☐
8 If you get to the station and a train is just leaving,… ☐

d Now match the examples 1–8 with A–H below.

A you'll spill coffee on it.
B it'll rain.
C they won't have it in your size.
D it'll be your train.
E the bus will come.
F it'll start working.
G you'll find it in the last place you look.
H the smoke will always go directly toward you.

e In pairs, look only at the first half of the sentences in the text. How many of the "laws" can you remember? Can you think of any others?

4 PRONUNCIATION vowels

a **6.2** Listen and repeat the pairs of vowels. Practice making the difference.

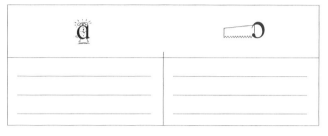

b Put these words into the chart.

beautiful	excuse	fall	got	if	law
leave	look	meet	move	opposite	push
seat	stop	talk	took	will	win

c **6.3** Listen and check. Practice saying the words.

d ⊃ p.157 Sound Bank. Look at the typical spellings for these sounds.

5 SPEAKING

In pairs or small groups, invent some new "Murphy's Laws" beginning with the sentence halves below.

If you're single and you meet somebody you really like,…

If you throw something away,…

If you park a long way from where you're going,…

If your baby goes to sleep late,…

If you're driving somewhere and you're in a hurry,…

If you arrive very early to catch a plane,…

If you get to work late,…

If you leave your cell phone at home,…

If you push a door,…

6 B

G *if* + past, *would* + base form (second conditional)
V animals
P stress and rhythm

> If I saw a bear, I'd run away.

Never smile at a crocodile

Would *you* survive?

We all enjoy seeing wild animals on television. But what would happen if we met one in real life? Take our animal quiz and see if you would survive.

1 What would you do ...

... **if you were in the middle of a river and suddenly you saw a crocodile swimming quickly toward you?**

a I would try to swim to the shore as quickly as possible. ☐
b I wouldn't move. I'd stay still and wait for the crocodile to go away. ☐
c I would try to hit the crocodile in the face. ☐

2 What would you do ...

... **if you were in a forest and a very large bear came toward you?**

a I would climb up the nearest tree. ☐
b I would lie on the ground and pretend to be dead. ☐
c I would run away as fast as I could. ☐

3 What would you do ...

... **if you were in the middle of a field and a bull started running toward you?**

a I would run. ☐
b I would throw something (e.g., my hat) in another direction. ☐
c I would shout and wave my arms. ☐

1 SPEAKING & LISTENING

a Read the quiz and put a check (✓) next to your answers, **a**, **b**, or **c**. Compare with a partner.

b **6.4** Now listen to a survival expert. Did you choose the right answer?

c Listen again. Why are the other two answers wrong? Compare what you heard with a partner.

2 GRAMMAR *if* + past, *would* + base form

a Look at question 1 in *Would you survive?* and answer these questions.

1 Is the crocodile situation...?
   a one that could easily happen to you
   OR
   b one that is not very probable
2 What tense of the verb goes after *if*?
3 What is the form of the other verbs in the question and in the answers?

b ○ **p.136 Grammar Bank 6B.** Read the rules and do the exercises.

3 PRONUNCIATION stress and rhythm

a **6.5** Listen and repeat the sentence halves and then the whole sentence. Copy the rhythm.

1 If I <u>saw</u> a <u>crocodile</u>,   I'd <u>climb</u> a <u>tree</u>.
2 What would you <u>do</u>   if you <u>saw</u> a <u>snake</u>?
3 We could <u>have</u> a <u>dog</u>   if we <u>had</u> a <u>yard</u>.
4 If a <u>bear</u> <u>attacked</u> me,   I wouldn't <u>move</u>.
5 If <u>I</u> were <u>you</u>,   I'd <u>go</u> on a <u>safari</u>.

b Cover the right-hand column. Try to remember the sentences.

4 VOCABULARY animals

a Answer the questions with a partner.

1 Do you (or did you ever) have a pet? What?
2 What's the most dangerous animal in your country?
3 What's your favorite movie about an animal?
4 What's your favorite cartoon animal?
5 If you went on a safari, what animal would you most like to see?
6 Are there any animals or insects that you are really afraid of?
7 If you were an animal, what would you like to be?

b ➡ **p.151 Vocabulary Bank** *Animals.*

c **6.6** Listen. Which animal can you hear?

5 SPEAKING

Choose five questions and ask your partner.

What would you do...

... if you saw a mouse in your bedroom?
... if you were driving and a bee flew into the car?
... if you saw a spider in the bathtub?
... if you were on a beach that was famous for shark attacks?
... if someone offered to buy you a fur coat?
... if you went to your friends' house for dinner and they gave you horse meat?
... if your neighbor's dog barked all night?
... if a friend asked you to watch their cat or dog?

6 READING

a Can you remember the best way to survive a crocodile attack?

b Read the article about crocodiles and mark the sentences T (true), F (false), or DS (doesn't say).

1 The Australian crocodile is bigger than all other kinds.
2 Crocodiles can run faster than horses.
3 Crocodiles only attack you if you are in the water.
4 The German tourist didn't know that there might be crocodiles in the lake.
5 The crocodile also attacked the woman's friends.
6 The Australian boy was killed when he and his friends went swimming in a river.
7 His friends escaped by climbing a tree.
8 Norman Pascoe's aunt was attacked by a crocodile.
9 She hit the crocodile on the nose, and it opened its mouth.

NATURE'S PERFECT KILLING MACHINE

THE AUSTRALIAN CROCODILE is the largest crocodile in the world. It can grow up to seven meters long, and the biggest can weigh up to 1,000 kilos. It has only two muscles to open its mouth but 40 to close it!

What makes crocodiles so dangerous is that they attack extremely quickly, and they take their victims under the water to drown them. They usually attack in the water, but they can suddenly come out of a river and attack animals or people. And they can run on land as fast as 17 kilometers per hour.

Every year in Australia there are crocodile attacks on humans. Two years ago a 24-year-old German tourist died when she went for a swim in a lake. Although there were signs warning people that there might be crocodiles, the woman and her friends decided to go for a midnight swim. The woman suddenly disappeared, and the next morning her body was found. Near it was a four-meter-long crocodile. And only last month two Australian boys watched in horror as their friend was killed by a crocodile when they were washing their bikes in a river. They climbed a tree and stayed there for 22 hours while the crocodile waited below.

But you CAN survive a crocodile attack. Last year Norman Pascoe, a 19-year-old, was saved from a crocodile when his aunt hit it on the nose. Norman's aunt said: "I hit it and I shouted, 'Help!' The crocodile suddenly opened its mouth and my nephew escaped."

c Cover the text. In pairs, can you remember what these numbers refer to?

| 7 | 1,000 | 40 | 17 | 24 | 22 | 19 |

d Read the text again and check your answers.

7 **6.7** SONG ♫ *Wouldn't it be nice?*

6C

G *may / might* (possibility)
V word building: noun formation
P sentence stress, *-ion* endings

I might go, but I might not.

Decisions, decisions

1 SPEAKING

a Complete the definitions with words from the box. Underline the stressed syllable.

decision   decisive   indecisive   decide

1 _____ /dɪˈsaɪd/ *verb* think about two or more possibilities and choose one

2 _____ /dɪˈsɪʒn/ *noun* from 1

3 _____ /dɪˈsaɪsɪv/ *adj* good at making decisions

4 _____ /ˌɪndɪˈsaɪsɪv/ *adj* not good at making decisions

b Interview your partner with the questionnaire. Ask for more information. Which of you is more indecisive?

Are you indecisive?

	Yes	No	Sometimes
Do you find it difficult to make decisions?			
Do you have problems deciding…			
– what to wear when you go out?			
– what to eat in a restaurant?			
– what to do in your free time?			
– where to go on vacation?			
– what to buy when you go shopping?			
Do you often change your mind about something?			
Do you think you are indecisive?			

Yes.   No.   I'm not sure.

2 GRAMMAR *may / might*

a 🔊 6.8 Cover the dialogue and listen. Who is indecisive, Roz or Mari? About what?

R Hi, Mari. It's me… Roz.

M Hi, Roz.

R Listen, Mari. It's about the party tonight.

M You're going, aren't you?

R I don't know. I'm not sure. I might _____ but I might not. I can't decide.

M Oh, come on. You'll love it. And you might _____ somebody new.

R OK. I'll go then.

M Good. So what are you going to wear?

R That's the other problem. I'm not sure what to wear. I might _____ my new black pants. Or maybe the red dress – what do you think?

M If I were you, I'd wear the red dress.

R But the red dress may _____ too small for me now…

M Well, wear the black pants then.

R OK. I'll wear the black pants.

M How are you getting there?

R I might _____ with Eduardo… or Ruth… or I may _____ there… I'm not sure yet.

M OK, I'll see you there. Bye.

R Bye.

M Hello?

R Mari? It's me again. Roz. Listen. I changed my mind. Sorry. I'm not going to go to the party.

b Listen again and complete the conversation.

c Underline the verb phrases in the dialogue with *may / might*. Do we use them for…?

1 an obligation   OR   2 a possibility

d ⊙ **p.136 Grammar Bank 6C.** Read the rules and do the exercises.

3 PRONUNCIATION & SPEAKING

a **6.9** Listen and repeat the *may* / *might* phrases from the dialogue. Copy the <u>rhythm</u>. Are *may* and *might* stressed?

b **○ Communication** *Decisions, decisions A p.110 B p.115.* In pairs, role-play being indecisive.

4 READING

a You are going to read some tips to help people make decisions. Before you read, cover the text. In pairs, try to predict what one of the tips will be.

b Quickly look through the article. Is your tip there? Then complete the text with the verbs below.

ask	compare	confuse	feel	have
make (x2)	~~take~~	use	wait	

c Read the article again. In pairs, try to decide which tip is the best. Can you think of one other tip?

How to make decisions
When you have to choose between two possibilities:

- ¹ *Take* your time. The most important thing is not to make a decision in a hurry.

- ²_____ a list of the positive and negative points for both options. Then decide which points are most important and ³_____ the two lists.

- If you ⁴_____ other people for their advice, don't ask more than one or two. If you ask a lot of people, this will probably ⁵_____ you.

- ⁶_____ your imagination to help you. Imagine yourself in both situations. How do you ⁷_____? Relaxed or stressed?

- After you've made a decision, ⁸_____ a little while before you tell other people, to see how you feel. If you feel comfortable with your decision after an hour, then you have probably made the right decision.

- Finally, remember that you can't ⁹_____ everything. Choosing one of two possibilities always means that you can't have the one you didn't choose. And it's impossible to *always* ¹⁰_____ the right decision!

5 VOCABULARY noun formation

⚠ With some verbs you can make a noun by adding *-ion*, *-sion*, or *-ation*, for example, *decide > decision*; *imagine > imagination*

a Complete the chart.

Verb	Noun
confuse	confusion
decide	decision
imagine	imagination
inform	_____
elect	_____
invite	_____
organize	_____
educate	_____
translate	_____
communicate	_____

b **6.10** Listen and check. <u>U</u>nderline the stressed syllable in the verbs and nouns.

1 How do you pronounce *-sion* and *-tion*?
2 Where is the stress in nouns that finish in *-ion*?

c Complete the questions with a noun from **a**.

1 When was the last time you had to make a big _____?
2 What kind of _____ do you often get from the Internet?
3 When was the last time you had an _____ to a wedding?
4 Who won the last general _____ in your country?
5 Do you belong to any _____ (for example, Greenpeace, etc.)?
6 What do you think is the best form of _____, e-mail, telephone, or text-messaging?

d In pairs, ask and answer the questions in **c**. Ask for more information.

G *should / shouldn't*
V *get*
P /ʊ/, sentence stress

> You should talk to her.

What should I do?

1 LISTENING & READING

a Read this information about a radio show.

 1 What kind of program is it?
 2 Why do people call the program?
 3 Would you call a program like this?

RADIO guide

WHAT'S THE PROBLEM?

Weekdays 8:00–8:45 A.M.

Daily advice program with Jack Green. Whatever your problem, call the program and ask for help. Listeners can e-mail their suggestions to the *What's the Problem?* website. Today's subject is "friends."

b **6.11** Listen to three people calling *What's the Problem?* Then complete the sentences with one word.

 | clothes | jealousy | money |

 Barbara's problem is about _____.
 Kevin's problem is about _____.
 Catherine's problem is about _____.

c Now listen again. What exactly are their problems? Compare what you understood with your partner.

d Read the e-mails that listeners sent to the *What's the Problem?* website. Match two e-mails to each problem. Write Barbara, Kevin, or Catherine.

What's the Problem?   MESSAGE BOARDS

AUTHOR   MESSAGE

1 Aki

Hi _____,
I think you should talk to your girlfriend, not your friend. She might like the way your friend treats her. Maybe that's why he does it. Why don't you tell her to ask him to stop?
Aki

2 Marcia

Dear _____,
If I were you, I wouldn't say anything to your friend. I think you should lock your clothes in a closet. She'll soon get the message, and that way you'll stay friends.
Marcia

3 Darren

Hi _____,
You shouldn't be so sensitive. It's not really a problem; it just shows your friend thinks you have good taste. And don't argue with your friend. Women aren't worth it.
Darren

AUTHOR   MESSAGE

4 Silvia

Hi _____,
I think it depends on whether your friend is good company or not. If he is, then I think you should pay for him. If not, don't tell him where you're going when you go out.
Silvia

5 Lian

Dear _____,
When your friend gets home tonight, I think you should talk to her. Say "I'm really sorry but I'm a little bit obsessive about my things. I don't like other people touching them." That way she'll stop, but she won't get angry or offended.
Lian

6 Martyn

Hi _____,
You definitely shouldn't pay for him. When the waiter brings the check, pretend that nobody has money to pay for him. Then he'll have to make an excuse to the waiter, and maybe he'll learn that he has to pay for himself.
Martyn

e Now read the e-mails again. In pairs, say which advice you think is best for each person and why.

2 GRAMMAR *should / shouldn't*

a Highlight examples of *should* and *shouldn't* in the e-mails on page 70.

b Does *You should talk to your girlfriend* mean…?
1 You have to talk to your girlfriend.
2 I think it's a good idea if you talk to your girlfriend.

c ○ p.136 **Grammar Bank 6D.** Read the rules and do the exercises.

3 PRONUNCIATION & SPEAKING /ʊ/

a 6.12 Listen and repeat. Write the words.

1 /ʃʊd/   = *should*
2 /ˈʃʊdnt/ =
3 /wʊd/   =
4 /ˈwʊdnt/ =
5 /kʊd/   =
6 /ˈkʊdnt/ =

b 6.13 Listen and repeat these sentences. Copy the rhythm.
1 You should <u>talk</u> to your <u>friend</u>.
2 You <u>shouldn't</u> be so <u>sensitive</u>.
3 You should <u>lock</u> your <u>clothes</u> in a <u>closet</u>.
4 You <u>definitely</u> <u>shouldn't</u> <u>pay</u> for your <u>friend</u>.
5 <u>What</u> should I <u>do</u>?
6 <u>Should</u> I <u>write</u> to him?

4 WRITING & SPEAKING

a Choose one of the problems below and write a short note giving advice.

1 It's my girlfriend's birthday next week, and I want to surprise her with a special present or a special evening somewhere. What should I do?

2 My friend has gone away on vacation for two weeks, and I'm taking care of her cat. Yesterday I couldn't find the cat anywhere. My friend is coming home in three days. I'm desperate. Should I call her now and tell her? What should I do?

3 My best friend wants to borrow some money to help her buy a car. I have the money, and she says she'll pay me back next year. But I'm worried that it's not a good idea to lend money to friends. What should I do?

4 I really want to get in shape and exercise more. The problem is I hate going to gyms, and they're very expensive. And there are no parks near me to go running. What should I do?

b In pairs, read each other's notes. Decide which problem they refer to. Do you agree with the advice? Why (not)?

5 VOCABULARY *get*

a Look at these sentences from exercise 1. Match the examples of *get* with meanings A–D.

1 I'm sure you'll soon **get** some e-mails with good advice. ☐
2 When your friend **gets** home tonight, you should talk to her. ☐
3 She won't **get** angry with you. ☐
4 I **get along** very **well** with her. ☐

A receive	B be friendly with
C become	D arrive

b ○ p.152 **Vocabulary Bank** *get*

c In pairs, take the *get* questionnaire.

1 Do you ever **get to** school / work late? When was the last time?

2 When was the last time you **got lost**? Where were you trying to go? What happened?

3 What makes you **get angry**? When was the last time you got really angry? Why?

4 When was the last time you **got a present**? What was it? Who was it from?

5 Who do you **get along with** best in your family? Is there anybody you don't get along with?

6 What do you think is the best age to **get married**? Why?

7 Which problems in your country are **getting better**? Which are **getting worse**?

ASKING FOR HELP

6.14 Listen and <u>underline</u> the correct phrase.

1 Allie asks the receptionist for some **aspirin / painkillers**.
2 Allie has a **headache / backache**.
3 The receptionist **gives / doesn't give** her medicine.
4 Allie **wants / doesn't want** a doctor.
5 The pharmacy **is / isn't** near the hotel.

	US English	*pharmacy*
	UK English	*chemist's*

ASKING FOR MEDICINE

a **6.15** Cover the dialogue and listen. What does the pharmacist give her? How often does she have to take them? How much are they?

YOU HEAR	YOU SAY
Good morning. Can I help you?	I have a bad cold. Do you have something I can take?
What _____ do you have?	I have a headache and a cough.
Do you have a _____?	No, I don't think so.
Does your back _____?	No.
Are you allergic to any drugs?	I'm allergic to penicillin.
No problem. These are _____.	
These will make you feel _____.	How many do I have to take?
Two every four hours.	Sorry? How often?
Every four hours. If you don't feel better in _____ hours, you should see a doctor.	OK, thanks. How much are they?
$4.75, please.	Thank you.
You're welcome.	

b Listen again. Complete the **YOU HEAR** phrases.

aspirin	better	hurt	symptoms
temperature		twenty-four	

c **6.16** Listen and repeat the **YOU SAY** phrases. <u>Copy the rhythm</u>.

d In pairs, role-play the dialogue. **A** (book open) you're the pharmacist, **B** (book closed) you're Allie. Change roles.

SOCIAL ENGLISH talking about the party

a **6.17** Listen and mark the sentences T (true) or F (false).

1 Mark apologizes for getting angry last night.
2 Allie thinks Brad is annoying.
3 Brad isn't Allie's type of man.
4 Today is Allie's last day.
5 They're going to have dinner on a boat.

b Complete the **USEFUL PHRASES**. Listen again and check.

c **6.18** Listen and repeat the phrases. How do you say them in your language?

USEFUL PHRASES

M B_____ you!
M I'm really sorry a_____ (last night).
A What do you m_____?
M H_____ about (a boat trip around the bay)?
A That s_____ fantastic.

From: **Daniel**

To: Alessandra
Subject: Visit

Hi Alessandra!

Thanks for your last e-mail. I hope your exams went well. I have some exciting news, and I'm writing to [1] _ask_ for your advice.

I [2]_____ to go on vacation to Argentina next year. What do you [3]_____ is the best month for me to come? I can only come for three weeks, so which places do you think I should [4]_____? Do you think I should [5]_____ a car or travel around by bus or train?

I'm planning to [6]_____ a few days in and around Mendoza, and it would be great if we could [7]_____. Can you [8]_____ a good hotel (not too expensive)?

Hope to hear from you soon!
Best wishes,
Daniel

a Read the e-mail and complete it with these verbs.

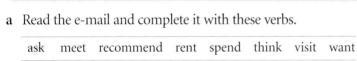

ask   meet   recommend   rent   spend   think   visit   want

b Imagine that Daniel has written to *you* about visiting *your* country. Plan how you're going to answer his questions. Compare with a partner.

c Look at the **USEFUL PHRASES**. What are the missing words?

USEFUL PHRASES
1 Thanks _____ your e-mail.
2 It was great to hear _____ you again.
3 I'm really happy that you want _____ visit my country.
4 I think you should come _____ July.
5 If I were you, I'd travel _____ bus.
6 I'm looking forward _____ seeing you soon.

WRITE an e-mail to Daniel. Use the phrases in c to help you.

Paragraph 1   Thank him for his e-mail, etc.
Paragraph 2   Answer his questions about your country. Give reasons.
Paragraph 3   Answer his question about your town. Give reasons.

CHECK your e-mail for mistakes (grammar , punctuation , and spelling).

GRAMMAR

Circle the correct answer, a, b, or c.

What's _____ name?

a yours   b your   c you

1 If we start walking, the bus _____ .
   a come
   b came
   c will come

2 Dario _____ come to the party if his ex-girlfriend is there.
   a won't
   b don't
   c doesn't

3 If we _____ lines, the first line will move more quickly.
   a change
   b will change
   c changed

4 What would you do if you _____ a bear?
   a saw
   b will see
   c see

5 If we had a yard, we _____ a dog.
   a 'll have
   b 'd have
   c had

6 I _____ go to the party. I'm not sure.
   a might
   b will
   c may to

7 The bank _____ open today. It's a holiday.
   a may not be
   b may not to be
   c may to

8 I think you _____ go to the doctor.
   a would
   b should to
   c should

9 She _____ come home so late.
   a not should
   b shouldn't
   c shouldn't to

10 If I _____ you, I'd talk to your girlfriend.
   a were
   b be
   c am

10

VOCABULARY

a confusing verbs

Cross out the wrong verb.

I don't **watch** / **look at** TV very often.

1 Where did you **know** / **meet** your husband?
2 Shh! They're **making** / **doing** their homework.
3 How much money does she **earn** / **win**?
4 He was **carrying** / **wearing** a black umbrella.
5 You **look** / **look like** your sister. You have the same eyes.

b animals

Write the names of the animals.

It's a popular pet and it barks. _____dog_____

1 It's a big cat and it lives in Africa. _____
2 It has eight legs and it eats flies. _____
3 People ride this animal in races. _____
4 It's the largest animal in the sea. _____
5 It's a male cow and it can be dangerous. _____

c noun formation

Make nouns from these verbs.

imagine _____imagination_____

1 communicate _____
2 organize _____
3 discuss _____
4 translate _____
5 decide _____

15

PRONUNCIATION

a Underline the word with a different sound

1	a	rob	lose	shopping	problem
2	i	we	meet	lion	sheep
3	æ	carry	camel	watch	happen
4	ɑr	garden	start	married	shark
5	u	zoo	food	you	mouse

b Underline the stressed syllable.

information

advice   crocodile   decision   happen   translation

10

CAN YOU UNDERSTAND THIS TEXT?

a Read the article and match the questions and answers.

A question of principles

The first of a new series in which celebrities answer questions on moral dilemmas. This week, radio presenter Stephen Bruce.

A ☐ If your girlfriend were allergic to the dog you've had for ten years, would you give your dog away?

B ☐ If your boss gave you tickets to the theater and you forgot to go, would you tell him the truth when he asked?

C ☐ If your young daughter's hamster died, would you buy an identical one or tell her the truth?

D ☐ If a coworker told everyone that he was 45, but you knew he was five years older, would you keep his secret?

E ☐ If a celebrity were having a secret romance with your neighbor, would you sell the story to a newspaper?

1 I'd tell everybody the truth, probably in front of him. I think telling lies about your age is ridiculous.

2 No, I'd say that it was the best show I've ever seen! I wouldn't want to offend him. But he would probably guess I was lying.

3 I'm afraid the dog would win! I'd tell my girlfriend that my dog and I had been together for a long time, but that she might not be here next week.

4 It would be an interesting story – my neighbor is a 92-year-old, bald Swedish man! No, I wouldn't. I'd just tell my girlfriend.

5 I'd buy another one. It happened to me once when the children's goldfish died. I bought another one, but they saw that it was different. I told them it had put on weight.

b Read the article again. Guess the meaning of the highlighted words or phrases. Check with the teacher or your dictionary.

CAN YOU UNDERSTAND THESE PEOPLE?

a **6.19** Listen and circle the correct answer, a, b, or c.

1 The man and woman decide to _____.
   a walk   b wait   c get a taxi
2 The woman _____ Deborah.
   a knows   b hasn't met   c wouldn't like to meet
3 Is the woman afraid of mice?
   a Yes.   b No.   c We don't know.
4 Where does the man decide to go?
   a home   b to the cafe   c to a movie
5 What pet does the woman think he should buy?
   a a fish   b a cat   c a hamster

b **6.20** Listen and mark the sentences T (true) or F (false).

1 Dave got married five years ago.
2 His wife just had a baby.
3 Dave's wife doesn't give him much attention.
4 Dave is more tired than his wife.
5 The advice he gets is to help his wife more.

CAN YOU SAY THIS IN ENGLISH?

a Can you...? Yes (✓)

☐ say three things you'll do if it rains tomorrow
☐ say what you would do if you were attacked by a crocodile
☐ say what you might do this weekend
☐ say what you should or shouldn't do if you have problems sleeping

b Write second conditional questions.

1 What / you do if / lose / wallet?
2 What / you do if / win the lottery?
3 What / you do if / find some money in the street?
4 What / you do if / have more free time?
5 What / you do if / can speak perfect English?

c Ask your partner the questions in **b**. Ask for more information.

G present perfect + *for* and *since*
V words related to fear
P /ɪ/ and /aɪ/, sentence stress

> I've been afraid of spiders since I was a child.

Famous fears and phobias

1 READING & VOCABULARY

a Match the words with the pictures.

flying ☐
heights ☐
closed spaces ☐
open spaces ☐
snakes ☐
spiders ☐
bees ☐
water ☐

b Are you afraid of any of these things? Why? Do you know any people who are?

> I'm afraid of flying.

> I have a friend who is afraid of water. He can't swim.

c Read the article and complete each paragraph with a word from **a**.

d Underline the four words in the text related to being afraid.

2 GRAMMAR present perfect + *for* and *since*

a Read about Winona Ryder again and answer the questions.

When did she begin to be afraid of water?
In _____.

Is she afraid of water now?   YES/NO

b Complete the answers with a year or a number of years.

How long has she been afraid of water?
She has been afraid of water **since** _____.
She has been afraid of water **for** _____ years.

c Complete the rule with *for* and *since*.

Use _____ with a period of time.
Use _____ with a point in time.

d ⊙ **p.138 Grammar Bank 7A.** Read the rules and do the exercises.

We're all afraid...

Famous people have phobias like the rest of us, and sometimes they seriously affect their lives.

Winona Ryder, American actress

Winona Ryder has been afraid of _____ since 1983. When she was 12 years old, she fell into a lake and almost died. Luckily someone pulled her out, and after a few minutes she came back to life again. It can be a real problem when she's making a movie. For example, in some of the scenes in *Alien III*, she had to get into a boat, and she was terrified.

Rupert Grint, British actor

Rupert Grint has been afraid of _____ since he was a child. In this respect he is like the character he played in the *Harry Potter* movies, Ron Weasley, who is also frightened of them. Rupert had a very hard time in the second *Harry Potter* movie, when he and Harry had to fight a giant one (the size of an elephant) with very hairy legs!

Dennis Bergkamp, former soccer player

Dennis Bergkamp has been afraid of _____ since 1994. He was on a plane in the US with the Dutch national team during the World Cup tournament. A journalist said that there was a bomb on the plane (there wasn't), and everybody started to panic, including Dennis. He decided never to travel by plane again. Because of his fear, Bergkamp could not play in many important matches for Holland, Inter Milan, and Arsenal.

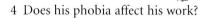

3 LISTENING

a 🔊 **7.1** Listen to Scott, a doctor, talking about his cat phobia. What happens if he sees a cat?

b Listen again and answer the questions.

1 What's the medical name of his phobia?
2 How long has he had his phobia?
3 How did it start?

4 Does his phobia affect his work?
5 What treatment is he getting?
6 Does he think his phobia will disappear?

4 PRONUNCIATION /ɪ/ and /aɪ/, sentence stress

a Put these words in the correct column.

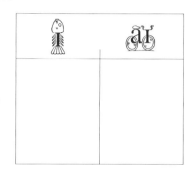

child	children	in	I've	like	life	line
live (v)	mine	minute (n)	since	win		

b 🔊 **7.2** Listen and check. Practice saying the words.

c Practice saying the sentences.

I've lived here since I was a child.
I've liked rice since I lived in China.

d 🔊 **7.3** Listen and repeat the questions. Copy the rhythm.

1 lived here	have you lived here	How long have you lived here?
2 known her	have you known her	How long have you known her?
3 been married	have they been married	How long have they been married?
4 had his dog	has he had his dog	How long has he had his dog?

5 SPEAKING

Ask and answer in pairs.

A ask **B** six *How long …?* questions with a verb phrase.

B answer with *for* or *since*.
Give more information if you can.
Then change roles.

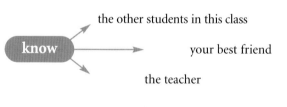

How long have you known your best friend?

Since we were in elementary school together.

the other students in this class

know → your best friend

the teacher

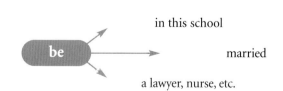

in this town

live → in your house or apartment

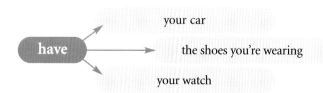

in this school

be → married

a lawyer, nurse, etc.

your car

have → the shoes you're wearing

your watch

7
B

G present perfect or simple past?
V biographies
P word stress

He was born in Knoxville, Tennessee.

Born to direct

1 VOCABULARY & PRONUNCIATION

a Underline the stressed syllable in the highlighted words below.

Events in your life

go to college	☐	fall in love	☐
be born	☐	get divorced	☐
go to elementary school	☐	have children	☐
start work	☐	get married	☐
graduate from college	☐	go to high school	☐
die	☐	separate	☐
retire	☐	graduate from high school	☐

b **7.4** Listen and check. Practice saying the phrases.

c Number the expressions in what you think is a logical order. Compare with a partner. Do you agree?

2 READING & SPEAKING

a Look at the movie photos. In pairs, answer the questions.

1 Who directed the movies?
2 Have you seen either of the movies? What kind of movies are they?

b Read fifteen facts about the lives of the two directors. In pairs, decide which eight are about Hitchcock, and which seven are about Tarantino. Write **H** or **T**.

c **A** re-read the facts about Hitchcock, and **B** about Tarantino.

d Work in pairs.

A (Book closed) in your own words say everything you can remember about Hitchcock.
B (Book open) listen and help. Then change roles. **B** Say everything you can remember about Tarantino.

3 GRAMMAR present perfect or simple past?

a Answer the questions.

1 Look at the eight facts about Hitchcock's life. What tense are all the verbs? Why?
2 Look at the seven facts about Tarantino's life. What three tenses are there? Why?

b ⟳ **p.138 Grammar Bank 7B.** Read the rules and do the exercises.

Hitchcock or Tarantino?

1 He appeared in small roles in almost all of his movies. [H]

2 He was a very intelligent child, but he had difficulties with reading and writing. He quit school when he was 15 and went to work in a movie theater, where he checked tickets at the entrance. ☐

3 He was born in London in 1899. ☐

4 His muse is Uma Thurman, who he has directed in several of his most successful movies. ☐

The Birds

5 He was married, and his daughter Patricia appeared in several of his movies. ☐

6 He went to school at St. Ignatius College, in London, and later studied art at the University of London. ☐

7 He was famous for not liking actors. He once said, "All actors are children and should be treated like cattle." ☐

8 He was born in Knoxville, Tennessee, in 1963. ☐

Kill Bill

Alfred Hitchcock

9 He spent a short time in prison because he could not pay a parking ticket. ☐

10 His muse was Grace Kelly (later Princess Grace of Monaco), who he directed in several of his movies. ☐

11 He died in 1980. ☐

12 He began his career as an actor. His biggest role was in an episode of the TV series *The Golden Girls*. He played the part of a man who impersonated Elvis Presley. ☐

Quentin Tarantino

13 He never won an Oscar for Best Director, although he was nominated five times. When the Academy finally gave him an honorary Oscar, he received a standing ovation. He just said, "Thank you" and left the stage. ☐

14 He has been nominated for an Oscar for Best Director, but he hasn't won one yet. ☐

15 He says he hates drugs and violence, but they appear a lot in his movies. ☐

4 SPEAKING

a Think about a member of your family (who is alive), for example, a parent, uncle, aunt, or grandparent. Prepare to answer the questions below about their life.

The past
Where / born?
Where / go to school?
When / start work?
When / get married?

The present
Where / live now?
   How long / live there?
Is he / she married?
   How long / be married?
Is he / she retired?
   How long has he / she be retired?
How many children / have?

b A interview B about their person. Ask for more information. Then change roles.

5 LISTENING

a Look at the photo of Sofia Coppola and her father. What do they both do?

b You're going to listen to part of a TV program about Sofia Coppola. Look at the information below. Before you listen, guess what the connection is with her.

Francis Ford Coppola   **Sofia Coppola**

I think she directed *The Godfather*.   No, she was too young.

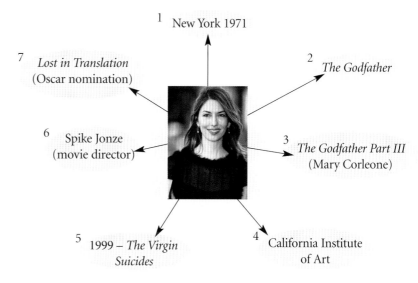

1 New York 1971

2 *The Godfather*

3 *The Godfather Part III* (Mary Corleone)

4 California Institute of Art

5 1999 – *The Virgin Suicides*

6 Spike Jonze (movie director)

7 *Lost in Translation* (Oscar nomination)

c **7.5** Now listen and take notes. Compare with a partner.

d In pairs, ask and answer the questions.

Have you seen any of the movies in **b**? Which one(s)? Did you like it/them?
Have you seen a good movie recently? Which one? Who was in it?
What's the best movie you've seen this year? Who directed it?
What's the worst movie you've seen this year? Who directed it?

7C

G used to
V school subjects: *history, geography,* etc.
P sentence stress: *used to / didn't use to*

Did you use to like elementary school?
Yes, I did.

I used to be a rebel

1 READING

a Look at the picture. Does it make you think of your school days? Why (not)?

b Look at the photos and read the article about Mick Jagger. Do you think he was *really* a rebel when he was in school? Why (not)?

c Read the text again. In pairs, guess the meaning of the highlighted words.

2 GRAMMAR used to

a Underline six phrases with *used to / didn't use to* in the text. Does *used to* refer to…

 1 the present or the past?
 2 things that happened once or for a long time?

b ⬭ **p.138 Grammar Bank 7C.** Read the rules and do the exercises.

A famous rebel – but was he really?

MICK JAGGER went back to his old school recently – for the first time since he graduated in 1961. He was invited to the school to open the Mick Jagger Performing Arts Centre, a new music and drama department at Dartford Grammar School.

Jagger said that he was "honored" that the center was named after him. But in a newspaper interview two days earlier he told a journalist that in fact he hated school and that he used to be a rebel.

He didn't use to do the homework – "there was far too much"– and he was continually at war with the teachers. He used to break the rules all the time, especially rules he thought were stupid, about how to wear the school uniform and things like that. Once he even organized a mass protest against "appalling" school dinners. "It was probably the greatest contribution to school I ever made," he said. Although he made a good start at school, Jagger said his school work deteriorated because of "music and girls."

However, according to one of his old school friends, musician Dick Taylor, this is not true. He says that Mick didn't use to be a rebel at all – he was very bright and used to work hard. He also used to play a lot of sports.

Also Mick's school records show that he was a very good student. So maybe Dick's memory is better than Mick's...

Mick Jagger with his school basketball team

3 LISTENING

a Look at the photos of Melissa when she was in school and today. How has she changed?

b **7.6** Listen to her talking about her school days. Was she a rebel or a "good girl" in school? What does she do now?

c Listen again. Mark the sentences T (true) or F (false).

1 Melissa is a teenager in the photo.
2 She used to write things on the walls.
3 She didn't like any of the subjects at school.
4 Her least favorite subject was PE.
5 The PE teacher made them try to do difficult things.
6 She used to break the rules about the school uniform.
7 She wanted to be a doctor.
8 Her parents wanted her to be a teacher.

4 PRONUNCIATION sentence stress

> ⚠ *used to* and (*didn't*) *use to* are both pronounced /ˈyustə/.

a **7.7** Listen and <u>underline</u> the stressed words. Then listen and repeat.

1 I used to go out a lot.
2 He used to hate school.
3 They didn't use to be friends.
4 She didn't use to like him.
5 Did you use to wear glasses?

b **7.8** Now listen and write six more sentences.

5 VOCABULARY school subjects

a Match the words with the pictures.

PE (=physical education) ☐
geography ☐
computer science ☐
math ☐
history ☐
foreign languages (English, etc.) ☐
literature ☐
science (physics, chemistry, and biology) ☐

b **7.9** Listen and practice saying the words.

c Think about when you were 11 or 12 years old. Talk about each subject with one of the expressions below. Say why.

I used to / didn't use to like _____ .

> I didn't use to like math. I was really bad at it.

6 SPEAKING

a Think about when you were 11 or 12. Were these things true or false about you? Why?

I used to be a rebel.	I used to play a lot of sports.
I used to work hard.	I used to wear glasses.
I used to like all the teachers.	I used to wear a uniform.
I used to hate school.	I used to have longer hair.

b Work in groups of three.

A tell **B** and **C** about how you used to be. **B** and **C** listen and ask for more information. Then change roles. Did you have anything in common?

> I didn't use to be a rebel. I was well-behaved.

7 **7.10 SONG** ♩ *It's all over now*

7 D

G passive
V verbs: *invent, discover*, etc.
P *-ed*, sentence stress

It was invented by a woman.

The mothers of invention

the dishwasher

disposable diapers

nylon stockings

the vacuum cleaner

the bulletproof vest

white-out

1 LISTENING

a Look at the photos. Five of these things were invented by women. In pairs, decide which five you think they are.

b **7.11** Now listen to a radio program about inventions. Were you right? Complete the sentences with the invention.

1 _____ was invented by Josephine Cochrane in 1886.
2 _____ were invented by Mary Anderson in 1903.
3 _____ were invented by Marion Donovan in 1950.
4 _____ was invented by Bette Nesmith Graham in 1956.
5 _____ was invented by Stephanie Kwolek in 1966.

c Listen again and answer the questions.

1 What happened after Josephine Cochrane's dinner parties?
2 What was the problem with cars before 1903 when it rained or snowed?
3 How many disposable diapers are used every day?
4 What was Bette Nesmith Graham's job?
5 What was special about the material Stephanie Kwolek invented?

d Which of the five inventions do you think was the best?

2 GRAMMAR passive

a Make five true sentences using the words in the chart.

The dishwasher	is called	white-out today.
Disposable diapers	was invented	by Marion Donovan.
More than 55 million diapers	are protected	every day.
Ms. Graham's invention	were invented	by the bulletproof vest.
Police officers all over the world	are used	by an American woman.

The dishwasher was invented by an American woman.

b Look at these two sentences and answer the questions.

a An American woman invented the dishwasher.
b The dishwasher was invented by an American woman.

1 Do the sentences have the same meaning?
2 Do the sentences have the same emphasis?
3 Which sentence is in the passive?

c **⊙ p.138 Grammar Bank 7D.** Read the rules and do the exercises.

windshield wipers

the ballpoint pen

the washing machine

3 READING & VOCABULARY

a Complete the text below with the correct verb in the right form.

> base   create   design (x2)   discover   invent   name   use   write

Did you know...?

Text-messaging was ¹*invented* by the Finnish company Nokia. They wanted to help Finnish teenagers, who were very shy. They found it easier to text their friends than to call them.

The first bikini was ²_____ by two Frenchmen. It was ³_____ after Bikini Atoll, the island where the atomic bomb was first tested. The Frenchmen thought that the bikini would have a similar effect on men as a bomb exploding.

Light bulbs are ⁴_____ specially to last only a certain number of hours. It would be possible to make light bulbs that lasted forever, but then the manufacturers wouldn't make so much money.

The first Harry Potter book was ⁵_____ in a cafe in Edinburgh, Scotland. J.K. Rowling was unemployed, and she didn't have enough money to pay for heat, so she wrote it in the cafe, where it was warmer.

Although penicillin was ⁶_____ by Alexander Fleming, he didn't know how to make it into a medicine. It was first made into a medicine ten years later, by Australian scientist Howard Florey.

Spiders were ⁷_____ as a cure for toothaches in the 17th century. They were first made into a paste, and then put on the bad tooth.

Sherlock Holmes, the great detective, was ⁸_____ by writer Arthur Conan Doyle. Holmes was ⁹_____ on a real person – Doyle's teacher at medical school, who was famous for saying to his students, "What can you tell me by just observing the patient?"

b Read the facts again. In pairs, say which one is the most surprising.

4 PRONUNCIATION *-ed*, sentence stress

a How is the *–ed* pronounced in these past participles? Put them in the correct column.

> based   designed   directed   discovered   invented
> named   painted   produced   used

d	t	/ɪd/

b **7.12** Listen and check. Underline the stressed syllable in each multisyllable verb.

c **7.13** Listen and repeat the sentences. Copy the rhythm. Which words are stressed?

1 The movie was based on a true story.
2 These clothes were designed by Armani.
3 This cheese is produced near here.
4 My sister was named after our grandmother.
5 These pictures were painted by my aunt.
6 Garlic and ginger are used a lot in Chinese cooking.

5 SPEAKING

○ **Communication** *Passives quiz A p.111 B p.115.* Make sentences for your partner to decide if they are true or false.

HOW TO GET THERE

7.14 Listen to Mark and Allie and mark the sentences T (true) or F (false).

1 Allie is feeling worse.
2 Mark thinks Allie might get cold.
3 They're going to get a taxi to the bay.
4 Allie wants to be at the hotel again at 1:00 p.m.
5 She's expecting an important visitor.

BUYING TICKETS

a **7.15** Cover the dialogue and listen. Complete the sentences.

The next boat leaves at ___ a.m. The trip takes ___ hour(s) and costs ___.

YOU SAY	YOU HEAR
Good morning.	Good morning, sir.
What time does the next boat leave?	At 10 o'clock.
How long does it take?	_____ an hour.
Where exactly does the boat go?	It goes _____ the bridge, _____ Angel Island and _____ Alcatraz, and then _____ here.
Can we get anything to eat or drink on the boat?	Yes, ma'am, there's a _____ bar.
Can I have two tickets, please?	Sure. Two _____.
How much is that?	That's $40.
Here you are.	Thank you, sir.
Thank you.	

b Listen again and complete the **YOU HEAR** phrases.

c **7.16** Listen and repeat the **YOU SAY** phrases. Copy the <u>rhythm</u>.

d In pairs, role-play the dialogue. **A** (book open) you're the ticket seller, **B** (book closed) you're Mark and Allie. Change roles.

SOCIAL ENGLISH on the boat

a **7.17** Listen and answer the questions.

1 Does Allie prefer San Francisco to London?
2 Does she think she could live there? Why (not)?
3 What did the building on Alcatraz use to be?
4 What's the weather like?
5 What does Mark ask the boatman to do?

b Complete the **USEFUL PHRASES**. Listen again and check.

c **7.18** Listen and repeat the phrases. How do you say them in your language?

USEFUL PHRASES

M What do you t_____ of (San Francisco)?
A Why do you a_____?
M Oh, no reason. I j_____ wondered.
A I'm really l_____ forward to it.
M C_____ you take a photo of us, please?
B Are you r_____?

a Read the description and complete it with words from the box.

cathedral completed designed roof steps statue view windows

b Match the questions with paragraphs 1–6.

Is there a view from the building? ☐
Describe the building outside. ☐
Describe the building inside. ☐
How much does it cost to go in? ☐
What's the most beautiful building in your city? Where is it? ☐
Who was it designed by? When was it built? ☐

c Find one spelling mistake in each paragraph and correct it.

WRITE a description of a building in your city.
Answer the questions in **b** in the correct order.

CHECK your description for mistakes (grammar ,
punctuation , and spelling).

---

1 The most bea/utiful building in my city is
the ¹_cathedral_ (the Duomo). It is in the
center of Milan, in the Piazza del Duomo.

2 Nobody knows who it was ²_____ by,
but peopel think it was an architect from
northern Europe. Construction began in
1386, but the building wasn't ³_____
for another 500 years.

3 It is one of the largest cathedrals in the
world, and it has 135 spires and 3,400
statues. On top of the Duomo there is
a gold ⁴_____ of the Madonna, which
watches over the city. The statue is called
the "Madonnina," or the little Madonna,
althought it is four meters tall.

4 Inside the Duomo it is fairly dark. There
are beautiful big ⁵_____ and a lot of
intresting statues and monuments. In the
chapel of St. Fina there are some
wonderful frescoes by Ghirlandaio.

5 One of the best things you can do in Milan
is to go up to the ⁶_____ of the Duomo.
The ⁷_____ is fantastic—on a cleer day
you can see the Italian Alps. You can take
the elevator, or if you are feeling energetic,
you can walk up the 250 ⁸_____ .

6 It is free to go in, but you must
dress apropriately.

What do you remember?

GRAMMAR

Circle the correct answer, a, b, or c.

What's _____ name?

a yours   (b) your   c you

1 I _____ in this house since I was a child.
   a live
   b 'm living
   c 've lived

2 My father has had his car _____.
   a for two years
   b since two years
   c two years ago

3 How long _____ afraid of flying?
   a are you
   b have you been
   c you have been

4 Tom Cruise and Nicole Kidman _____ married for ten years, but divorced in 2001.
   a are
   b have been
   c were

5 When _____?
   a did Alfred Hitchcock die
   b is Alfred Hitchcock dead
   c has Alfred Hitchcock died

6 My brother _____ glasses.
   a used to wear
   b use to wear
   c used to wearing

7 I _____ like vegetables when I was a child.
   a don't use to
   b didn't use to
   c didn't used to

8 Radium _____ discovered by Pierre and Marie Curie.
   a is
   b were
   c was

9 *The Lord of the Rings* _____ by J. R. R. Tolkien.
   a wrote
   b was wrote
   c was written

10 Paper _____ the Chinese.
   a was invented by
   b invented for
   c was invented for

`10`

VOCABULARY

a time expressions

Complete the sentences with *for* or *since*.

I've lived here ___*since*___ 1998.

1 I've had this pen _____ I was a child.
2 He's been married _____ last June.
3 They've known each other _____ a long time.
4 She's studied French literature _____ three years.
5 You've worn that sweater every day _____ New Year's!

b verb phrases

Complete the phrases with a verb.

be	get	fall	~~have~~	graduate	retire

___*have*___ children
1 _____ in love
2 _____ from school / college
3 _____ married / divorced
4 _____ when you're 65
5 _____ born

c school subjects

Complete the sentences with a school subject.

If you study ___*computer science*___, you learn to use computers.

1 If you study _____, you learn about what happened in the past.
2 If you study _____, you learn about countries, mountains, rivers, etc.
3 If you study _____, you learn to add, multiply, etc.
4 If you study _____, you learn physics and chemistry.
5 If you study _____, you learn about plants and animals.

`15`

PRONUNCIATION

a <u>Underline</u> the word with a different sound.

1		since	time	child	life
2		school	food	cartoon	book
3		use	ugly	university	uniform
4		scene	science	scarf	since
5		change	teacher	school	children

b <u>Underline</u> the stressed syllable.

infor<u>m</u>ation

afraid	favorite	directed	discovered	invented

`10`

CAN YOU UNDERSTAND THIS TEXT?

a Read the article quickly. What is surprising about Lady Morton?

The world's most experienced driver?

One of Scotland's most active [1] centenarians, Lady Morton, has been a driver for almost 80 years, although she has never taken a driving test. But last week she had her first-ever accident – she hit a traffic island when she took her new car for a drive in Edinburgh.

Lady Morton, who celebrated her 100th birthday in July, [2] was given the Nissan Micra as a surprise present. Yesterday she talked about the accident. "I wasn't going fast, but I hit a traffic island. I couldn't see it because it had no lights, which I think is [3] ridiculous. But I am all right, and luckily my car wasn't badly [4] damaged."

[5] In spite of the accident, she is not planning to stop driving. "Some people are just born to drive, and I think I am one of them. I've never taken a test, but I've been a good driver since the first time I got in a car. I'm musical, so I listen to the sound of the car to know when to change gears. Some people are very rude – they ask me if I'm still driving at my age. [6] It really annoys me."

Lady Morton bought her first car in 1927. The [7] main change she has noticed since then is the traffic. "It's [8] appalling. I don't mind it, because I am experienced, but I feel very sorry for beginners."

Adapted from a newspaper

b Put a check (✓) next to the things the article says.

1 Lady Morton has had a lot of accidents.
2 She bought a Nissan Micra recently.
3 She couldn't see the traffic island because she didn't have her lights on.
4 She wasn't badly hurt.
5 After her latest accident, she needs a new car.
6 She thinks she's a safe driver.
7 The amount of traffic isn't a problem for her.

c Read the article again. Guess the meaning of the highlighted words or phrases. Check with the teacher or your dictionary.

CAN YOU UNDERSTAND THESE PEOPLE?

a 7.19 Listen. Circle a, b, or c.

1 How long has Matt lived in Chicago?
  a Since he was in college. b For six months. c For a year.
2 John's sister _____ married.
  a is b is going to get c was
3 He started running _____.
  a a few years ago b in school c a few days ago
4 What's her favorite subject?
  a geography b literature c math
5 When was the Lincoln Memorial completed?
  a In the 19th century. b In 1914. c In 1922.

b 7.20 Listen and complete the table with a number or one word.

Main floor:	[1] a collection of _____ by Margaret Kennedy.
Second floor:	[2] children's _____
Entrance hall:	[3] the museum _____
Price of guidebook:	[4] _____
Museum closes at:	[5] _____

CAN YOU SAY THIS IN ENGLISH?

a Can you...? Yes (✓)

☐ say how long you have lived in your town, had your job, etc.
☐ talk about the life of an old person in your family
☐ say three things you used to do when you were in (elementary) school
☐ describe a famous building in your town

b Complete the questions with an auxiliary verb.

1 How long _____ you been in this class?
2 Where _____ your grandparents born?
3 What TV programs _____ you use to watch when you were a child?
4 What's the oldest building in your town? When _____ it built?

c Ask your partner the questions in **b**. Ask for more information.

8 A

G *something, anything, nothing, etc.*
V adjectives ending in *-ed* and *-ing*
P /ɛ/, /oʊ/, /ʌ/

I didn't do anything on the weekend.

I hate weekends!

Most people say that Saturdays or Sundays are their favorite days of the week – but not everybody. For some people weekends are not much fun...

Marco from Brazil is a _____

"I hate the weekend. The weekend is when I'm busiest. I never go ¹ **any**_where_ and I don't really do ² **any**_____ except work. On Friday and Saturday nights we're usually full, and I have to be on my feet for seven or eight hours both days. We're supposed to close at 1:00, but people often don't leave until 1:30 or even later – they never think that we might want to go home. Luckily we close after lunch on Sunday, but when I get home, usually at about 5:30, I'm so tired that I don't want to see ³ **any**_____ or do ⁴ **any**_____ except lie on the sofa and watch TV. The best day of the week for me is Wednesday – that's my day off."

Mara from the US is a _____

"I must admit that for me now the weekends are more tiring than the week. During the week I have ⁵ **some**_____ to help me, but on the weekends we're on our own. My husband is always exhausted from his job and wants to relax, but ⁶ **no**_____ can relax with two small kids around. Our apartment isn't very big, so there's ⁷ **no**_____ you can go to have some peace and quiet. Before we had children, I used to work, too, and weekends were perfect. We had ⁸ **no**_____ to do except enjoy ourselves. Now I'm really happy when it's Monday morning."

Sergio from Colombia is a _____

"My weekend is usually very stressful, more stressful than during the week. If we're playing at home, I can't go out on Friday night. All my friends know that, so ⁹ **no**_____ invites me out on a Friday. I have ¹⁰ **some**_____ light to eat, watch TV, and go to bed early. Very boring! On Saturday morning I usually relax and prepare myself mentally, as our home games are usually at 3:00 in the afternoon. What I do on Saturday night depends on whether we win or lose. If we win, I have to go out with the team to celebrate. If we lose, we're too depressed to go ¹¹ **any**_____. When we play away, the weekend doesn't exist. We travel ¹² **some**_____, play, and then travel back again. I look forward to having a weekend just for me."

1 READING

a Is the weekend your favorite part of the week? Why (not)?

b Read the article. In pairs, guess what the three people do.

c **8.1** Listen and check.

d Complete the sentences with **Marco**, **Mara**, or **Sergio**.

1 _____ always gets home late on Saturdays.
2 _____ goes to bed early on Friday night.
3 _____ usually spends the weekend with the family.
4 _____ sometimes goes out on Saturday night.
5 _____ used to love the weekend.
6 _____ prefers Wednesdays to Saturdays.

e Read the texts again. Complete the words 1–12 with *-thing*, *-body*, or *-where*.

2 GRAMMAR *something, anything, nothing, etc.*

a Look again at 1–12 in the text. Complete the rules with *things*, *places*, and *people*.

Use *something*, *anything*, and *nothing* for _____.
Use *somebody*, *anybody*, and *nobody* for _____.
Use *somewhere*, *anywhere*, and *nowhere* for _____.

b ➲ **p.140 Grammar Bank 8A.** Read the rules and do the exercises.

3 PRONUNCIATION /ɛ/, /oʊ/, /ʌ/

a What are sounds 1–3?

   1   2   3

b What sound do the pink letters make in each sentence? Write 1, 2, or 3.

1 Nobody knows where he goes. ☐
2 Somebody's coming to lunch. ☐
3 I never said anything. ☐
4 I've done nothing since Sunday. ☐
5 Don't tell anybody about the message. ☐
6 There's nowhere to go except home. ☐

c **8.2** Listen and check your answers. Practice saying the sentences.

4 VOCABULARY adjectives ending in *-ed* and *-ing*

a Look at the two sentences from the article. What's the difference between *tired* and *tiring*?

I'm so **tired** that I don't want to see anybody.
Weekends are more **tiring** than weekdays.

b Look at the adjectives in **bold** in these sentences. How do you pronounce them?

1 Friday night is **bored** / **boring**. I never go out.
2 I'm **bored** / **boring** with my job. It's always the same.
3 If we lose, we feel **depressed** / **depressing**.
4 My team never wins. It's **depressed** / **depressing**.
5 Reading is very **relaxed** / **relaxing**.
6 I feel very **relaxed** / **relaxing** on the weekend.
7 His latest movie is really **interesting** / **interested**.
8 I'm not very **interesting** / **interested** in sports.
9 I'm very **excited** / **exciting** about my vacation.
10 It was a really **excited** / **exciting** soccer game.

c Cross out the wrong word in each sentence.

5 SPEAKING

Ask and answer these questions with a partner. Ask for more information, too.

Every weekend

/ you usually have to work or study on weekends?
/ there anything you always watch on TV?
/ you usually have to buy anything on Saturdays?
/ have to do anything in the house (clean, etc.)?

Last weekend

/ you go anywhere exciting on Friday night?
/ do anything tiring on Saturday morning?
/ you meet anybody on Saturday night?
/ you do anything relaxing on Sunday?

Next weekend

/ you go out of town?
/ you do anything special on Saturday?
/ you go anywhere interesting on Sunday?

6 LISTENING

a **8.3** Listen and number the pictures 1–8.

b In pairs, use the pictures 1–8 to retell the story.

G quantifiers, *too, not enough*
V health and lifestyle: *use sunscreen*, etc.
P /ʌ/, /u/, /aɪ/, /ɛ/; linking

> I eat too much meat.
> I don't drink enough water.

How old is your body?

How old are you? How old is your body? The answer to these two questions isn't always the same. Our body age can be much younger or much older than our calendar age (even eighteen years different!). We can now calculate our body age by answering questions about the way we live. If our body age is older than our calendar age, we should change our lifestyle.

EXERCISE

I know I'm too heavy because I don't get enough exercise. I spend too much time sitting in studios. All I do is play squash, but I don't play very often – about once a month. I would go to a gym if I had more time.

DIET

I eat a lot of fresh food and a lot of fruit, but I probably eat too much meat. My girlfriend says I don't drink enough water. I drink a little alcohol – just a glass of red wine with my dinner. But I don't drink any beer. I drink a lot of coffee. It goes with the job.

LIFESTYLE

Like everybody, I'm too busy! There aren't enough hours in the day. I love my job, but I work too much (sometimes I spend 14 hours a day in the studio – that's too many). I often feel a little bit tense and irritable. I smoke a few cigarettes when I go out, but I'm not a regular smoker. I only use sunscreen when I go to the beach. My skin is fairly dark, so I don't think it's a problem.

PERSONALITY

I'm often pessimistic. I always think that things will go wrong – and they usually do, especially at work.

SOCIAL LIFE

I don't have much free time, but I have a few close friends and I try to see them regularly. If I'm too busy, then I call them.

DOCTOR'S VERDICT:

Tariq should get more exercise, for example, he could walk to work. This would help him control his stress. His diet is fairly healthy, but he should drink more water and less coffee. He must give up smoking. Although his skin is fairly dark, he should use sunscreen all year round, even in winter. And he should try to be more positive.

Tariq, a music producer
Calendar age 32 **Body age** ▢

1 READING

a Read the introduction to the article and answer the questions.

1 Is our body age the same as our calendar age?
2 How can we calculate our body age?
3 What should we do if our body age is older than our calendar age?

b Look at the photo of Tariq and read about him. <u>Underline</u> the things he does that are good. Circle the things he does that are bad. Compare with a partner.

c Cover the *Doctor's verdict*. What do you think Tariq should do?

d Now read the *Doctor's verdict*. Was the advice the same as yours? What do you think Tariq's body age is?

2 GRAMMAR quantifiers, *too, not enough*

a Can you remember how to use *much, many*, etc.? In pairs, choose the correct word or phrase for each sentence. Say why the other one is wrong.

1 How **much / many** coffee do you drink?
2 I don't eat **much / many** vegetables.
3 I eat **a lot of / many** bread.
4 I smoke **a lot / a lot of**.
5 **A** How much tea do you drink?
  B Any / None. I don't like it.

b Match the phrases 1–6 with the meanings A–F.

1 ▢ I drink **too much** coffee. A I don't drink much.
2 ▢ I'm **too** heavy. B I need to get more.
3 ▢ I work **too many** hours. C I have two or three.
4 ▢ I don't get **enough** exercise. D I work more than I want.
5 ▢ I drink **a little** alcohol. E I should be a little thinner.
6 ▢ I have **a few** close friends. F I drink more than I should.

c ⬧ **p.140 Grammar Bank 8B.** Read the rules and do the exercises.

3 PRONUNCIATION /ʌ/, /u/, /aɪ/, /ɛ/; linking

a Cross out the word with a different pronunciation.

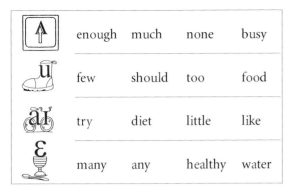

/ʌ/	enough	much	none	busy
/u/	few	should	too	food
/aɪ/	try	diet	little	like
/ɛ/	many	any	healthy	water

b **8.4** Listen and check. Practice saying the words.

⚠ Remember! When people speak quickly, they don't separate the words.

c **8.5** Listen and write the six sentences.

d Listen and repeat the sentences. Copy the rhythm.

4 SPEAKING

a Read the questionnaire and circle your answers.

b Interview your partner and <u>underline</u> his / her answers. Ask for more information.

How much exercise do you get?
A lot.

What do you do for exercise?
I go to the gym three times a week.

c ○ **Communication** *Body age p.111.* Figure out your body age.

d Look at your partner's answers. Give him / her some good advice.

I think you should get more exercise. For example...

What's your body age?
Take our quiz and find out

EXERCISE

1 How much do you walk each day?
  a a lot   **b** a fair amount   **c** not much   **d** very little

2 How much exercise do you get each week?
  a a lot   **b** a fair amount   **c** a little   **d** none

DIET

3 How much fast food (processed and pre-prepared) do you eat?
  a I eat too much.   **b** I eat some.
  c I don't eat much.   **d** I don't eat any.

4 How many portions of fruit and vegetables do you eat per day?
  a only a few   **b** some   **c** a lot

5 How much water do you drink?
  a a lot   **b** some   **c** a little

6 What's your worst diet habit?
  a I eat too much fat.   **b** I eat (or drink) too many sweet things.
  c I eat (or drink) too much.   **d** none of these

LIFESTYLE

7 How many cigarettes do you smoke a day?
  a none   **b** a few   **c** a lot

8 How would you describe yourself mentally?
  a I am a very positive person.   **b** I am not positive enough.
  c I'm very pessimistic.

9 How would you describe your stress level?
  a I am too stressed.   **b** I am stressed, but it's under control.
  c I am very relaxed.

10 How often do you use sunscreen?
  a all year   **b** only when I'm on vacation   **c** when it's sunny

SOCIAL LIFE

11 How many close friends do you see regularly?
  a a lot   **b** some   **c** not many / none

12 How much time do you have for yourself?
  a none   **b** not enough   **c** a lot

8 C

G word order of phrasal verbs
V phrasal verbs
P /g/ and /dʒ/

I wake up and I turn on the radio.

Waking up is hard to do

1 VOCABULARY phrasal verbs

a Match the questions 1–7 with the pictures A–G.

1 What time do you wake up in the morning? ▢ D
2 Do you use an alarm clock to wake up? ▢
3 Do you turn off the alarm clock immediately? ▢
4 What's the first thing you turn on after you wake up? ▢
5 Do you get up immediately after you wake up? ▢
6 How do you feel when you first get up? ▢
7 When you get dressed, what's the last thing you put on? ▢

b Cover the questions and look at the pictures. Try to remember the questions.

c In pairs, use the pictures to ask and answer the questions.

d ○ **p.153 Vocabulary Bank** *Phrasal verbs.*

2 GRAMMAR word order of phrasal verbs

a Look at the pictures 1–3 and underline the object of the phrasal verb in each sentence.

b Complete the rules about separable phrasal verbs with *noun* or *pronoun*.

1 If the object of a phrasal verb is a _____, you can put it **after** the verb +*up*, *on*, etc.
  OR **between** the verb and *up*, *on*, etc.
2 If the object of a phrasal verb is a _____, you **must** put it **between** the verb and *up*, *on*, etc.

c ○ **p.140 Grammar Bank 8C.** Read the rules and do the exercises.

d Match the sentences. Then cover the sentences on the right. Try to remember them.

1 Your cell phone is ringing. ▢ E   A You need to give it up.
2 This is an important rule. ▢   B Put them away.
3 I can't hear the music. ▢   C Turn it up.
4 If you don't know what the words mean, ▢   D Throw it away.
5 This is an immigration form. ▢   E ~~Turn it off.~~
6 Coffee is bad for you. ▢   F Please fill it out.
7 Your clothes are on the floor. ▢   G Write it down.
8 That's trash. ▢   H look them up.

3 READING

a Do you know what these scientific words and expressions mean?

> a gene   DNA   your "body clock"   research

b Read the article about morning and evening people. Choose **a**, **b**, or **c**.

1 Scientists say that if we are bad at getting up in the morning, this is because
   a we are born like that.
   b we go to bed too late.
   c we drink too much coffee.

2 Researchers asked people questions about
   a the way they lived.
   b science.
   c sports and exercise.

3 They discovered that people who have a short "clock" gene
   a are better in the morning than in the evening.
   b get tired very early.
   c are better in the evening than in the morning.

4 They recommend that people who have a long "clock" gene
   a should work only in the afternoon and evening.
   b should start work early and finish early.
   c should start work late and finish late.

Are you allergic to mornings?

Are you somebody who can't wake up in the morning? Do you need two cups of coffee before you can start a new day? Do you feel awful when you first wake up? Scientists say it's all because of our genes. How did they find this out? Researchers interviewed 500 people. They asked them questions about their lifestyle, for example, what time of day they preferred to exercise and how difficult they found it to wake up in the morning. Scientists then compared their answers to the people's DNA.

They discovered that we all have a "clock" gene, also called a Period 3 gene. This gene can be long or short. People who have the long gene are usually very good in the morning but get tired fairly early at night. People who have the short gene are usually more active at night but have problems waking up early in the morning. How does it help us to know if we have the long or short gene? Scientists say that, if possible, we should try to change our working hours to fit our "body clock." If you are a "morning person," then you could start work early and finish early. But if you are bad in the morning, then it might be better to start work in the afternoon and work until late at night. So maybe, instead of nine to five it should be seven to three or twelve to eight.

4 LISTENING & SPEAKING

a **8.6** Listen to David being interviewed by a researcher. Is he a morning or evening person?

b Listen again and write down David's answers.

1 What do you do?
2 When do you work?
3 What time do you get up in the morning?
4 If you have a test, do you study best in the morning, afternoon, or at night?
5 If you exercise, when do you prefer to do it?
6 Do you like your work/class schedule?
7 Why (not)?
8 Would you like to change it? How?

c Interview your partner using the questions in **b**. Is he / she a morning or evening person?

5 PRONUNCIATION /g/ and /dʒ/

a How is the letter *g* pronounced in these words? Put five words in each column.

> gene   get   go   change   energetic
> gym   good   give   hungry   age

b **8.7** Listen and check. Practice saying the words.

c Now practice saying the sentences.
   1 She gets up early to go to the gym.
   2 George and Greta are good at German.
   3 I'm allergic to mornings. It's in my genes.
   4 I generally feel hungry and energetic.

6 **8.8** SONG ♩ *I say a little prayer*

8 D

G *so/neither* + auxiliaries
V similarities
P vowel and consonant sounds, sentence stress

I like dogs.
So do I.

"I'm Jim." "So am I."

1 LISTENING

a Look at the photos and describe the two men.

b Read about the two men and answer the questions.

1 Who are Jim Springer and Jim Lewis?
2 Why didn't they know each other?
3 When did they meet?

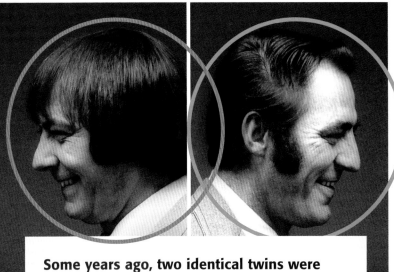

Some years ago, two identical twins were born in Minnesota, USA. They were adopted by two different families. The two new families both called their babies Jim. Jim Springer never knew that Jim Lewis existed. But when they were 39 years old, they met for the first time and they had a conversation something like this…

c **8.9** Cover the dialogue. Listen once. Try to remember **three** things they have in common.

d Uncover the dialogue. Listen again and fill in the blanks.

A Hi! I'm Jim.

B So ____ I. Great to meet you. Are you married, Jim?

A Yes…well, I've been married twice.

B Yeah? So ____ I. Do you have any children?

A I have one son.

B So ____ I. What's his name?

A James.

B That's amazing! My son's name is James, too.

A Did you go to college, Jim?

B No, I didn't.

A Neither ____ I. I was a terrible student.

B So ____ I. What do you like doing in your free time, Jim?

A I like making things, especially with wood.

B That's incredible! So ____ I.

A But I don't get any exercise at all. Look at me.

B Don't worry. Neither ____ I.

A Say, do you have any pets?

B Yes. I have a dog.

A So ____ I! What kind of car do you have?

B A Chevrolet.

A Me too! Hey, let's go and have a hamburger, OK?

B Sure. You know, I once worked in a hamburger restaurant.

A Unbelievable! So ____ I!

2 GRAMMAR *so, neither* + auxiliaries

a Look at the dialogue again. Write one phrase that the twins use…

when they have something ⊞ in common. ____
when they have something ⊟ in common. ____

b ⬭ **p.140 Grammar Bank 8D.** Read the rules and do the exercises.

3 READING & VOCABULARY

a Read the text and answer the questions.

1 Who reunited the two Jims?
2 What did Dr. Bouchard want to find out?
3 What was he very surprised by?
4 What are their sons and their dogs called?
5 What do they both do for their wives?
6 What does Dr. Bouchard believe, as a result of the case of the two Jims?

b Complete the phrases with these words.

as   both   like   neither   so   similar

Similarities

1 Jim Springer looks exactly _____ Jim Lewis.
2 Jim Springer's son has the same name _____ Jim Lewis's son.
3 The two Jims _____ have dogs.
4 Jim Springer likes baseball and _____ does Jim Lewis.
5 Jim Lewis doesn't like basketball and _____ does Jim Springer.
6 Dr. Bouchard didn't expect them to be so _____ to each other.

c Complete the sentences about you and your family. Tell your partner.

1 I have the same color eyes as my _____.
2 I look like my _____.
3 My personality is very similar to my _____'s.
4 My _____ and I both like _____.
5 I like _____ and so does my _____.
6 I don't like _____ and neither does my _____.

JIM SPRINGER AND JIM LEWIS were reunited after 39 years by Dr. Thomas Bouchard, Professor of psychology at the University of Minnesota. He was investigating how much of our personality depends on genes. Dr. Bouchard was amazed by how many things the twins had in common. He had expected them to look identical and to have similar medical histories. But he and his team were very surprised to find the enormous similarities in the two Jims' personalities, their lifestyle, their hobbies, their religion, even their political beliefs.

Some of the similarities are incredible: Jim Springer's son is called James Allen, and Jim Lewis's is called James Alan. They both have dogs named Toy. They like and hate the same sports and they voted for the same president. And both Jims have the same romantic habit of leaving little love letters for their wives around the house.

Dr. Bouchard is convinced that genes are probably much more important in determining our personality and preferences than people used to think.

4 PRONUNCIATION vowel and consonant sounds, sentence stress

a The same or different? Circle the word with a different sound in each group.

1 so	no	do
2 they	neither	both
3 two	twice	twins
4 identical	incredible	immediately
5 food	good	wood
6 now	know	how
7 speak	great	each
8 been	free	weekend

b **8.10** Listen and check. Practice saying the words.

c **8.11** Listen and repeat the dialogues. Underline the stressed words.

1 **A** I like tea.　　**B** So do I.
2 **A** I'm tired.　　**B** So am I.
3 **A** I don't smoke.　　**B** Neither do I.
4 **A** I'm not hungry.　　**B** Neither am I.

d **8.12** Listen and respond. Say you're the same. Use *So _____ I / Neither _____ I.*

5 SPEAKING

a Complete the sentences so they are true for you.

ME	WHO ELSE?
I love _____. (a kind of music)	_____
I don't like _____. (a TV program)	_____
I'm a _____. (star sign)	_____
I'm not very good at _____. (a subject)	_____
I'm going to _____ this weekend. (an activity)	_____
I have to _____ every day. (an obligation)	_____
I don't eat _____. (a kind of food)	_____
I'm not very _____. (adjective of personality)	_____

b Move around the class saying your sentences. For each sentence try to find someone like you, and write down their name. Respond to other people's sentences. Say *So do I / So am I* or *Neither do I / Neither am I* if you are like them.

I love classical music.

So do I.

CHECKING OUT

8.13 Listen to Allie talking to the receptionist. Answer the questions.

1 When is she leaving the hotel?
2 When does she want to pay?
3 What time is her flight?
4 What time does she have to be at the airport?
5 What is the message for her?

MAKING PHONE CALLS

a   **8.14**   Cover the dialogue and listen. Who does Allie want to speak to? What happens the first time she calls? Is the news good or bad? What is it?

YOU HEAR	YOU SAY
Hello.	Hello. Is that MTC?
Sorry, you've got the _____ number.	Oh sorry.
MTC New York. How can I help you?	Hello. Can I speak to Lisa Formosa, please?
Just a moment. I'll _____ you _____.	
Hello.	Hi, is that Lisa?
No, I'm sorry. She's not at her desk right now.	Can I leave a message, please?
Sure.	Tell her Allie Gray called. I'll call back in five minutes.
MTC New York. How can I help you?	Hello. Can I speak to Lisa Formosa, please?
Just a moment. I'm sorry, the line's _____.	
Do you want to _____?	OK, I'll hold.
Hello.	Hi, Lisa. It's Allie Gray.
Allie, hi. How's California?	Great, great. Well? Is it good news or bad news?
It's good. You got the job in Paris!	Oh wonderful! That's fantastic!

b Listen again and complete the **YOU HEAR** phrases.

c   **8.15**   Listen and repeat the **YOU SAY** phrases. Copy the rhythm.

d In pairs, role-play the dialogue. **A** (book closed) you're Allie, **B** (book open) you're all the other people. Change roles.

SOCIAL ENGLISH   saying good-bye?

a   **8.16**   Listen and mark the sentences T (true) or F (false).

1 Mark thinks that their relationship has a future.
2 Allie thinks it's a problem that Mark is very different from her.
3 Mark tells Allie he's going to move to another company.
4 Allie is very surprised.
5 Allie is going to be Mark's wife.

b Complete the **USEFUL PHRASES**. Listen again and check.

c   **8.17**   Listen and repeat the phrases. How do you say them in your language?

USEFUL PHRASES

A   Thanks for e_____.
M   C_____! To us.
A   What do you m_____?
M   I_____ that amazing?
M   What's the m_____?
M   I don't b_____ it.

a Read the article and complete it with these words.

| above all   although   another   but   general   however   secondly   which   who |

The weekend

The good side

For me the first good thing about the weekend is that I don't have to go to work. I like my job, [1] _but_ I have to spend all day inside, in an office, and I'm a person [2] _____ loves being outside. [3] _____ good thing is that I don't have to get up early. During the week I have to get up at half past six every day. It's not too bad in the summer, but I hate it in the winter when it's dark in the morning. But [4] _____, I like the weekend because I have time to do all the things I really enjoy doing, like listening to music, reading, or going out with friends.

The bad side

[5] _____, there are some things I don't like about the weekend. First of all, I have to go shopping on Saturday morning, and the supermarket is always crowded. [6] _____, on Sundays we always have lunch with my husband's family. [7] _____ my mother-in-law is a good cook and her food is delicious, I don't usually have a good time. The family always argues, and we end up watching TV, [8] _____ I think is boring.

But in [9] _____ I love the weekend – I often get a little bit depressed on Sunday afternoon when I know that the weekend is almost over.

b Read the article again. Now cover it and, from memory, mark the sentences T (true) or F (false).

1 She works outside.
2 She has to get up early during the week.
3 She enjoys shopping on Saturdays.
4 Her husband always makes lunch on Sundays.
5 She doesn't like watching TV.

What do you think of the weekend? **WRITE** two paragraphs.

Paragraph 1   The good side
For me the best thing about the weekend is…

Paragraph 2   The bad side
However, there are some things I don't like. For example,…

Final paragraph   Do you love it or hate it?
But in general,…

CHECK your article for mistakes (grammar , punctuation , and spelling).

GRAMMAR

Circle the correct answer, a, b, or c.

What's _____ name?

a yours   (b) your   c you

1 **A** What did you do this weekend?

  B _____

  a Nothing.

  b Nobody.

  c Anything.

2 We didn't go _____ on Sunday.

  a somewhere

  b anywhere

  c nowhere

3 She spoke to _____ in the office.

  a anybody

  b somebody

  c nobody

4 He eats _____ potato chips.

  a too

  b too much

  c too many

5 I can't go. I'm _____ busy.

  a enough

  b too

  c too much

6 You don't drink _____.

  a water enough

  b enough water

  c a few water

7 Here are your shoes. Put _____.

  a on them

  b them on

  c it on

8 I can't find my keys. Can you help me
_____?

  a look them for

  b look for them

  c for them look

9 **A** My father loves jazz.

  B _____

  a So I do.

  b So am I.

  c So do I.

10 **A** I didn't go to college.

  B _____

  a Neither do I.

  b Neither did I.

  c Neither I did.   **10**

VOCABULARY

a   adjectives ending in *-ed* and *-ing*

Complete the sentences with an adjective.

The movie was very e*xciting*.

1 We had a very r_____ vacation – we just lay in the sun.

2 I only got three hours' sleep – I'm really t_____.

3 I saw a really i_____ TV program last night.

4 She failed all her exams, so she feels a little bit d_____.

5 My job's very b_____ – I have to do all the photocopying.

b   health and lifestyle verbs

Complete the sentences with a verb.

She   *drinks*   a lot of coffee.

1 I don't _____ enough exercise.

2 You should _____ sunscreen if you're going to the beach.

3 He _____ too many cookies.

4 I _____ my friends every weekend.

5 You should _____ smoking; it's a terrible habit.

c   phrasal verbs

Complete the sentences with a verb.

I   *get*   up at 7:00.

get   look   put   take   turn   wake

1 Please _____ off the TV when you go to bed.

2 You should _____ up new words in a dictionary.

3 _____ up. It's 7:00 a.m.

4 _____ on a coat. It's cold.

5 I have to _____ care of my little brother today.   **15**

PRONUNCIATION

a <u>Underline</u> the word with a different sound.

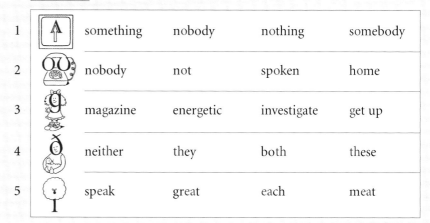

1	⬆	something	nobody	nothing	somebody
2	☎	nobody	not	spoken	home
3	👧	magazine	energetic	investigate	get up
4	👶	neither	they	both	these
5	🌳	speak	great	each	meat

b <u>Underline</u> the stressed syllable.

infor<u>ma</u>tion

somebody   relax   diet   enough   identical

   10

CAN YOU UNDERSTAND THIS TEXT?

Born to run

The Ethiopian runner, Haile Gebreselassie, the "Emperor," is probably the greatest athlete of all time. He has won two Olympic titles and seven world titles. He has also broken numerous world records in the 5,000 and 10,000 meter races. The journalist Paul Kimmage went to interview him at his home in Addis Ababa.

Haile's routine has not changed since he became an athlete. Every morning he gets up at 5:45 and runs for two hours. He takes a nap after lunch and then goes out running again.

Haile was brought up in a very poor family. Although today he is a multimillionaire, he has never been comfortable with being a rich man in such a poor country. "The thing that really offends me," he says, "is that the most important value in the 21st century is how much money you have."

In the future, when he retires from athletics, Haile may go into politics. "I want to do something to help the people of Ethiopia. I have traveled to many countries. I have experience and I want to share that experience." What Haile can't understand is why Europe is so rich and Ethiopia so poor. "I was in Germany a week ago and it was freezing! Minus five. We have a much better climate. But we don't have enough water, and so we don't have enough food, and there are too many people."

As we drive through the city in his ten-year-old Mercedes, everybody recognizes him and shouts his name. A truck carrying soldiers waits to let us pass. "Even soldiers in the army are your fans," I say. "No," replies Haile. "That was because there is a white man sitting in the front seat of the car with me."

Adapted from a newspaper

a Read the article and mark the sentences T (true), F (false), or DS (doesn't say).

1 Haile Gebreselassie is a runner.
2 He runs twice a day.
3 He enjoys being rich.
4 His family is also very rich.
5 He can't understand why Europe is richer than his country.
6 The soldiers stop because Haile is famous.

b Find a word or phrase in the article that means:

1 a short sleep (paragraph 1)
2 took care of when he was young (paragraph 2)
3 give something you have to other people too (paragraph 3)
4 very cold (paragraph 3)
5 calls in a loud voice (paragraph 4)

CAN YOU UNDERSTAND THESE PEOPLE?

a 🔊 8.18 Listen and circle the correct answer, a, b, or c.

1 Where did the woman go on the weekend?
   a to the movies   b nowhere   c to the beach
2 The man doesn't eat enough _____.
   a fruit   b fish   c vegetables
3 How often does the woman go to the gym?
   a only on Friday   b twice a week   c every day
4 What time does the woman get up?
   a 7:00   b 7:15   c 7:30
5 What do the men have in common?
   a They drink coffee.   b They used to be married.
   c They're teachers.

b 🔊 8.19 Listen and write M (the man), W (the woman), or B (both).

Who...?

1 went to bed late   ____
2 is good in the mornings   ____
3 went to Cal State   ____
4 studied economics   ____
5 knows Anna   ____

CAN YOU SAY THIS IN ENGLISH?

a Can you...? Yes (✓)

☐ talk about why you like / don't like the weekend
☐ talk about your lifestyle (food, exercise, etc.)
☐ talk about your typical morning

b Tell your partner about food you like / don't like. Find three things you have in common.

9A

G past perfect
V adverbs: *suddenly, immediately*, etc.
P review of vowel sounds, sentence stress

She had left the door open, so the man went into her house.

What a week!

Fact is always stranger than fiction.

Here is a selection of true stories that happened around the world last week.

Prize of the week.

1 James Bolton, who is unemployed, was very excited when he won first prize in a raffle last week. The prize was a weekend for two at a hotel on the coast of England. Unfortunately, he was less excited when he saw the name of the hotel. ☐

Mistake of the week

2 A 33-year-old Norwegian man came home late one night and got into bed next to his wife. The woman immediately woke up, screamed, and jumped out of bed. "Who are you?" asked the man. "You aren't my wife." ☐

Helpful advice of the week

3 An Italian man was driving along the highway when his cousin called him on his cell phone. He told him to drive more slowly, because the police were waiting a few kilometers ahead to catch drivers who were going too fast. The driver slowed down, but two kilometers later the police stopped him and gave him a ticket. ☐

Animal story of the week

4 Nurse Katie Parfitt from Manchester, UK, couldn't understand why her cat was behaving so strangely. The cat came home, attacked her bed, and then jumped on her plate while she was having her dinner. Then it fell asleep and began snoring. The next day when she spoke to her neighbor, the mystery was solved. ☐

Honest citizen of the week

5 A man in Baltimore, US, was arrested when he tried to become a police officer. When he filled out his application form for the job, he answered "yes" to the question, "Have you ever committed a crime?" ☐

Romantic hero of the week

6 The passengers on a bus in Germany were amazed when their driver suddenly stopped the bus, got out, and began hitting a man who was making a phone call in a public phone booth. First, the bus driver hit the man twice. Then the other man hit the bus driver very hard with the phone. The passengers were left sitting in the bus, and the bus driver was taken to the hospital. ☐

Adapted from a newspaper.

1 SPEAKING & READING

a Look at the pictures 1–6 on page 100. In which picture can you see…?

somebody **screaming** ☐
someone getting a **ticket** ☐
somebody winning a **raffle** ☐
something **snoring** ☐
somebody being **arrested** ☐
some passengers looking **amazed** ☐

b Read the stories and look at the pictures. Then in pairs, match them with their endings A–F.

A They had seen him using his cell phone while he was driving.

B He had discovered the day before that his girlfriend was dating the man in the phone booth.

C When they questioned him, the man admitted he had stolen a car a few months before and had robbed five people.

D The neighbor had seen it earlier that evening in a nearby cafe. One of the customers had given it a drink of rum. Luckily, it has not become an alcoholic!

E It was the hotel where he had worked as a porter the previous month. He had lost his job there.

F The man had accidentally gone into his neighbor's house. The neighbor had left the back door open because she was waiting for her husband to come home.

c Read the stories again. Look at the pictures. Can you remember the stories?

2 GRAMMAR past perfect

a Look at these sentences from story 3. Answer the questions.

 a The police stopped the driver.
 b They had seen him using his cell phone.

 1 Which action happened first, **a** or **b**?
 2 What is the form of the verb in sentence **b**?

b Read the endings of the other five stories again and underline examples of *had* + past participle. Did these actions happen *before* or *after* the main part of the story?

c ➲ **p.142 Grammar Bank 9A.** Read the rules and do the exercises.

3 PRONUNCIATION vowel sounds, sentence stress

a What sound do the pink letters make in each sentence? Match the sentences with the sound pictures.

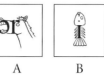

A   B   C   D   E   F

 1 He suddenly understood why his brother hadn't come. ☐
 2 I didn't know Linda hadn't written since the spring. ☐
 3 The police had seen me on the street. ☐
 4 George had taken the course before, so he was bored. ☐
 5 We hadn't heard a word about the third murder. ☐
 6 We'd waited for ages to see the famous painting. ☐

b ⬭ **9.1** Now listen and repeat the sentences. Copy the rhythm, and practice making the sounds.

4 VOCABULARY adverbs

a Circle the adverbs in these five sentences from the stories in **1**. Underline the stressed syllable. Which two adverbs are opposites?

The man had accidentally gone into his neighbor's house.

Unfortunately, he was less excited when he saw the name of the hotel.

The passengers were amazed when their driver suddenly stopped the bus.

Luckily, it has not become an alcoholic!

The woman immediately woke up, screamed, and jumped out of bed.

b Complete the sentences with one of the adverbs.

 1 I _____ took the office keys home with me.
 2 They were having a relaxing dinner when _____ the baby started to cry.
 3 The boss left, and everyone _____ started talking again.
 4 _____, the weather was terrible when we were on vacation.
 5 Last week I had a car crash. _____, nobody was hurt.

c In pairs, finish the sentences with your own ideas.

 1 She got to work very late. Luckily…
 2 I was watching a good movie on TV when suddenly…
 3 When we got out of the car, it was raining. Unfortunately, we…
 4 I got home, took a shower, and immediately…
 5 I'm really sorry about the book you lent me. I accidentally…

5 SPEAKING

➲ **Communication** *What had happened? A p.111 B p.115.*
Try to say your partner's sentences.

9

B

G reported speech
V *say*, *tell*, or *ask*?
P rhyming verbs

He said that he loved me.

Then he kissed me

1 SPEAKING & LISTENING

A

B

Mom, Dad, this is Millie.

C

Do you want to dance?

D

Will you marry me?

Yes

E

F

G

H

I love you, too.

I love you.

Then he kissed me

ask	dance	say	walk (x2)	want

1 Well, he ¹ *walked* up to me and he ² _____ me if I ³ _____ to dance.
He looked kind of nice, and so I ⁴ _____ I might take a chance.
When he ⁵ _____ he held me tight
And when he ⁶ _____ me home that night
5 All the stars were shining bright
And then he kissed me.

can't	don't know	is	say	see

Each time I ⁷ _____ him I ⁸ _____ wait to see him again.
I wanted to let him know that he ⁹ _____ more than a friend.
I ¹⁰ _____ just what to do
10 So I whispered "I love you"
And he ¹¹ _____ that he loved me, too
And then he kissed me.
He kissed me in a way that I've never been kissed before,
He kissed me in a way that I wanna be kissed forever more.

ask	feel	give	know	take

15 I ¹² _____ that he was mine, so I ¹³ _____ him all the love that I had.
And one day he ¹⁴ _____ me home to meet his mom and his dad.
Then he ¹⁵ _____ me to be his bride
And always be right by his side
I ¹⁶ _____ so happy I almost cried
20 And then he kissed me.

a Number the pictures A–H in a logical order.

b Complete the song with the verbs in the simple past. Use the glossary to help you.

c **9.2** Listen and check. Were your pictures in the correct order?

Glossary	
L.2 *He looked kind of nice*	He looked like a nice person.
L.2 *take a chance*	try something to see if you are lucky
L.3 *hold somebody tight*	put your arms around somebody strongly
L.5 *shining bright*	with a very strong light
L.14 *wanna*	want to

2 GRAMMAR reported speech

A "I love you, too."

B "Do you want to dance?"

C He said he loved me, too.

D He asked me if I wanted to dance.

a Look at the sentences. In pairs, answer the questions.

1 Which sentences are the speaker's exact words (direct speech)? ☐ ☐
2 Which sentences describe what the speaker said (reported speech)? ☐ ☐
3 What tense are the verbs in direct speech? simple p_____
4 What tense are the verbs in reported speech? simple p_____

b ⟳ **p.142 Grammar Bank 9B.** Read the rules and do the exercises.

c Change these sentences from direct speech to reported speech.

1 "My name is Dean." He said that _his name was Dean_ .

2 "Do you want a drink?" He asked her if _____ .

3 "I'm not thirsty." She said _____ .

4 "Will you go out with me?" He asked _____ .

5 "Can I walk you home?" He asked _____ .

6 "Where do you live?" He asked _____ .

7 "I live nearby." She said _____ .

8 "I fell in love at first sight." He told Millie _____ .

3 VOCABULARY say, tell, or ask?

Complete the sentences with *said*, *told*, or *asked*.

1 Jane _____ me if I could lend her some money.
2 I _____ him that I couldn't meet him tonight.
3 I _____ that I was too busy to go out.
4 We _____ the man if he could help us.
5 Annie _____: "I have a problem."
6 Annie _____ us that she had a problem.
7 She _____ her husband that she was leaving him.
8 He _____ the teacher that he had forgotten his homework.

4 PRONUNCIATION rhyming verbs

a Match a verb in the past tense from A with a rhyming one in B.

b **9.3** Listen and check.

A	B
said	slept
paid	read
caught	knew
kept	stood
spent	meant
told	played
flew	sold
heard	bought
could	preferred

5 SPEAKING

a Put a check (✓) next to five questions below to ask your partner. Ask your questions and write down his / her answers.

Do you like flying?

What's your favorite color? ☐

Can you play a musical instrument? ☐

Do you like flying? ☐

Where are your parents from? ☐

How long have you lived here? ☐

What languages do you speak? ☐

What kind of computer do you have? ☐

Do you have any phobias? ☐

Where do you buy your clothes? ☐

b Change partners. Tell partner 2 what you asked partner 1 and what his / her answers were.

I asked him what his favorite color was, and he told me that it was blue.

FILE 1 Grammar Bank p.126

In pairs or small groups, circle a, b, or c.

1 Where _____?
   a is from your sister   b your sister is from
   c is your sister from

2 **A** What _____?
   B He's a doctor.
   a does Ricardo do   b is Ricardo do   c does Ricardo

3 My father never _____ TV.
   a watch   b watchs   c watches

4 In the painting two women _____ at a table.
   a are sitting   b sits   c are sit

5 **A** What's that?
   B It's the thing _____ connects my camera to the computer.
   a who   b that   c where

FILE 2 Grammar Bank p.128

In pairs or small groups, circle a, b, or c.

1 Where _____ last summer?
   a you went   b did you went   c did you go

2 The exercise was very difficult. We _____ do it.
   a didn't can   b didn't could   c couldn't

3 When I opened the door, I saw it _____.
   a was raining   b rained   c were raining

4 Who _____ this song? I like it.
   a write   b wrote   c did write

5 _____ it was dark, I could read the map.
   a Because   b But   c Although

FILE 3 Grammar Bank p.130

In pairs or small groups, circle a, b, or c.

1 _____ take a vacation this year.
   a I don't going to   b I'm not going to
   c I'm not going

2 **A** What _____ this evening?
   B Nothing special.
   a do you do   b are you doing   c are you going

3 **A** My final exam is tomorrow.
   B You _____.
   a won't pass   b don't pass   c aren't passing

4 **A** It's hot in here.
   B _____ open the window.
   a I'll   b I   c Will

5 In my dream I saw a man. He _____ the violin.
   a was played   b playing   c was playing

FILE 4 Grammar Bank p.132

In pairs or small groups, circle a, b, or c.

1 _____ any of his movies?
   a Have you ever saw   b Did you ever seen
   c Have you ever seen

2 **A** Do you want some coffee?
   B No thanks, _____ some.
   a I've already had   b I've yet   c I already have

3 **A** Is your brother here?
   B No, he _____.
   a hasn't already arrived   b yet hasn't arrived
   c hasn't arrived yet

4 She doesn't work _____ Mary.
   a as hard as   b as hard than   c as hard

5 This is _____ city I've ever been to.
   a the nicest   b the nicer   c the most nice

FILE 5 Grammar Bank p.134

In pairs or small groups, circle a, b, or c.

1 He went to the supermarket _____ some milk.
   a for to get   b for get   c to get

2 We're thinking of _____ a new office.
   a opening   b to open   c open

3

Tomorrow's a holiday. We _____ work.

   a don't must to   b must not   c don't have to

4 You _____ show your passport when you enter the country.
   a must to   b must   c have

5 He _____ the stairs and opened the door.
   a ran   b up   c ran up

FILE 6 Grammar Bank p.136

In pairs or small groups, circle a, b, or c.

1 What will you do if you _____ the exam?
  a won't pass b don't pass c will pass

2 If we had a yard, I _____ a dog.
  a would buy b bought c 'll buy

3 I wouldn't camp near a river if I _____ there were crocodiles there.
  a would thought b thought c think

4 A What are you going to do this weekend?
  B I don't know. I _____.
  a might to go away b might go away
  c may to go away

5 You _____ coffee late at night.
  a shouldn't to drink b don't should drink
  c shouldn't drink

FILE 7 Grammar Bank p.138

In pairs or small groups, circle a, b, or c.

1 I've known my best friend _____.
  a since ten years b for ten years c for 1999

2 How long _____ your car?
  a do you have b have you c have you had

3 He's divorced now, but he _____ for 20 years.
  a has been married b was married
  c is married

4 He _____ have a lot of friends in school. He wasn't very popular.
  a didn't used to b didn't use to
  c doesn't use to

5 The radio _____ by Marconi.
  a invented b is invented c was invented

FILE 8 Grammar Bank p.140

In pairs or small groups, circle a, b, or c.

1 When I'm tired, I don't want to see _____.
  a anybody b nobody c somebody

2

I can't come tonight. I've got _____ work.

  a too many b too much c too

3 I don't eat _____. I should eat more.
  a fruit enough b some fruit c enough fruit

4 There's a towel on the floor. Please _____.
  a pick up b pick it up c pick up it

5 A I hate football.
  B _____
  a So am I. b So do I. c Neither do I.

FILE 9 Grammar Bank p.142

In pairs or small groups, circle a, b, or c.

1 We were too late. When we arrived, the game _____.
  a had finished b has finished c finished

2 They couldn't open the door because they _____ the key.
  a didn't brought b hadn't brought c haven't brought

3 "I love you." She said she _____ me.
  a love b loved c is loving

4 I asked her if _____ to dance.
  a he wanted b she wants c she wanted

5 She asked the boy what _____.
  a was his name b is his name c his name was

Do the exercises in pairs or small groups.

a Circle the word that is different.

	car	train	(station)	bus
1	funny	friendly	lazy	generous
2	eye	mouth	nose	toe
3	feet	legs	knees	fingers
4	see	hear	ear	smell
5	foggy	windy	sunny	cloudy
6	dress	cap	skirt	blouse
7	socks	shoes	pajamas	boots
8	get an e-mail	get a message	get home	get a present
9	duck	chicken	butterfly	swan
10	dolphin	whale	eagle	shark

b Complete the phrases.

carry do get go know make
meet spend sunbathe wear

1 _____ on the beach
2 _____ a coat
3 _____ a bag
4 _____ a noise
5 _____ housework
6 _____ somebody for a long time
7 _____ somebody for the first time
8 _____ swimming
9 _____ angry
10 _____ time (with your friends)

c Complete with *on, up, back,* etc.

1 I was born _____ April 2nd.
2 The bank is closed _____ weekends.
3 We always go on vacation _____ July.
4 I don't agree _____ you.
5 Wait _____ me. I'm nearly ready.
6 Don't throw _____ those newspapers.
7 I always try _____ clothes before I buy them.
8 Hurry _____. We're late.
9 I have to take care _____ my little sister today.
10 I'll pay you _____ the money tomorrow.

d Write the opposite verb or adjective.

1 friendly _____
2 talkative _____
3 crowded _____
4 rude _____
5 patient _____
6 lend money _____
7 pass an exam _____
8 push the door _____
9 find your keys _____
10 buy a house _____

e Label the pictures.

1 _____   6 _____

2 _____ the river   7 _____

3 _____   8 _____

4 _____ the tunnel   9 _____ the factory

5 _____   10 _____

Do the exercises in pairs or small groups.

a Underline the word with a different sound.

1	ʌ	nothing	enough	mouse	must
2	u	shoes	house	through	few
3	aɪ	since	nice	might	eyes
4	ɛ	many	already	friends	secret
5	oʊ	although	clothes	come	most
6	ɑ	won't	rob	father	body
7	ɚr	worn	shirt	dirty	worst
8	aʊ	mouth	how	slowly	round
9	ɔr	bored	four	story	work
10	æ	fast	pass	ask	walk
11	h	who	hour	holiday	hate
12	dʒ	age	just	enjoy	glasses
13	g	gym	argue	forget	goal
14	y	used	yet	years	very
15	w	which	where	twin	whose

b Underline the stressed syllable.

    information

1 biography
2 exercise
3 university
4 divorced
5 borrow
6 decision
7 always
8 promise
9 dangerous
10 polite
11 under
12 afraid
13 education
14 interesting
15 along
16 important
17 anything
18 depressing
19 language
20 unfortunately

c Write the words.

1 /ʃʊd/ _____
2 /ˈkwaɪət/ _____
3 /luz/ _____
4 /ɔlˈðoʊ/ _____
5 /ˈtitʃər/ _____
6 /ˈnʌθɪŋ/ _____
7 /ˈrili/ _____
8 /ˈhaʊswərk/ _____
9 /ɪnˈdʒɔɪ/ _____
10 /læf/ _____

1B Claire and Rosa **Student A**

a Ask B questions and complete the chart for Rosa.

Name	Claire	Rosa
Age?	25	
From?	Toronto, Canada	
Lives in?	Seattle, Washington	
Job?	Journalist	
Smokes?	No	
Likes?	movies, especially comedies; cats	
Doesn't like?	men who smoke	

b Answer B's questions about Claire.

c In pairs, decide who is the best girlfriend for Richard. Why?

1C Describe and draw **Student A**

a Look at your painting for a minute. Then describe it for B to draw.

b Listen to B describing his / her painting. Try to draw it. **Don't look at it.** Ask B questions to help you.

c Now compare your drawings with the original paintings!

1D Crossword **Student A**

a Ask B for the definitions of your missing words. Guess the words and complete your crossword.

What's 2 across? What's 5 down?

b Give definitions of the words B asks for.

2B Famous photos **Student A**

The Eiffel Tower painter
Marc Riboud 1953

┃ **T WAS 1953**. The photographer was living in Paris. He didn't have much money, and he was living in a small room and taking photos of the city every day. One day he saw that some people were painting the Eiffel Tower, and he decided to take some photographs. He went up the tower, and suddenly he saw the man in the photo. The man was painting. The photographer was very nervous because he was sure that the painter was going to fall. He took his photo, and a few weeks later the photo was in *Life* magazine.

The photo became very famous, and they made postcards and a poster with it. Later the company that paints the Eiffel Tower called him and invited him to lunch. They told him that the painter was an acrobat. His name was Zazou.

Leaving for Newfoundland
Willy Ronis 1949

a Look at the photos and read the text about *The Eiffel Tower painter*. Try to remember the information.

b Tell **B** the story of *The Eiffel Tower painter*. Try to tell it from memory.

c Now **B** will tell you about *Leaving for Newfoundland*.

2C Music quiz **Student A**

a Write your questions.

1 **Which singer (PLAY) soccer for Real Madrid?**
Which singer played soccer for Real Madrid _____?
  a Julio Iglesias   **b** Enrique Iglesias   **c** Placido Domingo

2 **Which group Beyoncé (SING) in?**
_____?
  a Destiny's Child   **b** The Spice Girls   **c** En Vogue

3 **Who (SING) *Livin' La Vida Loca*?**
_____?
  a Bruce Springsteen   **b** Marc Anthony   **c** Ricky Martin

4 **What kind of music the Sex Pistols (INVENT)?**
_____?
  a reggae   **b** punk   **c** hip-hop

5 **When MTV (BEGIN)?**
_____?
  a 1971   **b** 1981   **c** 1991

6 **Which of these groups (NOT HAVE) brothers or sisters in it?**
_____?
  a Oasis   **b** The Corrs   **c** Red Hot Chilli Peppers

7 **Whose daughter Michael Jackson (MARRY) in 1994?**
_____?
  a Elvis Presley's   **b** Frank Sinatra's   **c** Paul McCartney's

8 **Which Spice Girl David Beckham (MARRY) in 2000?**
_____?
  a Posh Spice   **b** Sporty Spice   **c** Ginger Spice

9 **Which group (SING) *Losing my Religion*?**
_____?
  a Blur   **b** REM   **c** Evanescence

10 **Which instrument Sting (PLAY) in the song *Every Breath you Take*?**
_____?
  a piano   **b** guitar   **c** double bass

b Ask **B** your questions. Give your partner one mark for each correct answer. Answer **B**'s questions. Who got the most correct answers?

Communication

3D Dreams Student A

a Last night you dreamed about these things. Prepare to tell **B** about your dream.

b **B** is a psychoanalyst. Tell him / her about your dream. He / she will tell you what it means.

> Last night I dreamed about a river…

c Change roles. Now you are a psychoanalyst. Listen to **B**'s dream. Number the things below in the order he / she talks about them.

> **Ice cream** – You will get some money (from the lottery or from a relative).
>
> **Long hair** – You want to be free. Perhaps you have problems with your family or your boyfriend/girlfriend.
>
> **A key** – You have a problem, and you are looking for a solution.
>
> **People speaking other languages** – You think your life is boring – you would like to have a more exciting life.
>
> **Traveling by bus** – You are worried about a person who is controlling your life.

d Now use the information in **c** to interpret **B**'s dream.

> First you dreamed about… This means…

4D The best and the worst Student A

a Write names in at least **SIX** of the ovals on p.47.

In **1**, one of the best books you've ever read.

In **2**, the coldest place you've ever been to.

In **3**, the most generous person you know.

In **4**, the most beautiful modern building you've ever seen.

In **5**, the worst program currently on TV.

In **6**, the most frightening movie you've ever seen.

In **7**, the best restaurant you've ever been to.

In **8**, the messiest person in your family.

b Go back to page 47.

5A Guess the infinitive Student A

a Look at sentences 1–6. What do you think the missing infinitives are?
Don't write anything yet!

$\boxed{+}$ = affirmative infinitive $\boxed{-}$ = negative infinitive

1 I don't like my job. I've decided _____ another one. $\boxed{+}$

2 Oh no! I forgot _____ the lights. $\boxed{+}$

3 I promise _____ anybody your secret. $\boxed{-}$

4 Your sister's really friendly. It was very nice _____ her. $\boxed{+}$

5 I was sorry _____ you when you were here last week. $\boxed{-}$

6 You don't need _____ an umbrella. It's not going to rain. $\boxed{+}$

b Read your sentence 1 to **B**. If it's not right, guess another verb until **B** says "That's right." Then write in the infinitive. Continue with 2–6.

c Listen to **B**'s sentence 7. If it's the same as 7 below, say "That's right." If not, say "Try again" until **B** gets it right. Continue with 8–12.

7 Remember **to call** your father on his birthday.

8 It's often difficult **to understand** movies in English.

9 It's a very formal dinner, so it's important **not to be** late.

10 I'm going to Australia **to visit** some friends.

11 The jacket was really expensive, so I decided **not to buy** it.

12 My phone number is very easy **to remember**.

6C Decisions, decisions Student A

a Imagine that you are a very indecisive person. **B** is going to ask you some questions. Answer **B**'s questions. Give two possibilities each time, using *I may* or *I might*. Then **B** will help you make a decision.

> I don't know. / I'm not sure. I might… or I may…

b Change roles. Now **B** is indecisive. Ask **B** question 1 below. Help **B** make a decision using *If I were you, I'd …* Say why. Continue with the other questions.

1 Where are you going to go on vacation next summer?

2 What are you going to do after class?

3 What are you going to wear tomorrow?

4 What are you going to buy when you next go shopping?

5 Where are you going to have lunch on Sunday?

7D Passives quiz **Student A**

a Complete your sentences with the verb in the passive and the right answer.

1 **Until 1664 New York** _____ (call) _____ .
   a New Amsterdam   **b** New Hampshire   **c** New Liberty

2 **Pasta** _____ (invent) by _____ .
   a the Egyptians   **b** the Italians   **c** the Chinese

3 **The Italian flag** _____ (design) by _____ .
   a Garibaldi   **b** Mussolini   **c** Napoleon

4 **The first Levi's jeans** _____ (wear) by _____ .
   a farmers   **b** miners   **c** cowboys

5 **The first credit card** _____ (use) in _____ .
   a 1950   **b** 1960   **c** 1970

6 **The Indiana Jones movies** _____ (direct) by _____ .
   a Steven Spielberg   **b** George Lucas   **c** Stanley Kubrick

7 **Penguins** _____ (find) _____ .
   a in Alaska   **b** at the North Pole   **c** at the South Pole

8 **In the world 15,000 babies** _____ (be born) _____ .
   a every second   **b** every hour   **c** every day

b Read your sentences to **B**. **B** will tell you if you are right.

c Now listen to **B**'s sentences. Tell him / her if he / she is right.

B's answers
1 The MP3 player was invented in Germany.
2 The *Star Wars* movies were directed by George Lucas.
3 Alexander the Great was born in Macedonia.
4 The book that is stolen most often from libraries is *The Guinness Book of Records*.
5 The electric chair was invented by a dentist.
6 Modern soccer was first played by the British.
7 In 1962 the original London Bridge was bought by an American.
8 The noun that is used most frequently in conversation is *time*.

9A What had happened? **Student A**

a Look at sentences 1–6 and think of the missing verb ([+] = affirmative verb, [-] = negative verb). **Don't write anything yet!**

1 Diana was very angry because her husband _____ dinner. [-]

2 He couldn't catch his plane because he _____ his passport at home. [+]

3 We went back to the hotel where we _____ on our honeymoon. [+]

4 The telephone wasn't working because they _____ the bill. [-]

5 Miriam was surprised to hear that she _____ the exam. [+]

6 The salesperson agreed to exchange the sweater because I _____ it. [-]

b Read your sentence 1 to **B**. If it's not right, try again until **B** tells you "That's right." Then write in the verb. Continue with 2–6.

c Listen to **B** say sentence 7. If it's the same as 7 below, say "That's right." If not, say "Try again" until **B** gets it right. Continue with 8–12.

7 We went back to see the house where we **had lived** when we were children.

8 The apartment was very dirty because nobody **had cleaned** it for a long time.

9 The crocodile was hungry because it **hadn't eaten** anything for a long time.

10 I ran to the station, but the last train **had left**.

11 I didn't want to lend him the book because I **hadn't read** it yet.

12 They got to the theater late and the movie **had started**.

8B Body age **Students A+B**

a Start with your calendar age. Add [+] or subtract [-] years according to your answers.

	a	b	c	d
1	−2	−1	0	+1
2	−2	−1	0	+2
3	+2	+1	0	−1
4	+1	−1	−2	
5	−2	−1	+1	
6	+1	+1	+2	0
7	−3	+1	+5	
8	−3	+1	+2	
9	+ 3	0	−2	
10	−2	+1	+1	
11	−2	−1	+2	
12	+2	+1	−1	

Communication

1B Claire and Rosa **Student B**

a Answer A's questions about Rosa.

Name	Claire	Rosa
Age?		23
From?		Mexico
Lives in?		Vancouver, Canada
Job?		Painter
Smokes?		No
Likes?		good food, music
Doesn't like?		sports

b Ask **A** questions and complete the chart for Claire.

c In pairs, decide who is the best girlfriend for Richard. Why?

1D Crossword **Student B**

a Ask **A** for the definitions of your missing words. Guess the words and complete your crossword.

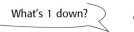

What's 1 down? | What's 6 across?

b Give definitions of the words **A** asks for.

```
        ¹
   ²M A R K E T        ³G ⁴A M E
              ⁵B     |   |
 ⁶D            I     |   |
  A       ⁷O U T G O I N G
  R           E
  K    ⁸K          ⁹      ¹⁰H
        I      ¹¹M        O
        C       O   ¹²    U
      ¹³K ¹⁴    V         S      ¹⁵
              ¹⁶I         E
               E         W
 ¹⁷                      I
                         F
 ¹⁸P O L I T I C I A N   E
              ¹⁹G E N E R O U S
```

1C Describe and draw **Student B**

a Look at your painting for a minute.

b Listen to **A** describing his / her painting. Try to draw it. **Don't look at it.** Ask questions to help you.

c Now describe your painting for **A** to draw.

d Now compare your drawings with the original paintings!

2B Famous photos **Student B**

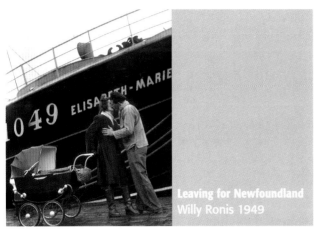

Leaving for Newfoundland
Willy Ronis 1949

HE TOOK THIS PHOTO in 1949 in France. He was working for a magazine. They wanted photos of fishermen. The people in the photo were a fisherman called Marcel, his wife, and their little baby boy. Marcel was leaving to go to Canada, and the photographer wanted to take a photo of him and his wife in front of the boat. He said, "Kiss your wife good-bye. I need a photo with a kiss." But Marcel was very shy, and he gave his wife a very cold kiss. So the photographer said, "Is that how you kiss your wife?" So he kissed her again, very naturally. This time he forgot about the photographer. The photo became very famous. Many years later Marcel saw his photo in my book, and he wrote to the photographer. He said that his son (the baby in the photo) was now 30 years old and was a fisherman, too.

The Eiffel Tower painter
Marc Riboud 1953

a   Look at the photos and read about *Leaving for Newfoundland*.

b   A will tell you about *The Eiffel Tower painter*.

c   Now tell **A** about *Leaving for Newfoundland*. Try to tell it from memory.

2C Music quiz **Student B**

a   Write your questions.

1 Which song Celine Dion (SING) in the movie *Titanic*?
Which song did Celine Dion sing in the movie Titanic _____?
a *I Will Always Love You*   **b** *My Heart Will Go On*   **c** *Love Is in the Air*

2 Who (SEND) *A Message in a Bottle* in 1979?
_____?
a The Beach Boys   **b** Dire Straits   **c** The Police

3 Who (WRITE) the song *Nothing Compares 2U*?
_____?
a Prince   **b** Sinead O'Connor   **c** Bono

4 Which "boy band" Justin Timberlake (SING) with?
_____?
a Backstreet Boys   **b** NSYNC   **c** BoyzIIMen

5 Which Beatle (DIE) in 2001?
_____?
a Ringo Starr   **b** John Lennon   **c** George Harrison

6 Who (BE) a *Material Girl*?
_____?
a Mariah Carey   **b** Madonna   **c** Christina Aguilera

7 Which heavy metal band Ozzy Osbourne (SING) with in the 1970s?
_____?
a Black Sabbath   **b** Deep Purple   **c** Led Zeppelin

8 Who (SAY) "I don't know anything about music. In my line you don't have to"?
_____?
a Eminem   **b** Arnold Schwarzenegger   **c** Elvis Presley

9 How reggae singer Bob Marley (DIE)?
_____?
a He drowned in the ocean.   **b** In a car accident.   **c** He had cancer.

10 Which song Elton John (REWRITE) for the funeral of Princess Diana in 1997?
_____?
a *Sacrifice*   **b** *Candle in the Wind*   **c** *Your Song*

b   Answer A's questions. Then ask A your questions. Give your partner one mark for each correct answer. Who got the most correct answers?

Communication

3D Dreams **Student B**

a Last night you dreamed about these things. Prepare to tell A about your dream.

b You are a pyschoanalyst. Listen to A's dream. Number the things below in the order he / she talks about them.

Taking a bath – You have a secret that nobody knows about.

Dogs – You are looking for friends.

Losing hair – You are going to lose some money.

Lost and Found – A problem you have will soon get better.

A river – You are going to be very lucky.

c Now use the information in **b** to interpret A's dream.

> Well, first you dreamed about… This means…

d Change roles. Now A is a psychoanalyst. Tell him / her about your dream. A will tell you what it means.

> Last night I dreamed that I had long hair…

4B Has he done it yet? **Students A+B**

a Work individually. Look at the list of things Max does every morning. Which ones has he already done? Try to remember what was in the picture. Write sentences.

He's already made the bed. OR *He hasn't made the bed yet.*

make the bed	turn off the computer
wash his coffee cup	put his clothes in the closet
clean up his desk	take a shower
pick up towels	have breakfast
take the dog for a walk	

b Work in pairs. Compare your sentences with your partner. Are they the same? Then go back to page 116 and compare your sentences with the picture. Were you right?

4D The best and the worst **Student B**

a Write the names in at least **SIX** of the ovals on page 47.

In **1**, the healthiest person you know.
In **2**, the best concert you've ever been to.
In **3**, the most dangerous sport or activity you've ever done.
In **4**, the cheapest person you know.
In **5**, the most boring sport you've ever watched.
In **6**, the most beautiful old building you've ever seen.
In **7**, the hottest place you've ever been to.
In **8**, the worst movie you've seen this year.

b Go back to page 47.

5A Guess the infinitive **Student B**

a Listen to A say sentence 1. If it's the same as 1 below, say "That's right." If not, say "Try again" until A gets it right. Continue with 2–6.

1 I don't like my job. I've decided **to look for** another one.
2 Oh no! I forgot **to turn off** the lights.
3 I promise **not to tell** anybody your secret.
4 Your sister's really friendly. It was very nice **to meet** her.
5 I was sorry **not to see** you when you were here last week.
6 You don't need **to take** an umbrella. It's not going to rain.

b Look at sentences 7–12. What do you think the missing infinitives are? **Don't write anything yet!**

[+] = affirmative infinitive [−] = negative infinitive

7 Remember _____ your father on his birthday. [+]
8 It's often difficult _____ movies in English. [+]
9 It's a very formal dinner, so it's important _____ late. [−]
10 I'm going to Australia _____ some friends. [+]
11 The jacket was really expensive, so I decided _____ it. [−]
12 My phone number is very easy _____. [+]

c Read your sentence 7 to A. If it's not right, guess another verb until A says "That's right." Then write in the infinitive. Continue with 8–12.

114

6C Decisions, decisions **Student B**

a A is a very indecisive person. You are going to help him / her make some decisions. Ask **A** question 1 below. Help **A** make a decision using *If I were you, I'd …* Say why. Continue with the other questions.

1 What's the next movie you're going to see?
2 What are you going to cook for dinner tonight?
3 What are you going to do on Saturday night?
4 What kind of car are you going to buy next?
5 How are you going to celebrate your next birthday?

b Change roles. Now imagine that <u>you</u> are a very indecisive person. Answer **A**'s questions. Give two possibilities each time, using *I may* or *I might* … **A** will help you make decisions.

> I don't know. / I'm not sure. I might… or I may…

7D Passives quiz **Student B**

a Complete your sentences with the verb in the passive and the right answer.

1 **The MP3 player** _____ (invent) in _____ .
  a Japan   **b** the US   **c** Germany

2 **The *Star Wars* movies** _____ (direct) by _____ .
  a George Lucas   **b** Steven Spielberg   **c** Stanley Kubrick

3 **Alexander the Great** _____ (be born) in _____ .
  a Greece   **b** Macedonia   **c** Egypt

4 **The book that** _____ (steal) **most often from libraries is** _____ .
  a The Bible   **b** *The Guinness Book of Records*   **c** *The Lord of the Rings*

5 **The electric chair** _____ (invent) by _____ .
  a a teacher   **b** a dentist   **c** a politician

6 **Modern soccer** _____ **first** _____ (play) by _____ .
  a the British   **b** the Romans   **c** the Greeks

7 **In 1962 the original London Bridge** _____ (buy) by _____ .
  a an American   **b** a museum   **c** the British royal family

8 **The noun that** _____ (use) **most frequently in conversation is** _____ .
  a *money*   **b** *time*   **c** *work*

b Now listen to **A**'s sentences. Tell him / her if they are right.

A's answers
1 Until 1664 New York was called New Amsterdam.
2 Pasta was invented by the Chinese.
3 The Italian flag was designed by Napoleon.
4 The first Levi's jeans were worn by miners.
5 The first credit card was used in 1950.
6 The Indiana Jones movies were directed by Steven Spielberg.
7 Penguins are found at the South Pole.
8 In the world 15,000 babies are born every hour.

c Read your sentences to **A**. **A** will tell you if you are right.

9A What had happened? **Student B**

a Listen to **A** say sentence 1. If it's the same as 1 below, say "That's right." If not, say "Try again" until B gets it right. Continue with 2–6.

1 Diana was very angry because her husband **hadn't cooked** dinner.
2 He couldn't catch his plane because he **had left** his passport at home.
3 We went back to the hotel where we **had stayed** on our honeymoon.
4 The telephone wasn't working because they **hadn't paid** the bill.
5 Miriam was surprised to hear that she **had failed** the exam.
6 The salesperson agreed to exchange the sweater because I **hadn't worn** it.

b Look at sentences 7–12 and think of the missing verb (+ = affirmative verb, − = negative verb). **Don't write anything yet!**

7 We went back to see the house where we _____ when we were children. +
8 The apartment was very dirty because nobody _____ it for a long time. +
9 The crocodile was hungry because it _____ anything for a long time. −
10 I ran to the station, but the last train _____ . +
11 I didn't want to lend him the book because I _____ it yet. −
12 They got to the theater late and the movie _____ . +

c Read your sentence 7 to **A**. If it's not right, try again until **A** tells you "That's right." Then write in the verb. Continue with 8–12.

3A Where are you going on vacation? **Students A+B**

FIJI

Spend two or four weeks in the South Pacific with tropical beaches, sun, water sports, etc. An unforgettable experience.

Departure June 1st

Return June 15th or 30th

Fly Quantas Airways (via Honolulu) or Air New Zealand (via Los Angeles)

Hotels Blue Lagoon (small beach hotel) Tropics (modern luxury hotel)

KENYA

Go on a two- or four-week safari for the experience of a lifetime. In a 4x4 you will see lions, zebras, and elephants in their natural habitat.

Departure June 1st

Return June 15th or 30th

Fly British Airways (via London) or KLM (via Amsterdam)

Accommodation in luxury campsites or in hotels

a Read the ads and choose a vacation. Decide:

Where are you going? _____
How are you getting there? _____
When are you leaving? _____
Where are you staying? _____
When are you coming back? _____

b Now find a partner who has planned exactly the same trip as you:

A *Where are you going?*
B *To Fiji.*
A *Me too. How are you getting there?*
B *I'm flying Air New Zealand.*
A *I'm flying Quantas Airways, so we can't go together.*

4B Has he done it yet? **Students A+B**

Look at the picture for one minute and try to remember what's in it. ➡ **p.114**

3C   *I'll* game

Follow your teacher's instructions to play the game.

5D   Cross country   **Students A+B**

a   You are the organizer of a cross-country race. You have to plan the race for the runners. Draw a route on the map marked **MY RACE**, beginning at **START** and finishing at the **FINISH** line. Your route <u>must</u> include all the things in the picture, but you can choose the order.

b   Take turns. A describe your route to your partner.
   B must draw it on your map marked **MY PARTNER'S RACE.**

   You have to go down the hill, around the lake...

c   Change roles.

d   Compare the two routes. Which is the most difficult?

Audioscripts

1.2 🔊

1 **A** When's the test?
  B Next week.
  A Yeah, I know, but what day? Is it Wednesday or Thursday?
  B Neither one. It's Tuesday.
2 **A** The weekend goes so quickly.
  B I know. I can't believe that tomorrow is Monday.
3 **A** Excuse me! Do you have the time?
  B Yes, it's twenty-five to nine.
  A Thanks.
4 **A** We're going to be late for class.
  B Relax. It doesn't start until a quarter after ten. It's only five after.
5 **A** When was she born?
  B Let's see. She was born on August 23rd, 1977.
  A Where?
  B In Colombia.
6 **A** Do you have any tickets left for the 5th of June?
  B Let's see… yes, we do. How many would you like?
  A Two, please.
  B OK, that's forty dollars, please.
7 **A** Hello?
  B Hi, it's me. I'm on your street, but I can't remember the number of your house. Is it 117?
  A No, it's 170.
8 **A** How much are those flowers?
  B Fifty dollars.
  A Fifty? That's not cheap.

1.3 🔊

Richard
I was very optimistic when I went to meet Claire. My first impression was that she was very friendly and outgoing. Physically, she was my type – she was rather slim and not very tall, with long dark hair – *very* pretty. And she was very funny, too. She had a great sense of humor. We laughed a lot. But the only problem was that Claire was *very* talkative. She talked all the time and I just listened. She wasn't very interested in me. At the end of the evening, I knew everything about her, and she knew nothing about me. Claire was the kind of woman I could have as a friend but not as a girlfriend.

1.4 🔊

When I first saw Rosa, I couldn't believe it. I thought, "Wow! Thanks, Mom." She's very attractive – she has short dark hair and she's fairly tall. She's Mexican, from Guadalajara, but her English was fantastic.
  At first, she was a little shy, but when we started talking, we found we had a lot of things in common – we both like music, good food, and traveling. We got along really well – we didn't stop talking for the whole evening. When it was time to go, I knew I really wanted to see Rosa again, and I asked her to go on another date. But… she just smiled at me and said in her beautiful

Mexican accent, "Richard, you're very sweet, but I'm sorry, you're not my type."

1.8 🔊

OK, now… the painting we're looking at now is by the French painter Toulouse-Lautrec. The painting is called *At the Moulin Rouge*. As you probably know, the Moulin Rouge is a nightclub in Paris. Maybe some of you remember the movie *Moulin Rouge*? In the nineteenth century, the nightclub was very famous for its beautiful dancers and singers. Toulouse-Lautrec did a lot of paintings and posters of the Moulin Rouge. He especially loved painting the dancers. And in these paintings he sometimes included his friends, too.
  In the middle of the picture, there are five people who are sitting at a table having a drink. The woman who's wearing a black and white hat is a dancer – her name is La Macarona – and the man sitting next to her on the left is a friend of Toulouse-Lautrec's. He was a photographer. On the right, here, there's a woman with blond hair, blue eyes, and very red lips. Her face looks very white. That's another famous dancer called Jane Avril. At the back of the picture, on the right, there are two women who are standing together. One of them is touching her hair. That's La Goulue, and she was one of the most famous singers at the Moulin Rouge at that time.
  Now this is very interesting. If you look carefully to the left of the two women, there are two men walking out of the nightclub. One of them is very tall and the other one is very short. The very tall man is Toulouse-Lautrec's cousin Gabriel, and the other man is Toulouse-Lautrec himself. Toulouse-Lautrec was only one meter 50 centimeters tall. He had very short legs and couldn't walk very well. Some people think that this is why he loved painting the dancers of the Moulin Rouge… because they all had beautiful, long legs.

1.10 🔊

Presenter Good evening, ladies and gentlemen, and welcome to *What's the word?* And our first contestant tonight is Adam. Hello, Adam. Are you nervous?
Adam A little bit.
Presenter Well, try and relax, Adam, and play *What's the word?* with us. In case you're watching the show for the first time, here's how we play the game. I have six cards with things, people, or places written on them. I'm going to give Adam definitions, and he's going to try and guess the words on my six cards. But of course, I can't use any of the words on the cards in my definitions. So, for example, if I have a card with *taxi driver*, I can't use *taxi* or *driver* in my definition. Are you ready, Adam?
Adam Uh…yes.
Presenter OK. You have two minutes to guess what's on the six cards starting now!

1.11 🔊

Presenter OK. You have two minutes to guess what's on the six cards starting now! OK, Adam. Card number 1. It's a person. It's somebody who works in a restaurant.
Adam A cook.
Presenter No, no. It's the person who takes the food from the kitchen to the tables.
Adam Oh, a _____.
Presenter That's right. Card number 2. It's a place. It's a place where you go when you want to buy something.
Adam A store.
Presenter Yes, but it's a very big store where you can buy almost anything.
Adam Is it a _____?
Presenter Yes, very good! OK, card number 3. It's a thing…uh. It's a thing that you use to talk to people.
Adam Your mouth?
Presenter No, no. It's a kind of machine. It's very small. Nearly everyone has one nowadays.
Adam _____!
Presenter That's it! Card number 4. It's an adjective. It's the opposite of *fat*.
Adam Thin?
Presenter It's like *thin*, but it means "thin and attractive."
Adam _____.
Presenter Yes! Number 5. It's an adjective again. Uh… It's how you feel when you have a lot of work.
Adam Worried?
Presenter No, but it's similar to *worried*. It's how you feel when you have a lot of things to do, but you don't have time to do them.
Adam Busy?
Presenter No!
Adam _____?
Presenter Yes, excellent! And card number 6, the last one. OK. It's a verb. For example, you do this with the TV.
Adam Watch?
Presenter No… It's the thing that you do when you finish watching the TV.
Adam Uh… go to bed?
Presenter No, you do it *to* the TV before you go to bed.
Adam Is it _____?
Presenter Yes!

1.15 🔊

Mark
Hi. My name's Mark Ryder. I'm American, and I live in San Francisco. I work for a music company called MTC. I'm divorced and I have a daughter.
  Last month I went to England on a work trip, and I met Allie. She's British, and she works for MTC in the UK. We had a great five days. We went out for coffee. We went shopping. It was my birthday, and she bought me a present. We went out for dinner. I really liked her, and I think she liked me, too.
  I invited her to a conference in San

Francisco, and she said yes. And now I'm at the airport. I'm waiting for her to arrive.

1.18

Mark Allie, hi!
Allie Hi, Mark.
Mark You look great!
Allie You too. How are you?
Mark I'm fine. How was the flight?
Allie Long! Eleven hours.
Mark You must be really tired.
Allie Yes. I couldn't sleep at all. The people next to me had a baby with them. What's the time here? I need to change my watch.
Mark It's seven in the evening.
Allie It's three in the morning for me.
Mark OK, I'm going to take you right to the hotel and you can rest.
Allie Fine. Sorry!
Mark You are going to love San Francisco! I'm so pleased you came!
Allie Me too. It's great to see you again.
Mark Come on. My car's in the parking lot. Let's go.

2.3

Presenter Hello and welcome to today's Travel Program. Today we've asked you to call in with your vacation horror stories – vacations where things went wrong. Our first caller today is Bill. Hi, Bill.
Bill Hello.
Presenter So where was this vacation?
Bill Well, this didn't happen to me; it happened to my aunt and uncle last summer.
Presenter Where did they go?
Bill To Ibiza, in Spain.
Presenter A fantastic place for a vacation.
Bill Yes, a fantastic place if you're seventeen – but they're nearly seventy!
Presenter Oh…
Bill And they wanted a quiet, relaxing vacation – you know. They like walking in the woods, sitting on quiet beaches – things like that. They don't go abroad very often, but they wanted to do something different.
Presenter So why did they choose Ibiza? It's "the party island."
Bill Yes, it is now, but they didn't know that. You see, they first went to Ibiza in the late sixties, when it was a beautiful, peaceful island with traditional cafes and restaurants, deserted beaches. And this was exactly what they wanted. So they looked on the Internet – my uncle loves using his computer – and they booked a hotel for a week in the same part of the island where they'd been before. And they found some cheap flights. It all seemed so perfect.
Presenter So what happened?
Bill Well, you can imagine. It was a complete disaster. Their hotel was in San Antonio, a resort that's full of bars and clubs.
Presenter Oh, no.
Bill Yeah… There was music until 5:00 in the morning, noise of car doors opening,

motorcycles, and people shouting. They couldn't sleep at all. They were too tired to do anything during the day. They tried to get some sleep, but they couldn't because it was too hot. When they came home, they were in a state of shock.
Presenter Oh, no… So, what are their plans for this year?
Bill I don't know. I think they'll probably stay at home this year… and next year… and probably the year after that…
Presenter Well, thank you, Bill. And now…

2.4

Marinette We didn't know that our picture was so famous until 30 years later. One day I was working in the cafe when the man from the bookstore next door came in. He was holding a new book, which had a photo on the cover. Suddenly I said, "I don't believe it! That's Henri and I when we were very young!"
   I remember that afternoon at the Bastille very well. When the man took that photo, we were arguing! Henri was standing very near me. I was saying, "Henri, don't stand so near me, there is somebody behind us."
Henri We didn't know that the photographer was taking a photo of us. We were arguing. I can't remember exactly what we were arguing about. I think I was trying to kiss Marinette and she didn't want to. Or I think maybe we were arguing about our wedding – we got married a few months after the man took the photo.
Marinette People who know this photo always think of us as the eternal lovers, like Romeo and Juliet. But life isn't like that. It's very difficult to stay in love when you see your husband every day at home, *and* you see him every day at work, too. And *I'm* very hardworking, but Henri is still a dreamer. Ah, those were the days…

2.15

Two hours later a police car arrived at Hannah's house. A policewoman knocked at the door. "Good evening, ma'am," she said. "Are you Hannah Davis? I'd like to speak to you. Can I come in?"
The policewoman came in and sat down on the sofa.
"Are you a friend of Jamie Dixon?" she said.
"Yes," said Hannah.
"I understand you were going to meet him this evening."
"Yes, at 5:30, at a coffee shop. But he didn't come, so I didn't see him."
"Well, I'm afraid I have some bad news for you," said the policewoman.
"What? What happened?"
"Jamie had an accident this evening."
"Oh no! What kind of accident?"
"He was crossing the street, and a car hit him."
"Is he ... Is he ...OK?"
"Well, he's going to be in the hospital for a long time."

"Oh no."
"But don't worry, He's going to be OK."
"When did this happen?"
"This evening at 5:25. He was crossing the street on Bridge Street."
"And the driver of the car?"
"She didn't stop."
"She?"
"Yes, it was a woman in a white car. The police are looking for her."
"Can I go to the hospital to see Jamie?"
"Yes, I can take you there now."
"I'll get my coat. OK, I'm ready."
"Is that your car, ma'am? The white one over there?"
"Yes, it is."
"Can I have a look at it? Did you know your front light is broken?"
"No, I didn't."
"What exactly were *you* doing at 5:25 this evening, ma'am?"

2.16

Clerk Good evening, ma'am. How can I help you?
Allie Good evening. I have a reservation. My name's Alison Gray. I'm here for the MTC conference.
Clerk Just a moment. Ah, here it is. Ms. Gray. For six nights?
Allie That's right.
Clerk OK, Ms. Gray. Here's your key. You're in room 419 on the fourth floor.
Allie Thank you. What time's breakfast?
Clerk From seven to nine, in the Pavilion Restaurant on the sixth floor.
Allie Thanks. Where's the lift?
Clerk The *elevators* are over there.
Allie Thanks.
Clerk Do you need any help with your bags?
Allie Yes, please.

2.19

Mark Here you go, Allie. A cappuccino – see, I remembered!
Allie Well done! Thanks.
Mark Did you sleep well?
Allie Yes, very well. How are things?
Mark They're fine.
Allie What are the plans for the week?
Mark Well, today we don't have any free time. But tomorrow I'm going to take you to this great little restaurant I know.
Allie That sounds good.
Mark And then on Wednesday night there's a cocktail party here at the hotel, and then a conference dinner on Thursday. Is there anything special you want to do?
Allie Well, I'd like to see the bay and the Golden Gate Bridge. And I'd like to go shopping if there's time.
Brad Hi, Mark, how are you doing?
Mark Hi, Brad. I'm fine, just fine.
Brad Aren't you going to introduce me?
Mark Oh, sure. Allie, this is Brad Martin. Brad works in the Los Angeles office. Brad, this is Allie Gray from the London office.
Allie Hello.

Audioscripts

Brad Hi, Allie, great to meet you. Mark told me you were very nice, but he didn't tell me you were so beautiful. So, is this your first time in San Francisco?
Allie Yes. Yes, it is.
Brad Has Mark shown you the sights?
Allie Well, not yet.
Brad Then maybe I can show you around. I love this city.
Mark Allie, it's time to go. Excuse us, Brad.
Brad Well, great to meet you, Allie. See you around.
Allie Yes. Nice to meet you, too. Good-bye.
Brad Bye.

3.1

Interviewer So Marina, did you find a job as an au pair?
Marina Well, I found a job, but not taking care of children. I'm working in a restaurant – a Mexican restaurant. I'm a waitress. I work very long hours!
Interviewer Was it difficult to find a job?
Marina No. There are lots of jobs in restaurants and hotels, things like that.
Interviewer Are you still living in your friend's apartment?
Marina Yes, because it's very expensive here and I can't afford my own apartment. New York is incredibly expensive!
Interviewer Your English is much better!
Marina Well, a bit better, but I don't go to classes, because I don't have time. As I said, I work very long hours in the restaurant. But I watch a lot of American TV, and I speak English at work.
Interviewer When are you going back to Brazil?
Marina I don't know. My plans have changed a little bit.
Interviewer Why?
Marina Well, I met someone at the restaurant. He's the chef. We're getting married next month.
Interviewer Congratulations! Is he from Brazil, too?
Marina No, he's Mexican. From Guadalajara. He's a fantastic cook.
Interviewer So, are you going to stay in New York?
Marina Yes. I'm very happy here now. We both really like New York. Our dream is to open a restaurant together someday.
Interviewer Is your family coming to the wedding?
Marina No! They don't even know I'm getting married! You see, they want me to go back to Brazil.
Interviewer Well, good luck with everything, Marina.
Marina Thank you.

3.7

Presenter Today's topic is "positive thinking." We all know that people who are positive enjoy life more than people who are negative and pessimistic. But scientific studies show that positive people are also healthier, get better more quickly when they're sick, and live longer. A recent study shows that people who are optimistic and think positively live, on average, nine years longer than pessimistic people who think negatively. So, let's hear what you the listeners think. Do you have any tips to help us be more positive in our lives?

3.8

Presenter And our first caller this evening is Andy. Hi, Andy. What's your tip for being positive?
Andy Hello. Well, I think it's very important to live in the present, not in the past. Don't think about mistakes you made in the past. You can't change the past. The important thing is to think about how you will do things better in the future.
Presenter Thank you, Andy. And now we have another caller. What's your name, please?
Julie Hi, my name's Julie. My tip is think positive thoughts, not negative ones. We all have negative thoughts sometimes, but when we start having them we need to stop and try to change them into positive ones. Like, if you have a test tomorrow and you start thinking "I'm sure I'll fail," then you'll fail the test. So you need to change that negative thought to a positive thought. Just think to yourself "I'll pass." I do this and it usually works.
Presenter Thank you, Julie. And our next caller is Rosa. Hi, Rosa.
Rosa Hi. My tip is don't spend a lot of time reading the newspapers or watching the news on TV. It's always bad news, and it just makes you feel depressed. Read a book or listen to your favorite music instead.
Presenter Thanks, Rosa. And our next caller is Mi-young. Mi-young?
Mi-young Hi.
Presenter Hi, Mi-young. What's your tip?
Mi-young My tip is every week make a list of all the good things that happened to you. Then keep the list with you, in your bag or in a pocket, and if you're feeling a little sad or depressed, just take it out and read it. It'll make you feel better.
Presenter Thanks, Mi-young. And our last call is from Michael. Hi, Michael. We're listening.
Michael Hi. My tip is to try to use positive language when you speak to other people. You know, if your friend has a problem, don't say "I'm sorry" or "Oh poor you." Say something positive like "Don't worry! Everything will be OK." That way you'll make the other person think more positively about their problem.
Presenter Thank you, Michael. Well that's all we've got time for. A big thank-you to all our callers. Until next week then, good-bye.

3.13

Patient So what does it mean, doctor?
Doctor Well, first the party. A party is a group of people. This means that you're going to meet a lot of people. I think you're going to be very busy.
Patient At work?
Doctor Yes, at work... you work in an office, I think?
Patient Yes, that's right.
Doctor I think the party means you are going to have a lot of meetings.
Patient What about the champagne?
Doctor Let me look at my notes again. Ah yes, you were drinking champagne. Champagne means a celebration. It's a symbol of success. So we have a meeting or meetings and then a celebration. Maybe in the future you'll have a meeting with your boss, about a possible promotion?
Patient Well, it's possible. I hope so... What about the garden and the flowers? Do they mean anything?
Doctor Yes. Flowers are a positive symbol. So, the flowers mean that you are feeling positive about the future. So perhaps you already knew about this possible promotion?
Patient No, I didn't. But it's true, I am very happy at work and I feel very positive about my future. That's not where my problems are. My problems are with my love life. Does my dream tell you anything about that?
Doctor Hmm, yes, it does. You're single, aren't you?
Patient Yes, well, divorced.
Doctor Because the violin music tells me you want some romance in your life. You're looking for a partner perhaps?
Patient Yes, yes, I am. In fact, I met a very nice woman last month – I really like her... I think I'm in love with her. I'm meeting her tonight...
Doctor In your dream you saw an owl... in a tree?
Patient Yes, an owl... a big owl.
Doctor The owl represents an older person. I think you'll need to ask this older person for help. Maybe this "older person" is me? Maybe you need my help?
Patient Well, yes, what I really want to know is... Does this person... this woman... love me?
Doctor You remember the end of your dream? You were feeling cold?
Patient Yes, my feet were very cold.
Doctor Well... I think perhaps you already know the answer to your question.
Patient You mean she doesn't love me.
Doctor No, I don't think so. I think you will need to find another woman. I'm sorry.

3.15

Waiter Are you ready to order?
Mark Yes, to start a tomato and mozzarella salad – is that right, Allie?
Allie Yes.
Mark And the mushroom soup for me.
Waiter And for your main course?
Allie I'll have the fried chicken.
Waiter With French fries or a baked potato?
Allie A baked potato, please.
Waiter And for you, sir?

Mark And I'd like the steak, with French fries.
Waiter How would you like your steak? Rare, medium, well-done?
Mark Rare, please.
Waiter And to drink?
Mark Could your bring us the wine list, please?

3.18

Waiter Your check, sir.
Mark Thanks.
Waiter Thank you.
Allie Thank you, Mark. That was a lovely dinner.
Mark I'm glad you enjoyed it.
Allie How's your daughter?
Mark Jennifer? She's fine. She's with her mother in Los Angeles.
Allie Mark?
Mark Yeah.
Allie Can I ask you something? Something personal?
Mark Sure. What?
Allie How long were you married?
Mark Three years.
Allie Why did you break up?
Mark There were a lot of reasons. We were very young when we had Jennifer. We were both working very hard. We didn't spend much time together… the usual story. What about you, Allie?
Allie Well, there was someone. I met him when I was at university. We were together for two years. We broke up.
Mark Why?
Allie I don't know. Usual story!
Mark Thank you. Listen, it's early – it's only nine o'clock. Shall we go for a walk?
Allie Good idea. Where shall we go?
Mark There's a place called Fisherman's Wharf – it's right on the bay. There are lots of cafes and bars. We could have another cup of coffee.
Allie Fine. Let's go.

4.2

1
Interviewer Excuse me, sir, I'm doing a … sir? Excuse me, ma'am, do you have a few minutes to answer…
Passer-by Sorry, I really don't have time.
Interviewer Excuse me. Could I ask you a few questions about Zara?
Woman 1 Yes, OK.
Interviewer Have you ever been to a Zara store?
Woman 1 Yes, many times.
Interviewer And when did you last go there?
Woman 1 About three weeks ago.
Interviewer And where was that?
Woman 1 Here in Houston. At the Galleria Mall.
Interviewer OK, thank you. What did you buy?
Woman 1 Uh, a white jacket.
Interviewer And are you happy with it?

Woman 1 Hmm…yes and no. I like the jacket, but the color was a mistake. It's already dirty.
Interviewer Thank you very much for your time.
2
Interviewer Hello. Do you mind if I ask you a few questions about Zara?
Woman 2 How long will it take?
Interviewer Only a few minutes.
Woman 2 Well, all right.
Interviewer Have you ever been to a Zara store?
Woman 2 Yes.
Interviewer When did you last go there?
Woman 2 Last month.
Interviewer Where?
Woman 2 In Spain.
Interviewer What did you buy?
Woman 2 Just a scarf. I tried on some pants, but I didn't buy them.
Interviewer Are you happy with the scarf?
Woman 2 Yes. I like it a lot.
3
Interviewer Have you ever been to a Zara store?
Man Yes, once.
Interviewer When did you go there?
Man In August.
Interviewer Where?
Man At an airport.
Interviewer Uh-huh. What did you buy?
Man Well, I *almost* bought lots of things, but in the end I didn't buy anything. But my girlfriend bought some shoes.

4.8

1 Definitely more. My daughter got married last year, and she and her husband live pretty far away. She calls me almost every day to tell me how everything is going, and we usually talk for hours. My phone bill is now double what it was when she was living at home.
2 I spend a lot less time than before. My youngest child just started school, and I've gone back to work, so I never make lunch now during the week – I just have a sandwich. And in the evenings we often get take-out pizza or Chinese food, or we heat something up in the microwave. I spend a little more time in the kitchen on weekends, though.
3 Well, I'd say less – though I'm not sure if my parents would agree. I get so much homework now that I never go to bed before 11:00 or 12:00, but I still get up at 7:00 in the morning. It's true I get up later on weekends, but that's only two days out of seven.
4 More, much more. Before, it only used to take me fifteen minutes to get to work, and now it takes me at least half an hour. It's mainly because there are just more cars on the road. Sometimes I think I should use public transportation, but it's so complicated from where I live.

4.9

Tim
First I did the photo test. I was near Charing Cross station. I stopped a man who was walking fairly slowly down the street and I said, "Excuse me, could you take my photo?" The man said, "No, no, I have no time for that," and just continued walking. Then I asked a woman in a business suit, who was walking toward the station. She took one photo, but when I asked her to take another one, she walked away quickly.

Next, it was the shopping test. I went to a souvenir shop and bought a key ring and a red bus. The red bus was very expensive. The total price was £40. I gave the man £100 – two fifty-pound bills. He gave me £60 back.

Finally, it was time for the accident test. For this test, I went down into the Tube (the London subway). As I went down the stairs, I purposely fell down and landed on the floor. A man immediately stopped and looked down at me. I thought he was going to help me, but he didn't. He just said, "Why don't you look where you're going?"

4.11

Clerk Good morning, ma'am. How can I help you?
Allie I want to go shopping. Where's the best place to go?
Clerk Well, all the big department stores are around Union Square.
Allie Can you tell me how to get there?
Clerk Yes, of course. Go out of the hotel and turn left. Go straight ahead, down Sutter Street. Turn left at Stockton – it's the third street on the left. Union Square will be right in front of you. You can't miss it.
Allie Thanks.

4.14

Allie Oh, where is it? Excuse me. Can you tell me the way to Union Square?
Brad Hey – don't I know you?
Allie I don't think so.
Brad Allie, I'm Brad! Brad Martin from the Los Angeles office. I'm Mark's friend, remember? We met yesterday at the hotel.
Allie Oh yes, that's right. Brad. I'm so sorry.
Brad No problem. What are you doing here?
Allie I want to go shopping. I'm looking for Union Square. But I'm lost.
Brad Where's Mark?
Allie He's at the hotel – he had a meeting, I think.
Brad Listen, Allie. I'm going to take you for a cup of coffee at Del Monico's – they have the best coffee in San Francisco, and amazing cookies. And then I'll walk with you to Union Square.
Allie That's really kind of you. Are you sure?
Brad Absolutely. It's my pleasure.
Allie OK. Great. I'm awful with new cities. I always get lost.
Brad Oh, I love your British accent…

5.1

1

Harry Hello, you're one of Peter's friends, aren't you?
Alan That's right. I'm Alan.
Harry Hi, I'm Harry. Are you enjoying the party?
Alan Yes, I am.
Harry So, what do you do for a living, Alan?
Alan I'm a doctor.
Harry A doctor? Oh, good. Listen, I have a problem with my back. Could you take a look at it? I've got a pain right here…
Alan I'm sorry, can you excuse me? I see Peter over there, and I want to wish him a happy birthday.

2

Man Jim, this is Sandra.
Jim Hi.
Sandra Nice to meet you.
Man Sandra's a math teacher in a high school.
Jim A teacher? Really? What a wonderful job! You're so lucky.
Sandra Why lucky?
Jim Well, you have really long summer vacations!
Sandra Yes, that's what people always say. Maybe you would like to teach my class sometime. When you teach teenagers all year, you *need* a long summer vacation.

3

Kate Hello. We haven't met before, have we?
Luke No, I don't think so.
Kate I'm Kate. I'm Peter's sister.
Luke Oh, hi, I'm Luke. I went to school with Peter.
Kate Ah, Luke! You're the travel agent, aren't you?
Luke Yes, I am.
Kate Peter's told me all about you. Listen, can you recommend a cheap vacation? I'd like to go somewhere hot. And I want to go in August. But when I say cheap, I mean cheap. Oh, and I can't fly because I'm terrified of flying.

4

Woman Deborah, can I introduce you to an old friend of mine, Laura?
Deborah Hi, Laura.
Laura Nice to meet you.
Woman Laura's my hairdresser.
Deborah Ah. You're just the person I want to talk to. Laura, what do you think of my hair color?
Laura Well…
Deborah Come on, tell me the truth. Is it too blond?
Laura Uh… no. I think it's fine.
Deborah Are you sure?
Woman Laura, what would you like to drink?
Laura Oh, a diet soda, please.
Deborah Do you think my hair would look better shorter?
Woman Deborah, Laura's not at work now.
Deborah Oh… sorry.

5

Andrea Hi. I'm Andrea. Nice to meet you.
Steve Hello. My name's Steve.
Andrea What do you do, Steve? No, don't tell me! Let me guess your job! Let me see. You look like a … professional athlete.
Steve No… I'm a psychiatrist.
Andrea A psychiatrist! Ooh, how fascinating! Steve …? Are you analyzing me?
Steve Uh, no, I'm not. Excuse me, uh, Andrea. I need to go to the restroom.

5.5

Interviewer Good evening and welcome. In today's program, we're going to talk about singing. In the studio we have Martin, the director of a singing school in Atlanta, and Jenny, a student at Martin's school. Good morning to both of you.
Martin & Jenny Good morning.
Interviewer First, Martin, can you tell us, why is it a good idea for people to learn to sing?
Martin First, because singing makes you feel good. And secondly, because singing is very good for your health.
Interviewer Really? In what way?
Martin Well, when you learn to sing, you need to learn to breathe correctly. That's very important. And you also learn to stand and sit correctly. As a result, people who sing are often in better shape and healthier than people who don't.
Interviewer Are your courses only for professional singers?
Martin No, not at all. They're for everybody. You don't need to have any experience singing. And you don't need to be able to read music.
Interviewer So how do your students learn to sing?
Martin They learn by listening and repeating. Singing well is really 95% listening.
Interviewer OK, Jenny. Tell us about the course. How long did it last?
Jenny Only one day. From ten in the morning to six in the evening.
Interviewer Could you already sing well before you started?
Jenny No, not well. But I *have* always liked singing. But I can't read music, and I never thought I sang very well.
Interviewer So what happened in the course?
Jenny Well, first we did a lot of listening and breathing exercises, and we learned some other interesting techniques.
Interviewer What kind of things?
Jenny Well, for example, we learned that it's easier to sing high notes if you sing with a surprised look on your face!
Interviewer Oh really? Could you show us?
Jenny Well, I'll try.
Interviewer And for those of you at home, I can promise you that Jenny looked *very* surprised. Were you happy with your progress?
Jenny Absolutely. By the end of the course, we were singing in almost perfect harmony. It was amazing. In just one day we really were much better.
Interviewer Could you two give us a little demonstration?
Martin & Jenny Oh, OK.

5.7

I arrived at São Paulo Airport with Fabiana, my guide. Test number one. I had to get a taxi to the hotel. I said to the taxi driver, in Portuguese, "To the Holiday Inn Hotel, please" – *"Vamos para o hotel Holiday Inn, por favor."* No problem. The driver understood me. But then he started talking to me in perfect English. I felt a little stupid.

We got to the hotel, checked in, and then we went to a cafe for test number two. A waitress came up to us and I said, *"Uma água mineral, por favor."* That is, a mineral water, please. Then the waitress said something in Portuguese and I understood her! She said, "A large or a small water?" "Large," I said. I was so happy that I could understand her. I really enjoyed that drink.

Next we went out into the street for test three: asking for directions. I decided to ask for directions to a drugstore because I knew the word for drugstore, *farmácia.* I stopped a woman who looked friendly and I said, in Portuguese, "Excuse me, please, is there a drugstore near here?" No problem. But then she started talking really fast and pointing. I tried to listen for *left* or *right* or anything I could understand, but no, I couldn't understand anything. I was sure that Fabiana was going to give me zero for this test!

I was feeling less confident now. We went back to the hotel for test four: making a phone call. Fabiana gave me a phone number and told me to ask to speak to her friend. His name was Adam. I dialed the number. A woman answered the phone. "Is Adam there?" I said hopefully. *"Não, ele não está,"* she said. I understood that! "No, he's not in." I wanted to say, "When will he be back?" but I could only say "When home?" *"Quando em casa?"* And I didn't understand her answer. So I said thank you and good-bye very politely. Fabiana smiled, so I thought, well, that wasn't bad.

Finally, test five: asking for the time. I *knew* this test was going to be easy. Numbers in Portuguese aren't too difficult for me, and I've always found telling the time very easy. I stopped a man in the street and said, "Excuse me, do you have the time?" Surprisingly, I couldn't understand the answer, but I had a great idea and said, "Can I see your watch, please?" He showed it to me. Seven forty. Perfect!

How well did I do on the tests? Well, Fabiana gave me five out of ten for language, and eight for imagination. So can you learn a language in a month? Not Portuguese, definitely!

5.12

Salesperson Can I help you?
Allie Yes, I really like this sweater. Do you have it in a medium?

Salesperson Let's see... um...we have it in red in a medium.

Allie No, I want it in black.

Salesperson Just a minute, I'll go and check. Here you are. A black medium. Do you want to try it on?

Allie No, thanks. I'm sure it'll be fine. How much is it?

Salesperson $43.38.

Allie It says $39.99.

Salesperson Yes, but that doesn't include sales tax – that's 8.5% extra.

Allie Oh, OK. Do you take MasterCard™?

Salesperson Yes, of course.

🔊 5.15

Mark Allie! You look great, as usual. How was your morning?

Allie Really good. First I went shopping, and then I went to the Museum of Modern Art.

Mark What did you think of it?

Allie It was wonderful. But I didn't have enough time to see it all. Never mind.

Mark Maybe next time.

Allie What a lovely evening!

Brad Hi, Allie. How was the shopping?

Allie Great, thanks.

Brad Hi, Mark. And did you like the museum? I hope you didn't get lost again!

Mark Hey, I didn't know you two were friends already.

Allie We met this morning. I got lost. I was trying to find Union Square – and suddenly Brad appeared.

Brad So I took her to my favorite coffee shop.

Mark Allie, what would you like to drink?

Allie I'd like a cocktail please. A margarita.

Brad What a good idea. I'll have one, too. Mark, could you get us a couple of margaritas?

Mark Oh, so now I'm the waiter, am I?

Brad So tell me about the museum, Allie. What was your favorite painting?

🔊 6.4

Interviewer OK, Michael, can you tell us what to do in these three situations? First, what about the crocodile attack?

Michael Well, once a crocodile has seen you, it will attack you. So doing nothing is not really an option. And a crocodile attacks so quickly that people never have time to swim to safety. The crocodile will try to get you in its mouth and take you under the water. Your only hope is to try to hit it in the eye or on the nose. If you did this and you were very lucky, the crocodile would open its mouth and give you time to escape. But I have to say that it's very difficult, although not impossible, to survive a crocodile attack.

Interviewer What about the bear attack?

Michael When a bear attacks someone, their natural reaction is always to try to run away or to climb up a tree. But these are both bad ideas. Bears can run much faster than we can and they're also much better and faster at climbing trees. The best thing to do in this situation would be to pretend

to be dead. A bear usually stops attacking when it thinks that its enemy is dead, and so, if you were lucky, it would lose interest in you and go away.

Interviewer And finally, the bull attack.

Michael Well, if you were in the middle of a field, forget about running. Bulls can run incredibly fast. And don't shout or wave your arms because bulls react to movement, and this will just make the bull come in your direction. The best thing to do is to try not to move, and just stay where you are, and then at the last moment to throw something, a hat or your shirt, away from you. If you were lucky, the bull would change direction to follow the hat or shirt and you'd be able to escape. By the way, it doesn't matter what color the shirt is. It isn't true that bulls like red. They don't see color; they only see movement.

🔊 6.11

Presenter Welcome to this morning's edition of *What's the problem?* Today we're talking about friends, so if you have a problem with one of your friends, call us now. And if you're listening to the program, and you think you can help with any of the problems, just send an e-mail to our website. Our e-mail address is what.problem@radiotalk.com. Our first caller today is Barbara. Hello, Barbara.

Barbara Hello.

Presenter So, Barbara, what's the problem?

Barbara Well, I have a problem with a friend called Jonathan. (That's not his real name.) Well, Jonathan often goes out with me and my friends. The problem is that he's really cheap.

Presenter Cheap?

Barbara Yes, he never pays for anything. When we have a drink, he always says he doesn't have any money or that he forgot to bring his wallet. So in the end one of us always pays for him. At first, we thought, "Poor Jonathan, he doesn't have much money." But it's not true. His parents work, and he works on Saturdays in a store – so he must have some money. Do you think we should say something to him?

Presenter Thanks, Barbara. I'm sure you'll soon get some e-mails with good advice. OK, our next caller is Kevin. Hello, Kevin.

Kevin Hi.

Presenter What's the problem?

Kevin Uh, my problem is with my best friend. Well, the thing is, he's always flirting with my girlfriend.

Presenter Your best friend flirts with your girlfriend?

Kevin Yes, when the three of us are together, he always says things to my girlfriend like, "Wow! You look fantastic today," or "I love your dress, Suzanne," things like that. And when we're at parties, he always asks her to dance.

Presenter Well, do you think he's in love with your girlfriend?

Kevin I don't know, but I'm really angry

about it. What can I do?

Presenter Well, let's see if one of our listeners can help, Kevin. And our last caller is Catherine. OK, Catherine, over to you. What's the problem?

Catherine Hello. I'm in college and I live on campus. I live in a dormitory, and I share a room with a roommate. She's really nice. I get along very well with her, but there's one big problem.

Presenter What's that?

Catherine Well, she always borrows things from me without telling me.

Presenter What does she borrow?

Catherine Well, first it was CDs and books, but then she started taking my clothes too... sweaters, jackets, and things. Yesterday she took a white sweater of mine and she didn't tell me. So when I wanted to wear it this afternoon, it was dirty. I don't want to lose her as a friend, but what should I do?

Presenter Thank you, Catherine. So... if you can help Barbara, Kevin, or Catherine, e-mail us at what.problem@radiotalk.com...

🔊 6.14

Clerk Hi. How can I help you?

Allie Do you have any painkillers? I have a headache.

Clerk I'm sorry. We can't give our guests medicine. But we can call a doctor for you if you like.

Allie No, it's OK. I don't need a doctor. It's just a cold. But is there a chemist's near the hotel?

Clerk Do you mean a pharmacy?

Allie Sorry, that's right, a pharmacy.

Clerk Sure. There's one right across the street.

Allie Thank you.

Clerk You're welcome.

🔊 6.17

Mark Bless you! Are you OK?

Allie It's just a cold. I had a bad headache this morning, but I feel better now.

Mark Listen. I'm really sorry about last night.

Allie What do you mean?

Mark At the party. I got kind of angry at Brad. He was really annoying me.

Allie Oh, I think he's very nice.

Mark Yeah, women always think so.

Allie Don't worry, Mark. Brad's not my type.

Mark So what is your type, Allie?

Allie You know what my type is. Dark hair, 34 years old, lives in San Francisco...

Mark Listen, tomorrow's your last day. I want to do something special. What would you like to do?

Allie I don't mind. You choose.

Mark How about a boat trip around the bay? We could do that in the morning, and then have a nice dinner in the evening.

Allie That sounds fantastic.

Mark It's too bad you can't stay longer.

Allie Yes, it's a pity – this week has gone so quickly. I feel I've just arrived and now

I'm going home.

Mark Well, I'm going to make sure tomorrow is a really special day.

7.1

Interviewer What exactly is your phobia, Scott?

Scott Well, the medical name is felinophobia or gatophobia.

Interviewer And what does that mean exactly?

Scott It means I'm afraid of cats.

Interviewer Cats?

Scott Yes.

Interviewer How long have you had this phobia?

Scott Since I was a child.

Interviewer And how did it start?

Scott When I was five or six years old, I remember going to a friend's house, and I saw a cat on the stairs. And the cat was looking at me, well, staring at me. I went to touch it, and it bit me. And since then I've always been afraid of cats.

Interviewer What happens if you see a cat?

Scott Well, I start to feel very nervous, and my heart beats quickly. And I have to go away very quickly from where the cat is. For example, if I see a cat on the street, I always cross to the other side.

Interviewer Hmm... What do you do?

Scott I'm a doctor.

Interviewer Is your phobia a problem for you in your work?

Scott Yes, sometimes. For example, if I go to a house and there is a cat, I have to ask the people to put the cat in another room. I can't be in the same room as a cat.

Interviewer Hmm. Have you ever had any treatment for your phobia?

Scott Yes, I just started going to a therapist. I've had three sessions.

Interviewer How's it going?

Scott Well, now I can look at a photo of a cat without feeling nervous or afraid. And I can touch a toy cat. The next step will be to be in a room with a real cat.

Interviewer Do you think you will ever lose your phobia of cats?

Scott I hope so. I'm optimistic. Who knows, maybe someday I'll have a cat as a pet.

7.5

Presenter Good evening and welcome to *Movie of the Week*. Tonight we are going to see Sofia Coppola's movie *Lost in Translation*. This movie came out in 2003, and it gave the young director her first Oscar nomination. Before it starts, Anthony, can you tell us a little bit about her?

Anthony Well, of course as you know, Sofia Coppola is the daughter of Francis Ford Coppola, so you could say that she was born with a camera in her hand. She was born in New York in 1971 while her father was making the movie *The Godfather*, and

in fact she actually appeared in the movie – she was the little baby in the baptism scene.

After she graduated from school, she decided to become an actress, but her career as an actress didn't last long. When her father made *The Godfather Part III*, he gave his daughter a part in the movie. She played Mary Corleone, the Godfather's daughter. But it was a disaster, and the movie critics wrote terrible things about her. So she stopped being an actress, and she went to the California Institute of Art, where she studied fine arts and photography. Then she decided to become a movie director.

Nineteen-ninety-nine was a really big year for her. She directed her first movie, *The Virgin Suicides*, and this time the critics thought she was great. She also got married, to the movie director Spike Jonze – but they separated after a few years.

And then in 2003 she made her next movie, which is the one we're going to see now, called *Lost in Translation*. *Lost in Translation* was the movie that made Sofia Coppola famous. For this movie she became the first American woman to be nominated for an Oscar for best director, although she didn't win it.

Presenter Thank you very much, Anthony. And now, let's watch *Lost in Translation*.

7.6

Interviewer How old are you in the photograph, Melissa?

Melissa Twelve or thirteen, I think.

Interviewer Did you like school?

Melissa Not really.

Interviewer Why not?

Melissa Because I didn't like any of the subjects. Well, that's not completely true; I liked English, but that was the only class I used to look forward to. I didn't like math, didn't like science at all, and I *hated* phys ed. I used to argue with the PE teacher all the time. She used to make us do impossible things, things we couldn't do, like climbing ropes and jumping over the horse. I think she just wanted to humiliate us.

Interviewer Were you "a good girl" at school?

Melissa It depends on what you mean by "good." I didn't smoke, I didn't use to write graffiti on the walls or anything like that. But I was a little bit of a rebel. I used to break rules all the time, and of course the teachers didn't like that.

Interviewer What kind of rules did you break?

Melissa Well, for example, the school was very strict about the school uniform – we had to wear a blue skirt, and the skirt had to cover our knees. I used to make the skirt shorter. And sometimes I used to wear blue socks and a black sweater, like in the photo, instead of a gray sweater, and gray socks. The teachers used to get really angry; I just thought it was silly.

Interviewer What did you want to be when you were in school?

Melisssa I wanted to be a lawyer.

Interviewer Why?

Melissa Well, I used to watch a lot of TV programs and movies about lawyers at the time, and I used to think it would be fun to argue with people all day.

Interviewer So why did you become an elementary school teacher?

Melissa Lots of reasons. But I think the main reason is that both my parents were teachers, and they both used to tell me, "When you grow up and get a job, *don't* be a teacher." So as I was a rebel, I did exactly the opposite.

7.11

Presenter Good afternoon, and welcome to another edition of *Science Today*. In today's program we are going to hear about women inventors. When we think of famous inventors, we usually think of men, such as Alexander Graham Bell, Guglielmo Marconi, Thomas Edison. But as historian Sally Brown will tell us, many of the things that make our lives easier today were invented by women.

Sally That's absolutely right. Let's take the dishwasher, for example. This was invented by a woman named Josephine Cochrane in 1886. She was a rich American woman who gave a lot of dinner parties. But she was annoyed that her servants used to break plates and glasses when they were washing them after the party. So, Josephine decided to try to invent a machine that could wash a lot of plates and glasses safely. Today the dishwasher is used by millions of people all over the world.

The car was invented by a man, but it was a woman, Mary Anderson, who in 1903 solved one of the biggest problems of driving. Until her invention, it was impossible for drivers to see where they were going when it was raining or snowing. The name of her invention? Windshield wipers.

A fantastic invention that definitely improved the lives of millions of people was disposable diapers. They were invented by a woman named Marion Donovan in 1950. Anybody who has a small baby will know what a big difference disposable diapers make in our lives. Today more than 55 million disposable diapers are used every day in the world.

A few years later in 1956, Bette Nesmith Graham was working as a secretary. She used to get frustrated and angry when she made typing mistakes. In those days if you made a mistake, you had to get a new sheet of paper and start again from the beginning. She had a brilliant idea, which was to use a white liquid to paint over mistakes. Her invention is called white-out today. Ms. Graham was a divorced mother, and her invention made her a very rich woman.

And finally… Police officers, soldiers, and politicians all over the world are protected by something that was invented by a woman. In 1966 Stephanie Kwolek invented kevlar, a special material that was very light but extremely strong, much stronger than metal. And this material is used to make the bulletproof vest. Her invention has probably saved thousands of lives.

Presenter Thanks very much, Sally. So… if you thought that everything was invented by men, think again.

🔊 **7.14**

Mark Hi, Allie. How are you feeling today?
Allie Much better.
Mark Good. Are you going to be warm enough with just that sweater? It might be a little cold on the boat.
Allie I'll be fine. Are we going to walk to the bay?
Mark No, it's too far. It's better if we get a cab.
Allie How long does it take by cab?
Mark About ten minutes.
Allie And how long's the boat trip?
Mark I'm not sure. I think it's an hour. Why?
Allie Well, I have to be back here by 1:00 – I'm expecting an important phone call.
Mark Not from Brad, I hope?
Allie Well, actually… No, of course not! From the New York office.
Mark OK. Let's go.

🔊 **7.17**

Mark So, what do you think of San Francisco?
Allie It's beautiful, Mark. I love it.
Mark Better than London?
Allie Not better. Different.
Mark Do you think you could live here?
Allie No, I don't think so.
Mark Oh. Why?
Allie Well, it's a long way from London. I think I'd miss all my family and friends.
Mark Could you live somewhere else – but in *Europe*?
Allie Maybe. Why do you ask?
Mark Oh, no reason. I just wondered.
On your left you can see the island of Alcatraz.
Mark Look, can you see that building? That used to be the prison, but it was closed in 1963. It's a museum now.
Allie Where are we going for dinner tonight?
Mark It's a surprise.
Allie I'm really looking forward to it.
Mark Me too.
Allie Brr. I'm cold.
Mark Do you want to borrow my coat?
Allie No. It's OK. I'm going to miss you, Mark.
Mark Hey, excuse me! Could you take a photo of us, please?
Man Sure. Are you ready?
Allie Ready.
Man Say cheese!

🔊 **8.3**

Newsreader And now for our top news story. Last Friday Steve Olson, a businessman from Seattle, was looking forward to a relaxing two days in the mountains. He and his wife had arranged a skiing weekend in a luxury hotel. But the weekend didn't work out exactly as they had planned.

Steve worked until late on Friday evening. His office was on the 12th floor. When he finished, at 8 o'clock, he locked his office and got into the elevator… and he didn't get out again until Monday morning!
Steve I pressed the button for the first floor, and the elevator started going down but then stopped. I pressed the button again, but nothing happened. I pressed the alarm and shouted, but nobody heard me. Most people had already gone home. I tried to call my wife, but my cell phone didn't work in the elevator… I couldn't do anything. I just sat on the floor and hoped maybe somebody would realize what had happened. But on Saturday and Sunday, I knew nobody would be there. I slept most of the time to forget how hungry I was.
Newsreader Meanwhile Steve's wife, Kate, was waiting for her husband to come home.
Kate I was very worried when he didn't come home on Friday evening, and I couldn't understand why his cell phone wasn't working. I called the police, and they looked for him but couldn't find him anywhere. I thought maybe he was with another woman.
Newsreader So Steve was in the elevator the whole weekend from Friday evening until Monday morning. At 8 o'clock, when the office workers arrived, they called the emergency number, and somebody came and repaired the elevator.
Steve I was very happy to get out. I hadn't eaten since Friday afternoon, and I was extremely hungry. It's lucky that I'm not claustrophobic because the elevator was very small. The first thing I did was to call my wife to say that I was OK.
Newsreader Steve will soon be the fittest man in his office – from now on he's going to take the stairs every day – even though it's 12 floors.

🔊 **8.6**

Interviewer Excuse me. Could I ask you a few questions? We're doing some research.
David Sure. What's it about?
Interviewer Well, we want to find out if you are a morning or an evening person.
David OK, fine.
Interviewer OK, and what's your name?
David David Cope.
Interviewer And, what do you do, David?
David I'm a magazine editor.
Interviewer OK, and when do you work?
David Monday to Friday, eight till four.
Interviewer What time do you get up in the morning?

David At 5:45. I have to get up early because I start work at 8:00, and it takes me an hour to get to work.
Interviewer What time do you go to bed?
David Probably around 10 o'clock.
Interviewer If you have a test, do you study best in the morning, afternoon, or at night?
David Let me think, I haven't taken a test for a long time, but when I was a student, I used to study better in the morning.
Interviewer And… if you exercise, when do you prefer to do it?
David In the morning, definitely. I love going for a long walk or cycling. It's really great early in the morning because you feel that you're the only person in the world who's awake at that time.
Interviewer Do you like your work schedule?
David I don't mind it. Finishing work early means I can pick up my daughter from school and take care of her in the afternoons. It's true that I can't really have a social life during the week because I go to bed at ten, but that's OK.
Interviewer All right, and the last question. Would you like to change your work schedule?
David Well, yes, I would. I'd like to work four days a week, maybe working more hours in the day and have a three-day weekend. Then I could spend three full days a week with my family.
Interviewer That's great. Thank you very much for your time.

🔊 **8.13**

Clerk Good afternoon. How can I help you?
Allie Hi. I'm leaving tomorrow morning very early. Could you prepare my bill so I can pay this evening?
Clerk Of course.
Allie And could you order me a cab?
Clerk For what time?
Allie My flight's at 9:15, so I have to be at the airport at 7:15.
Clerk Then you'll need a cab at six o'clock. I'll order one for you.
Allie Thanks. Oh, and has there been a phone call for me?
Clerk Oh, yes. There's a message for you. Can you call this number in New York?
Allie Right. Thanks.
Clerk You're welcome.

1

1A word order in questions

Questions with *do* / *does* / *did* in simple present and past

Question word	Auxiliary	Subject	Base form (= verb)
	Do	you	live with your parents?
	Does	Lian	like Chinese food?
Where	do	you	live?
What kind of food	does	Lian	like?

- In the simple present use the auxiliary verb *do* / *does* to make questions.
- In the simple past use the auxiliary verb *did* to make questions.
- In these questions the subject goes <u>after</u> the auxiliary verb.
- Remember to use the base form of the verb in questions with *do*, *does*, and *did*.

Questions with *be*, present continuous, and *going to*

Question word	*be*	Subject	(adjective, noun, verb + *-ing*, etc.)
	Is	Ana	a student?
What	are	they	doing?
	are	you	talking about?
Where	is	he	going to live?

- In questions with *be*, make questions by inverting the verb and the subject.

> ⚠ If a verb is followed by a preposition (*listen to*, *talk about*), the preposition goes at the end of the question.
> *What are you talking **about**?*
> NOT ~~About what are you talking.~~

1B simple present

	I / you / we / they	he / she / it
+	I usually **work** at home.	Danny **knows** me very well.
−	They **don't live** near here.	It **doesn't** usually **rain** here.
?	**Do** you **smoke**?	**Does** Rosa **like** music?
✔ ✘	Yes, I **do**. / No, I **don't**.	Yes, she **does**./No, she **doesn't**.

- Use the simple present for things you do every day, week, year, and for things that are always true.
- Remember the spelling rules for 3rd person singular *s*:
  work>work**s**   add *s*
  study>stud**ies**   consonant + y: *y* and add *ies*
  finish>finish**es**   *sh, s, ch, x*: add *es*
  go>go**es** do>do**es** have>**has**

adverbs and expressions of frequency

- We often use the simple present with adverbs of frequency (*always, often, sometimes, usually, hardly ever, never*).
- Adverbs of frequency usually go <u>before</u> the main verb, but <u>after</u> *be*.
  He **never** goes out. NOT ~~He goes never out.~~
  *She's **always** late.* NOT ~~She's late always.~~
- Expressions of frequency (*every day, once a week*, etc.) usually go at the end of a sentence.
  *I have English classes **twice a week**.*

1C present continuous: *be* + verb + *ing*

	I	you / we / they	he / she / it
+	I'm working	You We 're working They	He She 's working It
−	I'm not working	You We aren't working They	He She isn't working It
? ✔ ✘	**Are** you **working**? **Yes**, I **am**. **No**, I'm **not**. **Is** he **working**? **Yes**, he **is**. **No**, he **isn't**.		

- Use the present continuous for things happening now, at this moment.
  My brother is working in South America.
  A *What are you doing?*
  B *I'm sending a text message to Sarah.*
- Remember the spelling rules for the *-ing* form.
  cook>cook**ing**   study >study**ing**
  live >liv**ing**   run >run**ning**

> ⚠ Some verbs are not normally used in the present continuous, for example *like, want, have* (= possess), *need*.
> *I need to talk to you now.*
> NOT ~~I'm needing to talk to you now.~~

1D defining relative clauses with *who, that, where*

> A cook is a person **who** works in a restaurant.
> A clock is a thing **that** tells the time.
> A post office is a place **where** you can buy stamps.

- Use relative clauses to explain what a place, thing, or person is or does.
  That's the woman who won the lottery last year.
  This is the restaurant where we had dinner last week.
- Use *who* for a person, *that* for a thing, and *where* for a place.

> ⚠ You can use *that* instead of *who*.
> *She's the woman **who** / **that** works with my brother.*
> You can use *which* instead of *that* to talk about things.
> *It's a thing **which** / **that** connects two computers.*

1A

a Put the word or phrase in the right place in the question.

      old
   How/are you?   (old)
1 you going to go out this evening?   (are)
2 Where does your work?   (sister)
3 What song are you listening?   (to)
4 Does finish at 8:00?   (the class)
5 Why you write to me?   (didn't)
6 Do you to the movies a lot?   (go)
7 What this word mean?   (does)
8 What time did arrive?   (your friends)

b Put the words in the right order to make questions.

   you live where do?   *Where do you live?*
1 you a do have car?
2 older is brother your you than?
3 often he how to write does you?
4 this time start does what class?
5 last go where you summer did?
6 languages how you many do speak?
7 see you are going to evening her this?
8 for waiting who you are?

1B

a Write sentences and questions with the simple present.

   he / usually get up late ⊞   *He usually gets up late.*
1 Anna / like music ?   _____?
2 she / have a lot of hobbies ⊞   _____
3 I / get along well with my sister ⊟ _____
4 my brother / know me very well ⊟ _____
5 they / have any children ?   _____?
6 the movie / finish late ?   _____?
7 he / go out twice a week ⊞   _____
8 we / usually talk about politics ⊟ _____

b Complete with a verb in the simple present.

   get along not have listen ~~live~~ open not talk not work

   He *lives* in an apartment.

1 _____ the banks _____ in the afternoon?
2 My sister _____ many friends.
3 We hardly ever _____ to the news in the car.
4 She's very shy. She _____ much.
5 _____ Jane _____ well with her boss?
6 My cell phone is new, but it _____ very well.

1C

a Write sentences with the present continuous.

   It / rain. ⊟   *It isn't raining.*
1 Hey! you / stand on my foot! ⊞
2 they / play very well today ⊟
3 what / you study right now ?
4 we / think of you ⊞
5 she / wear makeup ?
6 they / make / a big mistake ⊞
7 your brother / work in Taipei now ?
8 she / talk on the phone right now ⊟

b Complete the sentences with the simple present or present continuous.

   The girl in the painting *is playing* the guitar.   (play)
1 My dog isn't dangerous. He _____.   (not bite)
2 Why _____ you _____ sunglasses? It _____!   (wear, rain)
3 You can turn off the radio. I _____ to it.   (not listen)
4 I _____ to go to the bank. I _____ any money.   (need, not have)
5 Be careful! The baby _____ that pencil in her mouth!   (put)
6 A _____ you usually _____ on weekends?   (cook, eat)
   B No, we always _____ out.
7 A What _____ you _____ here?   (do, meet)
   B I _____ Keiko. Look, there she is.

1D

a Complete the definitions with *who*, *that*, or *where*. A ☐ B ☐

   It's the person *who* serves you in a cafe.
1 They're people _____ make you laugh.
2 It's a machine _____ cuts the grass.
3 It's an animal _____ lives in the sea and has eight legs.
4 It's a room _____ people try on clothes.
5 He's the person _____ helps you with your luggage.
6 It's a kind of food _____ keeps vampires away.

b Match the definitions and the pictures.

C ☐   D ☐   E ☐   F ☐

c Write sentences with *who*, *that*, or *where*.

   that / the dog / always barks at night
   That's the dog that always barks at night.
1 she / the woman / lives next door to me
2 that / the store / I bought my dress
3 he / the actor / was in *Friends*
4 they / the children / broke my window
5 this / the restaurant / they have great pasta
6 that / the switch / controls the air-conditioning
7 he / the teacher / teaches my sister
8 that / the room / we have our meetings

2A simple past: regular and irregular verbs

⊕		⊖
I You He She It We They	**stayed** at a hotel. **went** on vacation.	**didn't stay** at a hotel. **didn't go** on vacation.

✔ ✘ ?			
Did you	**stay** at a hotel?	Yes I **did**.
Did you	**go** on vacation?	No, I **didn't**.

Base form	Past
work	work**ed**
stay	stay**ed**
like	lik**ed** (just add *d* if verb finishes in *e*)
study	stud**ied** (*y*>*i* after a consonant)
stop	stop**ped** (if a one-syllable verb ends in consonant–vowel–consonant, double the final consonant)

- Use the simple past to talk about finished actions in the past.
- The simple past is the same for all persons.
- Use the base form after *Did…?* and *didn't* for negatives and questions.

- To make the simple past ⊕ of regular verbs add *-ed*. Remember the spelling rules.
- Many common verbs are irregular in ⊕ simple past, for example, *go>went*. See the **Irregular verb list** on p.155.

2B past continuous: *was / were* + verb + *ing*

⊕	I He She It	**was working.**	You We They	**were working.**
⊖	I He She It	**wasn't working.**	You We They	**weren't working.**

? ✔ ✘				
Was he	**working?**	Yes, he **was.**	No, he **wasn't.**
Were they	**working?**	Yes, they **were.**	No, they **weren't.**

- Use the past continuous to describe an action in progress at a specific moment in the past.
  At six o'clock last night, I was driving home.
  On April 1st I was staying with some friends in the country.

simple past or past continuous?

> When I **took** the photo, they **were writing** a song.
> I **was sitting** on the sofa when I **saw** the news on TV.

- Use the simple past for a completed action.
  I took the photo. / I saw the news.
- Use the past continuous for an action in progress.
  They were writing a song. / I was sitting on the sofa.

2C questions with and without auxiliaries

Questions with an auxiliary

Question	Auxiliary	Subject	Base form
What music	do	you	like?
Which CD	did	he	buy?
Who	did	you	go with?

- To make questions in the simple past and simple present, we normally use the auxiliary verbs *do / does / did* + base form.
  What music do you like? NOT ~~What music you like?~~
- In these questions the subject goes <u>after</u> the auxiliary verb.

Questions without an auxiliary

Subject	Verb	
What	happened	after the concert?
Which team	won	the game?
Who	writes	their songs?

- When the question word (*Who? What? Which? How many?*) is the <u>subject</u> of the verb in the question, we do <u>not</u> use an auxiliary (*do, does, did*). The verb is in the third person.
  Who writes their songs? NOT ~~Who does write their songs?~~

2D *so, because, but, although*

because and *so*

> She was driving fast **because** she was in a hurry. (reason)
> She was in a hurry, **so** she was driving fast. (result)
>
> Hannah spoke to the DJ **because** they didn't like the music. (reason)
> They didn't like the music, **so** Hannah spoke to the DJ. (result)

- Use *because* to express a reason.
- Use *so* to express a result.

but and *although*

> She tried to stop, **but** she hit the man.
> **Although** she tried to stop, she hit the man.
>
> It was late, **but** she couldn't sleep.
> She couldn't sleep, **although** it was late.

- Use *but* and *although* to show a contrast.
- *Although* can go at the beginning or in the middle of the sentence.

2A

a Put the verbs in parentheses in the simple past.

Two summers ago we _took_ (take) our vacation in Vancouver.
We [1]_____ (drive) there from San Francisco, but our car
[2]_____ (break) down on the freeway and we [3]_____ (spend)
the first night in Seattle. When we [4]_____ (get) to Vancouver, we
[5]_____ (not can) find a hotel – they [6]_____ (be) all full.
We [7]_____ (not know) what to do, but we finally [8]_____ (find)
a bed and breakfast, and we [9]_____ (stay) there for the week.
We [10]_____ (see) the botanical gardens, [11]_____ (go) to
an arts festival, and [12]_____ (buy) a lot of souvenirs. We
[13]_____ (want) to go to Victoria, but we [14]_____ (not have)
enough time. The weather [15]_____ (be) good, but it
[16]_____ (start) raining the day we [17]_____ (leave).

b Reorder the words to make questions.

Where did you go on vacation? go where vacation you on did?
Chicago

1 _____? time did have you good a?
Yes, it was great.
2 _____? with did who go you?
With some friends.
3 _____? stay where did you?
At a hotel.
4 _____? you it why didn't like?
Because it was noisy and very expensive.
5 _____? how did cost plane much the ticket?
$500.

2B

a Complete with a verb in the past continuous.

1 He met his wife when he _____ in Japan. (work)
2 They _____ for us when we arrived. (wait)
3 _____ she _____ a coat when she went out? (wear)
4 What _____ you _____ at 7:30 last night? (do)
5 I _____ when you gave the instructions. (not listen)
6 I _____ when you called me. (drive)
7 It _____ when I woke up this morning. (not rain)

b Put the verbs into the simple past or past continuous.

She *arrived* when we *were having* dinner. (arrive, have)

1 I _____ my arm when I _____ soccer. (break, play)
2 _____ you _____ fast when the police _____ you? (drive, stop)
3 It _____ when we _____ the theater. (snow, leave)
4 I _____ the game because I _____. (not see, work)
5 When you _____ me, I _____ to my boss. (call, talk)

2C

a Cross out the wrong question.

What **you did** / **did you** do last night?
1 What **happened** / **did happen** to you?
2 What **means this word** / **does this word mean**?
3 How many people **came** / **did come** to this class?
4 Which bus **goes** / **does go** to the airport?
5 Which actor **won** / **did win** the Oscar this year?
6 What **said the teacher** / **did the teacher say**?

b Write the questions. Do you know the answers?

Who _said_, "Hasta la vista, baby?" (say)
1 How many Formula 1 world championships _____?
(Ayrton Senna / win)
2 Which US president _____ the Nobel Peace Prize in 2002? (win)
3 Who _____ the movie *The Godfather*? (direct)
4 When _____ president of South Africa?
(Nelson Mandela / become)
5 Who _____ *The Lord of the Rings*? (write)
6 What _____ before he became a singer? (Sting / do)

2D

a Complete with *so*, *because*, *but*, or *although*.

We couldn't find a taxi, _so_ we walked home.

1 _____ it was very cold, she wasn't wearing a coat.
2 I woke up during the night _____ there was a noise.
3 I called him, _____ his cell phone was turned off.
4 _____ she's very nice, she doesn't have many friends.
5 There was nothing on TV, _____ I went to bed.
6 All the cafes were full _____ it was a holiday.
7 She wanted to be a doctor, _____ she failed
her exams.

b Match the sentence halves and complete with *so*, *because*,
but, or *although*.

1 I was tired last night, _so_
2 She drove very fast _____
3 His English isn't very good, _____
4 I called him at his office, _____
5 She's not feeling very well, _____
6 I didn't write to you _____
7 He called the hotel, _____
8 I took her to a restaurant _____

E A I lost your e-mail address.
   B it was her birthday.
   C they didn't have any rooms.
   D he lived in Canada for two years.
   E ~~I went to bed early.~~
   F she was in a hurry.
   G he was in a meeting.
   H she can't go to class tonight.

3

3A *going to*

+	I'm **going to** work in a restaurant. She's **going to** meet me at the airport.
–	We **aren't going to** stay very long. He **isn't going to** like the weather there.
?	**Are** you **going to** find a job? When **is** your brother **going to** visit you?

- Use (*be*) *going to* + base form to talk about future plans and predictions.
  *I'm **going to work** in the US for six weeks.* (plan)
  *I think it's **going to rain** this afternoon.* (prediction)
- When you use *going to go*, you can omit *to go*.
  I'm going to go to college next year
  or *I'm going ~~to go~~ to college next year.*

present continuous for future arrangements

+	I'm **seeing** some friends tonight. We're **having** dinner at their house tomorrow.
–	She **isn't leaving** until Friday. They **aren't coming** to the party.
?	What **are** you **doing** this evening? **Is** she **meeting** us at the theater?

- You can also use the present continuous for future arrangements that you have planned for a fixed time or place.
- Don't use the simple present for this. NOT ~~I see some friends tonight.~~
- The present continuous is especially common with the expressions *tonight, tomorrow, this weekend*, etc. and with these verbs: *go, come, meet, see, leave*, and *arrive*.

3B *will, won't* + base form (predictions)

+	–
I You He She **'ll be** late. It We They	I You He She **won't be** late. It We They

Contractions: 'll = will; won't = will not

- Use *will* / *won't* + base form for future predictions. (You can also use *going to*. See 3A above.)
- The future of *there is* / *are* = *there will be*; the future of *I can* = *I'll be able to* NOT ~~I'll can.~~

?	✔	✘
Will I you he she **be** late? it we they	**Yes,** I you he she **will**. it we they	**No,** I you he she **won't**. it we they

- We often use *I think* / *I don't think* …+ *will*… *I think he'll fail the exam. I don't think he'll pass the exam.* NOT ~~I think he won't pass.~~

3C *will* (promises, offers, and decisions)

Decisions	I **won't have the** fish. I'**ll have** the steak. We'**ll take** the 6:30 train.
Offers	I'**ll help** you with your homework. I'**ll open** the door for you.
Promises	I'**ll always love** you. I **won't tell** anyone.

- Use *will* / *won't* + base form for making decisions, offering, and promising.
  I'll help you with those bags. NOT ~~I help you.~~

⚠ In ? sentences with *I* and *we*, *shall* (and not *will*) is sometimes used to offer to do something or to make a suggestion, but this is not a common use.
Shall we go for a walk?

3D review of tenses: present, past, and future

Tense	Example	Use
simple present	I **live** downtown. She **doesn't smoke**.	Things that happen always or usually.
present continuous	He's **looking** for a new job. I'm **leaving** tomorrow.	Things that are happening now or plans for a fixed time or place.
simple past	We **saw** a good movie last night. We **didn't do** anything yesterday.	Finished actions in the past.
past continuous	He **was working** in Taipei. What **were you doing** at 7:00?	Actions that were in progress at a past time.
going to + **base form**	I'm **going to see** Tom tonight. It's **going to rain**.	Future plans and predictions.
will / *won't* + **base form**	You'**ll love** Bangkok. I'**ll call** her later. I'**ll help** you. I'**ll pay** you back tomorrow.	Predictions, instant decisions, offers, and promises.

3A

a Complete with *going to* + a verb.

> be buy get married not go not pass see snow stay

> What movie __are__ you __going to see__ tonight?
1 He's very lazy. I'm sure he _____ his exams.
2 _____ your sister _____ a new house?
3 You _____ in my class next year.
4 We _____ camping next summer. We _____ at a hotel.
5 **A** When _____ they _____? **B** In October.
6 It's very cold, but I don't think it _____ today.

b Cross out the wrong form. Put a check (✔) if both forms are possible.

> ~~I see~~ / **I'm seeing** my boyfriend tonight.
1 What **are you doing** / **do you do** after class today?
2 Is it **going to rain** / **raining** tomorrow?
3 We're **going to go away** / **going away** this weekend.
4 **I'm meeting** / **I meet** Susan this evening.
5 Where are you **going to stay** / **staying** in Seoul?
6 Hurry up! We're **going to be late** / **being late**.
7 She's **going to come** / **coming** tonight.

3B

a Write sentences and questions with *will* / *won't*. Use contractions where you can.

> it / be difficult ⊞   *It'll be difficult.*
1 they / win ⊟
2 the meeting / be long ?
3 he / get the job ⊟
4 you / see him at the party ?
5 it / be impossible to park ⊞
6 you / like the movie ⊟
7 she / love the chocolates we bought her ⊞
8 there / be a lot of traffic at 6:00 ⊟
9 you / can find a good job ⊞

b Complete the predictions with *will* / *won't* + a verb.

> be do ~~have~~ last make

> "I don't think we_'ll have_ another war. This one is probably the last."
> Richard Nixon, 1971 (talking about the Vietnam War)
1 "He _____ never _____ anything important in life."
   Albert Einstein's teacher (said to his father), 1895
2 "No movie about the Civil War _____ ever _____ any money."
   An MGM executive, 1945 (about the movie *Gone With The Wind*.)
3 "It's a bad joke. It _____."
   Coco Chanel (about the miniskirt)
4 "I don't think there _____ a woman Prime Minister in my lifetime."
   Margaret Thatcher, 1973

3C

a Match the sentences.

> It's cold in here.   *G*   A I'll help you with it.
1 I'm thirsty.   B I'll make you a sandwich.
2 That music is too loud.   C I'll carry one for you.
3 This exercise is hard.   D I'll lend you some money.
4 I'm hungry.   F I'll send it by e-mail now.
5 These bags are heavy.   G ~~I'll shut the window.~~
6 I left my wallet at home.   H I'll turn it off.
7 I need that photo urgently.   I I'll get you a glass of water.

b Complete the sentences with *will* / *won't* + a verb.

> call forget ~~have~~ help pay take tell

> **A** What would you like? **B** I_'ll have_ the pasta.
1 **A** I can't open this window. **B** I _____ you.
2 **A** It's a secret. **B** I _____ anyone, I promise.
3 **A** When will I see you again? **B** I _____ you tonight.
4 Can I borrow $50? I _____ you back tomorrow.
5 **A** It's my birthday next week. **B** Don't worry. I _____.
6 **A** I don't feel very well. **B** I _____ you home.

3D

a Complete the sentences with an auxiliary verb.

> Where __did__ you have lunch yesterday?
1 _____ you usually remember your dreams?
2 When _____ your mother coming to stay?
3 _____ you see the game last night?
4 Who _____ you talking to a few minutes ago?
5 Who _____ you think _____ win the elections?
6 _____ your brother like classical music?
7 What _____ you going to cook tonight?
8 _____ it raining when you left?

b Put the verb in the right form.

A What __are__ we __doing__ tonight? (do)
B We [1] _____ dinner with my sister. (have)
A But we [2] _____ dinner with her last week! (have)
B Yes, but she [3] _____ to tell us some good news. (want)
A Oh, OK. I [4] _____ some champagne. (buy)
....
B It's 7:00! What [5] _____ to you? (happen)
A When I [6] _____ home, I [7] _____ to buy the champagne. (come, stop) And then I [8] _____ Jim at the store… (meet)
B Well, hurry up. We [9] _____ late! (be)

4A present perfect (experience) + *ever* and *never*

+			−		
I've (I **have**)			I **haven't**		
You've (You **have**)			You **haven't**		
He's (He **has**)	been to		He **hasn't**	worked in	
She's (She **has**)	Korea.		She **hasn't**	a bank.	
It's (It **has**)			It **hasn't**		
We've (We **have**)			We **haven't**		
They've (They **have**)			They **haven't**		

?		✔	✘
Have you ever **worked** in a bank?		Yes, I **have**.	No, I **haven't**.
Has he ever **been** to Korea?		Yes, he **has**.	No, he **hasn't**.

- Use the present perfect to talk about past experiences when you don't say exactly when they happened.
  I've been to London. NOT ~~I've been to London last year.~~
  My brother has worked abroad.
- For regular verbs the past participle is the same as the past simple (+ *ed*). For **Irregular verbs** see page 155.
- We often use the present perfect with *ever* (= in your life until now) and *never*.
  Have you ever been to London? No, I've never been there.

> ⚠ Compare the present perfect of *go* and *be*.
> *He's gone to Paris.* = He's in Paris now.
> *He's been to Paris.* = He went to Paris and came back.

present perfect or simple past?

A Have you ever been to Mexico?	**B** Yes, I have.		
A When did you go there?	**B** I went last year.		

- Conversations often begin in the present perfect (with a general question) and then change to the simple past (with questions asking for specific details, *when, where, who with,* etc.)
- Use the simple past to ask / say exactly when something happened.

4B present perfect + *yet* and *already*

yet

A Have you finished your homework **yet**?	
B No, not **yet**. I haven't finished **yet**.	

- Use *yet* + the present perfect in − and ? sentences to ask if something that you think is going to happen has happened or to say it hasn't happened.
- Put *yet* at the end of the sentence.

already

A Do you want to see this movie?	
B No, I've **already** seen it three times.	
A Do you want a newspaper?	
B No, I've **already** bought one.	

- Use *already* in + sentences to say that something happened before now or earlier than expected.
- Put *already* <u>before</u> the main verb.

4C comparative adjectives

Adjective	Comparative	
short	short**er**	one syllable: + *er*
big	big**ger**	one vowel + one consonant: double final consonant
busy	bus**ier**	consonant + *y*: *y* + *ier*
relaxed	**more** relaxed	two or more syllables: *more* + adjective
good	**better**	irregular
bad	**worse**	
far	**farther, further**	

comparative adverbs

Adverb	Comparative	Adverb	Comparative
Regular		**Irregular**	
quickly	**more quickly**	hard	**harder**
slowly	**less slowly**	well	**better**
		badly	**worse**

- Use comparative adjectives to compare people and things.
  My brother's taller than John.
- Use comparative adverbs to compare actions.
  He drives more slowly than my father.
- You can also use (*not*) *as* + (adjective / adverb) + *as*.
  John isn't as tall as my brother.
  He doesn't drive as fast as my father.

4D superlatives (+ *ever* + present perfect)

Adjective	Comparative	Superlative
cold	cold**er**	**the** cold**est**
hot	hot**ter**	**the** hot**test**
pretty	prett**ier**	**the** prett**iest**
beautiful	**more** beautiful	**the most** beautiful
good	**better**	**the best**
bad	**worse**	**the worst**
far	**further**	**the furthest**

- Use *the* + superlative adjectives to say which is the biggest, etc. in a group.
  It's the highest mountain in Asia.
  She's the best in the class.
- We often use a superlative with the present perfect.
  Russia is the coldest place we've ever been to.
  That's the most beautiful painting I've ever seen.

4A

a Write sentences or questions with the present perfect.

he / ever / be there ? *Has he ever been there?*

1 you / ever buy / clothes from that store?
2 I / not read / the newspaper today.
3 We / never be / to that shopping mall.
4 your brother / live abroad / all his life?
5 They / go / to live in South America.
6 She / never fly / before.
7 We / not save / enough for a vacation.
8 you / eat / in this restaurant before?

b Right (✔) or wrong (✗)? Correct the wrong sentences.

He's got up late this morning. ✗ *He got up late this morning.*

1 We've been to Pusan last year.   _____
2 Have you ever been to Chile?   _____
3 Jane's gone to the bank an hour ago.   _____
4 I like your shoes. Where did you buy them? _____
5 I've seen that movie last week.   _____
6 I spoke to him a minute ago.   _____
7 My sister's a writer. She's written five novels. _____
8 World War II has ended in 1945.   _____

4B

a Reorder the words to make sentences.

1 made have you yet your bed?
2 gone already to work she's.
3 yet we haven't a cup of coffee had.
4 I found a job haven't yet.
5 sent me yet an he hasn't e-mail.
6 house already sold they've their.

b Write sentences or questions with *already* or *yet*. Use the present perfect.

he / arrive (already)   *He's already arrived.*

1 you / finish your homework? (yet)
2 the movie / start (already)
3 I / not meet / his girlfriend (yet)
4 You're too late. He / go home (already)
5 you / speak to him? (yet)
6 I / not read his new book (yet)

4C

a Write comparative sentences.

Hong Kong is / expensive / Bangkok.
Hong Kong is more expensive than Bangkok.

1 Ana is / thin / my sister.
2 I'm / busy / this week / last week.
3 Quebec is / far from Toronto / Ottawa.
4 I did / bad / on the final exam / the midterm.
5 Our team played / well / theirs.
6 my new job is / boring / my old one.

b Rewrite the sentences so they mean the same. Use *as… as.*

Mike is stronger than Jim.   Jim isn't *as strong as Mike.*

1 Cindy is taller than Kelly.   Kelly isn't _____ .
2 Your laptop is heavier than mine.   My laptop isn't _____ .
3 Mexico City is bigger than Bogotá.   Bogotá isn't _____ .
4 Soccer is more popular
   than tennis.   Tennis isn't _____ .
5 Children learn languages faster
   than adults.   Adults don't _____ .
6 You work harder than John.   John doesn't _____ .
7 Brazil played better than Italy.   Italy didn't _____ .

4D

a Complete the sentences with a superlative.

Is this *the noisiest* city in the world? (noisy)

1 Yesterday was _____ day of the year. (hot)
2 This is _____ time of day to drive downtown. (bad)
3 She's _____ person in the class. (friendly)
4 This is _____ part of the test. (difficult)
5 The _____ month to visit is September. (good)
6 It's _____ city in the world. (polluted)
7 The _____ I've ever flown is to Australia. (far)

b Write sentences with *ever.*

it / hot country / I be to
It's the hottest country I've ever been to.

1 it / good movie / I / see
2 he / unfriendly person / I / meet
3 it / hard test / he / take
4 they / expensive shoes / she / buy
5 it / long book / I / read
6 she / beautiful woman / I / see
7 it / bad meal / I / eat

5A uses of the infinitive

infinitive

I want **to go** to the party.
I need **to buy** some new clothes.
It'll be nice **to meet** some new people.
It's important **not to be** late.

- Use the infinitive after:
  – some verbs (*want, need, would like,* etc.) See **Verb Forms** page 154.
  – adjectives
  It isn't easy to find a job. Nice to meet you.
- The negative infinitive is *not* + infinitive.
  Try not to be late tomorrow.

infinitive of purpose

A Why did you go to the party?   **B To meet** new people.
I went to the party **to meet** new people.

- Use the infinitive to say why you do something.
  I came to this school to learn English. NOT ~~for learn English~~.

5B uses of the *-ing* form

Eating outside in the summer makes me feel good.
I enjoy **reading** in bed.
I'm thinking of **buying** a new car.

- Use verb + *-ing*:
  – as the subject of a sentence
  Smoking is bad for you.
  – after some verbs, (*finish, practice, enjoy,* etc.) See **Verb Forms** page 154.
  Have you finished doing your homework?

- – after prepositions
  He left without saying good-bye.
- Remember the spelling rules for the *-ing* form (See page 126 1C)

5C *have to, don't have to, must, must not, can't* + base form

have to, don't have to

+	She **has to** get up at 7:00 every day. You **have to** drive on the left in Japan.
–	We **don't have to** wear a uniform at this school. He **doesn't have to** work on Saturdays.
?	**Do** I **have to** buy a grammar book? **Does** she **have to** study tonight?

Don't contract *have* or *has*.
I have to go. NOT ~~I've to go.~~

- Use *have to* + base form to talk about rules and obligations, or to say something is necessary.
- Use *don't have to* + base form to say there is no obligation, or something is not necessary.
- Use *do / does* to make questions and negatives.
  Do I have to go? NOT ~~Have I to go?~~

must / must not / can't

+	All traffic **must** turn right.
–	Passengers **must not** leave bags unattended.
–	You **can't** bring food into the library.

- Use *must* + base form to talk about rules and obligations.
  You must turn off your cell phone before coming into class.
- Use *can't / must not* + base form to say something is prohibited or to state a rule.
  You can't park here. / You must not park here.
- The words *can't* and *must not* have similar meanings, but *can't* is more common in speaking. You can also use *cannot*.
- The verbs *must / must not / can't* are the same for all persons.
- The verb *must* is not often used in questions (*have to* is more common).

⚠ *Must* and *have to* are <u>very</u> similar, but *have to* is more common, especially in speaking. *Must* is often used in official forms, notices, and signs.

Must not and *don't have to* have <u>completely different</u> meanings. Compare:
You must not go = You can't go. It's prohibited.
You don't have to go = You can go if you want, but it's not obligatory/necessary.

5D expressing movement: *go, run,* etc. + preposition

The man **went up** the steps and **into** the building.
I **ran over** the bridge and **across** the park.
She **drove out of** the garage and **along** the street.

- To express movement, use a verb of movement, for example, *go, come, run, walk,* etc. and a preposition of movement (*up, down,* etc.)

- Be careful with *in / into* and *out / out of*. Use *into / out of* + noun, but if there isn't a noun, only use *in* or *out*.
  *Come **into** the living room. Come **in**.*
  *He went **out of** the house. He **went out**.*

5A

a Complete with an infinitive.

I'm planning *to take* a vacation next month.

do   not drive   go   learn   leave   not make   meet

1 **A** Hi, I'm Su-jin.
  B I'm Renata. Nice _____ you.
2 What do you want _____ this evening?
3 I need _____ to the bank. I don't have any money.
4 Try _____ noise. Your father's asleep.
5 I'd really like _____ a new language.
6 Be careful _____ too fast on the way home.
7 She's decided _____ her husband.

b Match the sentence halves.

They want to go to Ecuador	*D*	A to celebrate getting the job.
1 He's going to have a party		B to get some gas.
2 You'll need a visa		C to buy stamps.
3 Don't forget to call the restaurant		D to visit their family there.
4 I stopped at the gas station		E to tell them where we are.
5 She's gone to the supermarket		F to go to China.
6 I went to the post office		G to make a reservation.
7 I'll send them a text message		H to get some food for tonight.

5B

a Complete the sentences with a verb in the *-ing* form.

be   do   go   learn   remember   study   talk   teach

I don't enjoy *doing* housework.
1 My mother is very bad at _____ names.
2 _____ teenagers is really hard work.
3 You can't sing well without _____ to breathe properly.
4 My sister spends hours on the phone _____ to her boyfriend.
5 I hate _____ the first to arrive at parties.
6 _____ by train is cheaper than by plane.
7 I'll keep on _____ until dinner time.

b Put the verbs in the *-ing* form or infinitive.

I feel like *listening* to a CD. (listen)
1 _____ yoga is good for your health. (do)
2 We decided _____ to the party. (not go)
3 We won't take the car. It's impossible _____. (park)
4 I'm not very good at _____ maps. (read)
5 You can borrow the car if you promise _____ slowly. (drive)
6 Have you finished _____ your homework? (do)
7 I don't mind _____ but I dislike _____ the dishes. (cook, do)

5C

a Write sentences with the correct form of *have to*.

I / work on Saturday ⊟ *I don't have to work on Saturday.*
1 Jane / work very hard ⊞
2 you / wear a uniform ?
3 my sister / go to school ⊟
4 I / finish this now ?
5 we / get up early tomorrow ⊟
6 Harry / work tomorrow ?
7 we / hurry or we'll be late ⊞

b Complete the sentences with *have to*, *don't have to*, or *can't*.

We *don't have to* work tomorrow. It's a holiday.
1 You _____ enter the country without a passport.
2 We _____ take the bus to school. It's too far to walk.
3 The concert is free. You _____ pay.
4 It's late. I _____ go now.
5 You _____ bring food into the library.
6 You _____ come if you don't want to. I can go by myself.
7 In Australia you _____ drive on the left.
8 You _____ be very tall to play soccer.

5D

a Cross out the wrong preposition.

My phone stopped working when we went **across / through** a tunnel.
1 She ran **to / down** the lake and jumped **into / out of** the water.
2 If you go **over / past** the school, you'll see my house on the left.
3 He walked **along / across** the street until he got to the drugstore.
4 The plane flew **on / over** the town and then landed.
5 The police officer walked **toward / to** me, but then he stopped.
6 We drove **over / out of** the bridge and **in / into** the city.
7 The cyclists went **around / under** the track three times.

b Complete the sentences with *in*, *into*, *out*, or *out of*.

She jumped *into* her car and drove away.
1 I like to go _____ on a Friday night.
2 Come _____. The door's open.
3 He took his passport _____ his jacket.
4 She walked _____ the cafe and ordered a coffee.

6

6A *if* + present, *will* + base form (first conditional)

> If I **miss** the bus, **I'll** get a taxi.
> She **won't be** angry if you **tell** her the truth.
> What **will** you **do** if it **rains**?

> ⚠ You can also use the imperative or *can*.
> *If you miss the bus, get a taxi.*
> *If you miss the bus, you can get a taxi.*

- Use *if* + present, *will* + base form to talk about a possible future situation and its consequence.
- The *if* clause can come first or second.
  I'll come if you like. OR *If you like, I'll come.*

6B *if* + past, *would* + base form (second conditional)

> If a bear **attacked** me, **I'd run** away.
> If I **didn't have** children, I **wouldn't live** in the country.
> **Would** you **take** the manager's job if they **offered** it to you?

- Use *if* + past, *would* + base form to talk about an improbable / impossible or hypothetical future situation and its consequence.
  If a bear attacked me, I'd run away. = I'm imagining this situation. It's very improbable.
- *would / wouldn't* is the same for all persons.
- The contraction of *would* is *'d* (*I'd, you'd, he'd*, etc.), and the contraction of *would not* is *wouldn't*.

- The *if* clause can come first or second.
  If I saw a bear, I'd run. OR *I'd run if I saw a bear.*
- Remember with *can*, use *could* + base form, not ~~would can~~.
  If I had a car, we could drive there.

> ⚠ With the verb *be* use *were* (instead of *was*) after *I* and *he / she / it*.
> *If he were here, he'd help you.*
> We often use the expression *If I were you...* for advice.
> *If I were you, I'd find a new roommate.*

First and second conditionals

Compare the first and second conditionals:
Use the **first conditional** for **possible** future situations.
If I have time tomorrow, I'll help you. (= maybe I will have time)
Use the **second conditional** for **improbable / impossible** or **hypothetical** situations.
If I had time tomorrow, I'd help you. (= I won't have time.)

6C *may / might* + base form (possibility)

> We **might** have a picnic tomorrow, but it depends on the weather.
> I **might not** go to the party. I haven't decided yet.
> I **may** go to the party, but I'm not sure.
> I **may not** have time to do everything today.
>
> *Might not* and *may not* aren't usually contracted.

> ⚠ You can also use *May I... / May we...* to ask for permission.
> *May I use your phone?* (Can I use your phone?)

- Use *might / may* and *might not / may not* + base form to talk about a future possibility.
  It might / may rain. = It's possible that it will rain.
- *Might / May (not)* is the same for all persons, *I might / may, he might / may, we might / may,* etc.

6D *should / shouldn't* + base form (advice)

> I think you **should** change your job.
> The government **should** do more for old people.

- Use *should / shouldn't* + base form to give somebody advice or say what you think is the right thing to do.
  You should cut your hair. = I think it would be a good idea.
- *should / shouldn't* + base form is the same for all persons.
- You can also use *ought to* instead of *should*. We don't usually use *ought to* in the negative form.
  You ought to change your job.

6A

a Match the sentence halves.

If you leave now,   C

1 It will be cheaper
2 If I don't see you later,
3 You'll learn more
4 If you get the job,
5 You won't have time
6 If I lend you this book,

A if you don't start now.
B will you give it back to me?
C ~~you'll catch the 8:00 train.~~
D if you go by bus.
E I'll see you on Friday.
F if you come to every class.
G will you earn more money?

b Complete with the correct form of the verbs.

If you _tell_ me your secret, I _won't tell_ anybody. (tell, not tell)

1 If we _____ walking, the bus _____. (start, come)
2 He _____ angry if you _____ him. (be, not tell)
3 If I _____ it down, I _____ it. (not write, not remember)
4 _____ you _____ me if you _____ any news? (call, hear)
5 If you _____ her nicely, she _____ you. (ask, help)
6 You _____ the test if you _____. (not pass, not study)

6B

a Match the sentence halves.

You'd feel much better   C

1 I'd enjoy the weekend more
2 If you stayed for another day,
3 Would you wear it
4 If I were you,
5 I wouldn't work
6 Would you come with me

A we could go shopping.
B I'd get a new job.
C ~~if you stopped smoking.~~
D if I went to live in China?
E if I bought it for you?
F if I didn't need the money.
G if I didn't have to work on Saturday.

b Complete with the correct form of the verbs.

If I _found_ a good job, I _would move_ to Mexico. (find, move)

1 We _____ the house if it _____ bigger. (buy, be)
2 If I _____ his number, I _____ him. (know, call)
3 You _____ more if you _____ harder. (learn, work)
4 If you _____ for a week, you _____ see everything. (stay, can)
5 We _____ our son more often if he _____ closer to us. (see, live)
6 I _____ to the doctor if I _____ you. (go, be)

6C

a Match the sentence halves.

Take your umbrella.   D

1 Let's buy a lottery ticket.
2 Call the restaurant.
3 Don't stand on the wall.
4 Let's take a map.
5 Try the shirt on.
6 Don't wait for me.
7 Be careful with that knife.

A You might fall.
B It might not be your size.
C We might get lost.
D ~~It might rain.~~
E I might be late.
F You might cut yourself.
G It might be closed on Sundays.
H We might win.

b Complete the sentences with *might* + a verb.

be cold	be sick	be in a meeting	~~go to the movies~~
not have time	not like it	win	

I'm not sure what to do tonight. I _might go to the movies._

1 Jong-mi wasn't in class today. She _____
2 Danilo isn't answering his phone. He _____
3 It's an unusual movie. You _____
4 I don't know if I'll finish it. I _____
5 It's a difficult game, but we _____
6 Take your coat. It _____

6D

a Complete the doctor's advice with *should* or *shouldn't*.

You _should_ stop smoking.

1 You _____ eat too much red meat.
2 You _____ work 12 hours a day.
3 You _____ lose some weight.
4 You _____ eat more fruit.
5 You _____ drink a lot of coffee.
6 You _____ get enough sleep.
7 You _____ start exercising.

b Complete the sentences with *should* or *shouldn't* + a verb.

drive	go	~~leave~~	relax	study	walk	wear

We _should leave_ early. There might be a lot of traffic later.

1 You _____ a jacket. It's cold outside.
2 I _____ tonight. I have a test tomorrow.
3 You _____ alone in that part of the city. Get a taxi.
4 She _____ more. She's very stressed.
5 People _____ so fast when it's raining.
6 You _____ to bed early tonight. You look really tired.

7A present perfect + *for* and *since*

A Where do you live now?	**B** In Tokyo.
A **How long have you lived** there?	**B** **I've lived** there **since** 1990.
A Where do you work?	**B** In an elementary school.
A **How long have you worked** there?	**B** **I've worked** there **for** five years.

> ⚠ You can't use the simple present here.
> NOT ~~How long do you live here?~~
> ~~I live in Tokyo since 1990.~~

- Use the present perfect + *for* or *since* to talk about actions and states that started in the past and are still true now.
  I've lived in Tokyo since 1990. = I came to live in Tokyo in 1990, and I live in Tokyo now.
- Use *How long?* to ask questions about the duration of an action or a state.

- Use *since* with the beginning of a period of time, for example, *since 1990, since last June,* etc.
  I've been afraid of water since I was a child.
- Use *for* + a period of time, for example, *for two weeks, for ten years,* etc.
  I've had this car for three months.

7B present perfect or simple past?

How long **has** Tarantino **been** a director?	He's **been** a director since the 1980s.
How many movies **has** he **made**?	He's **made** six movies.
How long **was** Hitchcock a director?	He **was** a director for 50 years.
How many movies **did** he **make**?	He **made** 52 movies.

> ⚠ Don't use *since* with the simple past.
> NOT ~~He was president since 1993.~~
> You have to use *from…to.*
> *He was president from 1993 to 2001.*

- Use the present perfect + *how long?, for,* and *since* to talk about a period of time from the past until now.
  How long have you been married? I've been married for 10 years. (= I'm married now.)
- Use the simple past + *how long?* and *for* to talk about a finished period of time in the past.
  How long was he married? He was married for two years. (= He's not married now.)

7C used to / didn't use to

+	**−**
I You He She **used to** wear glasses. It We They	I You He She **didn't use to** wear glasses. It We They

?	**✔**	**✘**
Did I you he she **use to** wear glasses? we they	**Yes,** I you he she **did.** we they	**No,** I you he she **didn't.** we they

- Use *used to / didn't use to* + base form for things that happened repeatedly or over a long period of time in the past but are usually <u>not</u> true now, for example, for things that happened when you were a child.
  I used to have long hair. I used to play in the street. I didn't use to have a cell phone.
- You can also use the simple past here: *I had long hair when I was a child.*

> ⚠ Don't use *use to* for present habits.
> Use the simple present + *usually.*
> *I usually cook in the evenings.*
> NOT ~~I use to cook in the evenings.~~

7D passive: *be* + past participle

Present

+	**−**	**?**
Risotto **is made** with rice.	It **isn't made** with pasta.	**Is** it **made** with meat?
These offices **are cleaned** every morning.	They **aren't cleaned** on Saturdays.	**Are** they **cleaned** on Sundays?

Past

+	**−**	**?**
Guernica **was painted** by Picasso.	It **wasn't painted** by Dali.	When **was** it **painted**?
The pyramids **were built** by the Egyptians.	They **weren't built** by the Greeks.	Why **were** they **built**?

- You can often say things in two ways, in the active or in the passive.
  Picasso painted Guernica. (**active**)   Guernica *was painted by Picasso.* (**passive**)
- In the active sentence, the focus is more on the person (e.g., *Picasso*).
- In the passive sentence the focus is more on the painting (e.g., *Guernica*).
- You can also use the passive when it's not known or not important who does or did the action.
  My car was stolen last week. (I don't know who stole it.)

- Make the present passive with *am / is / are* + the past participle.
- Make the past passive with *was / were* + the past participle.
- Use *by* to say who did the action.
  The Lord of the Rings was written by Tolkien.

7A

a Write questions with *How long* and the present perfect.

you / be married   *How long have you been married?*

1 he / have his car _____ ?
2 your parents / live in this house _____ ?
3 you / be a teacher _____ ?
4 she / know her boyfriend _____ ?
5 Poland / be in the EU _____ ?
6 you / have your dog _____ ?
7 Tim / be afraid of water _____ ?

b Answer the questions in **a**. Use the present perfect + *for* or *since*.

I've been married since 1986.

1 He _____ three years.
2 They _____ a long time.
3 I _____ 1990.
4 She _____ May.
5 It _____ 2004.
6 We _____ about two years.
7 He _____ he was a child.

7B

a Right (✔) or wrong (✘)? Correct the wrong sentences.

She is married since 1990. ✘ *She's been married since 1990.*

1 He has finished school last year.
2 I lived in Ottawa for two years, but then I moved to Toronto.
3 She lives in Hollywood since 2004.
4 My sister has had her baby yesterday!
5 I work in a bank. I work there for twenty years.
6 The city has changed a lot since I was a child.
7 They have been married for a year. They're divorced now.

b Complete with the present perfect or past simple.

1 **A** Where does Joanna live now?
   B In Washington.
   A How long _____ there? (she / live)
   B For six months. She _____ there in February. (move)
2 **A** When _____ ? (Picasso / die)
   B In 1973, in France, I think.
   A How long _____ in France? (he / live).
   B For a long time. He _____ Spain when he was 23. (leave)
3 **A** My sister and her husband get along very well.
   B How long _____ married? (they / be)

7C

a Look at how James has changed. Write five sentences about how he was **THEN**.

THEN

He didn't use to be slim.
1 _____ short hair.
2 _____ heavy.
3 _____ glasses.
4 _____ a school uniform.
5 _____ wine.

NOW

b Make sentences with *used to, didn't use to,* or *did … use to.*

you / have long hair [?]
Did you use to have long hair?

1 where / you / go to school [?]
2 I / like vegetables when I was a child [–]
3 my sister / hate math in school [+]
4 what / you / do in the summer [?]
5 they / live near here [–]
6 this building / be a theater [+]
7 your brother / study here [?]

7D

a Complete with present passive or past passive.

The Eiffel Tower *was built* in 1889. (build)

1 All the singer's clothes _____ specially for her. (make)
2 The grass _____ every month. (cut)
3 This morning I _____ up by the neighbor's dog. (wake)
4 Baseball _____ in the summer in the US. (play)
5 These songs _____ last year. (record)
6 Most children _____ in public schools. (educate)

b Rewrite the sentences in the passive.

Shakespeare wrote Hamlet.
Hamlet *was written by Shakespeare.*

1 Last night the police stopped us.
   Last night we _____.
2 American teenagers eat a lot of fast food.
   A lot of fast food _____.
3 Toulouse-Lautrec painted *At the Moulin Rouge.*
   At the Moulin Rouge _____.
4 The marketing manager organizes weekly meetings.
   Weekly meetings _____.
5 Oxford University Press published this book.
   This book _____.

8A something, anything, nothing, etc.

	+	? and − verb	✗ Short − answer
people	somebody	anybody	nobody
	someone	anyone	no one
things	something	anything	nothing
places	somewhere	anywhere	nowhere

Somebody's in the bathroom.

Is **anybody in** the bathroom?

There isn't **anybody** in the bathroom.

- Use *somebody, something, someone*, etc. when you don't say exactly who, what, or where.
  Somebody broke the window.
  I went somewhere nice last weekend.
- Use *anything, anybody, anywhere* in questions or with a − verb.
  I didn't do anything last night. NOT ~~I didn't do nothing.~~

- Use *nobody, nothing, nowhere* in short − answers or in a sentence (with a + verb).
  Who's in the bathroom?
  Nobody. Nobody's in the bathroom.
  NOT ~~Anybody is in the bathroom.~~
- *Somebody, nobody*, etc. are the same as *someone, no one*, etc.

8B quantifiers

too, too much, too many

I'm stressed. I have **too much** work.
My diet is unhealthy. I eat **too many** cookies.
I don't want to go out. I'm **too** tired.

- Use *too, too much, too many* to say "more than is good."
- Use *too* + an adjective NOT ~~I'm too much tired.~~
- Use *too much* + uncountable nouns (e.g., coffee, time).
- Use *too many* + countable nouns (e.g., cookies, people).

enough

Do you eat **enough** vegetables?
I don't drink **enough** water.
This dress isn't big **enough**.

- Use *enough* before a noun to mean "all that is necessary."
- Use *enough* after an adjective.

a little, a few

A Do you take sugar?   B Yes. Just **a little**.
A Do want some fries?   B Yes, but **just a few**.
I eat **a little** meat.   Can you buy **a few** bananas?
I drink **very little** coffee. He has **very few** friends.

- Use *a little / very little* and *a few / very few* to talk about small quantities.
- Use *a little / very little* with uncountable nouns and *a few / very few* with countable nouns.

8C word order of phrasal verbs

Every morning I **get up** at 8:00.
Then I **turn on** the radio.
I always have to **look for** my glasses.

- A phrasal verb = verb + particle (preposition or adverb) *get up, turn on, look for*.
  1 Some phrasal verbs don't have an object.
  Come in and sit down.
  What time do you get up?
  2 Some phrasal verbs have an object and are separable.
  Put on your coat.
  Turn off the TV.

- With these verbs you can put the particle (*on, off*, etc.) before or after the object.
  Put on your coat OR *Put your coat on.*
  Turn off the TV OR *Turn the TV off.*
- When the object is a pronoun (*me, it, him*, etc.), it always goes between the verb and particle.
  Here's your coat. Put it on. NOT ~~Put on it.~~
  I don't want to watch TV. Turn it off. NOT ~~Turn off it.~~
  3 Some phrasal verbs have an object and are inseparable.
  I'm looking for my keys.
  I'm looking for them.
  With these phrasal verbs, the verb (*look*) and the particle (*for*) are never separated.
  I looked through my notes. NOT ~~I looked my notes through.~~
  I looked through them. NOT ~~I looked them through.~~

8D so, neither + auxiliaries

A I love soccer.
B So do I.
A I went to college.
B So did I.
A I'm not married.
B Neither am I.
A I don't smoke.
B Neither do I.

- Use *So do I / Neither do I*, etc. to say that you have something in common with somebody.
- Use *So* + auxiliary + *I* with + sentences.
  A *I'm happy.* B *So am I.* NOT ~~So I am.~~
- Use *Neither* + auxiliary + *I* with − sentences.
  A *I'm not hungry.* B *Neither am I.*
  NOT ~~Neither I am.~~

- The auxiliary you use depends on the tense used in the sentence you are responding to.
  I love soccer.   *So do I.*
  I didn't like the movie.   *Neither did I.*
  I can swim.   *So can I.*
  I wasn't very tired.   *Neither was I.*
  I've been to Europe.   *So have I.*
  I wouldn't like to go there. *Neither would I.*

8A

a Complete with *something, anything, nothing,* etc.

Did you meet ___anybody___ last night?

1 Are you doing _____ tonight?
2 _____ called when you were out. He said he'd call back later.
3 I saw your car keys _____, but I can't remember where.
4 Did _____ happen while I was out?
5 Did you go _____ exciting last night?
6 I bought you _____ for your birthday.
7 I knocked at the door, but _____ answered.
8 We went shopping, but we didn't buy _____.

b Answer with *Nobody, Nowhere,* or *Nothing.*

1 What did you do last night? _____
2 Where did you go yesterday? _____
3 Who did you see? _____

c Answer the questions in **b** with a full sentence.

1 I didn't do _____
2 _____
3 _____

8B

a Cross out the wrong form.

How **much / many** meat do you eat?

1 I drink **too / too much** coffee.
2 I eat **too much / too many** cookies.
3 I don't drink **enough water / water enough**.
4 I can't go. I am **too / too much** busy.
5 You work **too much / too many**.
6 I only drink **a few / a little** coffee.
7 I don't have **enough time / time enough**.
8 She has **a few / a little** good friends.

b Complete the sentences with *too, too much, too many,* or *enough.*

My father's not in good shape. He doesn't get ___enough___ exercise.

1 You eat _____ red meat. It isn't good for you.
2 I can't walk to work. It's _____ far.
3 There are _____ cars on the roads today.
4 I don't get _____ sleep – only six hours, but I really need eight.
5 I was _____ tired to go out last night.
6 There were _____ people at the party, so it was impossible to dance.

8C

a Complete the sentences with a particle from the box.

away	back	down (x2)	for	off	on	out	up

Turn ___off___ your cell phone before you come into class. ✔

1 Turn _____ the radio. It's too loud.
2 What time do you usually get _____ in the morning?
3 John called when you were out. He'll call _____ later.
4 My sister is looking _____ a new job.
5 I think you should throw _____ those old jeans.
6 I always try _____ new clothes before I buy them.
7 Do you want to go _____ tonight or stay home?
8 You should write _____ new words in your book.

b Put a check (✔) next to the sentences in **a** where the particle (*on, off,* etc.) could also go after the object.

c Complete the sentences with *it* or *them* and a particle.

away	off (x2)	on	up (x3)

1 I can't hear the radio. Turn _____ _____.
2 Your clothes are all over the floor. Pick _____ _____.
3 Here's your coat. Put _____ _____.
4 What does this word mean? Look _____ _____.
5 Your shoes are wet. Take _____ _____.
6 I don't need those papers. Throw _____ _____.
7 Don't watch the TV now. Turn _____ _____.

8D

a Complete B's answers with an auxiliary verb.

A I like coffee. **B** So ___do___ I.

1 **A** I'm really hungry. **B** So _____ I.
2 **A** I didn't go out last night. **B** Neither _____ I.
3 **A** I was born in India. **B** So _____ I.
4 **A** I don't smoke. **B** Neither _____ I.
5 **A** I've been to Bangkok. **B** So _____ I.
6 **A** I can't swim. **B** Neither _____ I.
7 **A** I'd like to go to China. **B** So _____ I.
8 **A** I saw a movie last night. **B** So _____ I.

b Respond to A. Say you are the same.
Use *So…I* or *Neither…I*

A I don't like fast food. ___Neither do I.___

1 **A** I live near the school. _____
2 **A** I'm not afraid of snakes. _____
3 **A** I went to bed early. _____
4 **A** I haven't been to China. _____
5 **A** I don't have any children. _____
6 **A** I can speak three languages. _____
7 **A** I always have breakfast. _____

9

9A past perfect

+		**−**	
I You He She It We They	**'d seen** the play before.	I You He She It We They	**hadn't seen** the play before.

contractions: I'd = I had   I hadn't = I had not

?		**✔**		**✗**	
Had	I you he she we they **seen** it before?	**Yes,**	I you he she we they **had.**	**No,**	I you he she we they **hadn't.**

Suddenly he remembered that he had seen the movie before.

- Use the past perfect when you are already talking about the past, and want to talk about an earlier past action.
  When I woke up the yard was all white.
  It had snowed during the night.
  I arrived at the coffee shop twenty minutes late, and my friends had already left.
- Make the past perfect with *had / hadn't* + the past participle.
- The past perfect is the same for all persons.

⚠ Be careful: *I'd* can be *I had* or *I would*.

9B reported (or indirect) speech

reported sentences

Direct speech	Reported speech
"I love you."	He said (that) he loved her.
"I want to see you again."	He told her (that) he wanted to see her again.

- Use reported speech to say what another person said.

  I **love** you.   He said (that) he **loved** her.

- Other tenses change like this:

Direct speech	Reported speech
"I **can** help you."	He said (that) he **could** help me.
"I'**ll** call you."	He told me (that) he **would** call me.
"I **met** a woman."	He told me (that) he **had met** a woman.
"I'**ve been** at work since 8:00."	He said (that) **he had been** at work since 8:00.

- *that* is optional after *say* and *tell*.
- Pronouns also change in reported speech, for example: *I* changes to *he / she*, etc.

  I'm coming.   She told me that **she** was coming.

⚠ You can use *said* or *told* in reported speech, but they are used differently.
  - You can't use *said* with an object or pronoun.
    NOT ~~He said her he loved her~~
  - You *must* use *told* with an object.
    He told her that he loved her NOT ~~he told that…~~

reported questions

Direct speech	Reported speech
"**Do you want** to dance?"	He asked her **if she wanted** to dance.
"**Where do you live**?"	He asked her **where she lived**.

- In reported questions:
  – the tenses change in exactly the same way as in reported sentences, e.g., present to past, etc.
  – we don't use *do / did*.

  What **do** you **want**?
  *He asked me **what I wanted**.*

  NOT ~~He asked me what did I want.~~
  – if the question begins with *do, can*, etc., add *if*.

  Do you like the music?
  *He asked her **if she liked** the music.*

  Can you sing?
  *She asked him **if he could sing**.*

  – the word order is subject + verb.

  Are you a student?
  *He asked her if **she was** a student.*

  Have you seen the movie?
  *She asked him if **he had seen** the movie.*

142

9A

a Match the sentence halves.

I couldn't get into my house because   *D*   A He had made other plans.
1 When our friends arrived,   B I realized that I'd seen it before.
2 I took the sweater back because   C she hadn't flown before.
3 Jack didn't come with us.   D ~~I'd forgotten my keys.~~
4 I turned on the TV   E I hadn't turned off the stove.
5 Fumiko was nervous because   F he had bought me the wrong size.
6 When the movie started,   G we hadn't finished cooking the dinner.
7 At work I suddenly remembered that   H to see what had happened.

b Complete the sentences. Put the verbs in the simple past or past perfect.

We __*didn't get*__ a table in the restaurant because we __*hadn't made*__ a reservation. (not get, not make)

1 I _____ Maria because she _____ her hair. (not recognize, cut)
2 My friend _____ to tell me I _____ my jacket in the car. (call, leave)
3 When I _____ the TV, the game _____ . (turn on, finish)
4 She _____ me the book because she _____ it yet. (not lend, finish)
5 He _____ all his final exams because he _____ at all. (fail, not study)
6 When we _____ home, we saw that somebody _____ the kitchen window. (get, break)

9B

a Write the sentences in reported speech.

He said,   "I love you."   He told her that
                           he loved her .

1 "I'm tired."   She said that
                         _____ .

2 "I don't like   He told her
    rock music."   _____ .

3 "I'll make   He said
    a reservation."   _____ .

4 "I've seen that   Paul told us that
    movie twice."   _____ .

5 "I live in   She said that
    the city."   _____ .

6 "We can do it."   They said that
                         _____ .

7 "I saw the movie   Julie said that
    on TV."   _____ .

b Make reported questions.

Do you want to dance?   He asked her if she
                        wanted to dance .

1 "Do you like   Mike asked me if I
    football?"   _____ .

2 "What kind of   I asked her what kind of music
    music do you like?" _____ .

3 "Are you tired?"   She asked me
                         _____ .

4 "Have you been   I asked them
    to Brazil?"   _____ .

5 "Where did you   He asked me
    live before?"   _____ .

6 "Can you swim?"   She asked him
                         _____ .

7 "Where are   I asked him
    you from?"   _____ .

Classroom language

YOU HEAR

a Match the phrases and pictures.

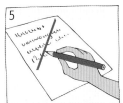

Ask and answer the questions.
Don't write.
Don't speak (*Spanish*).
Go to page 33.
Write down the words.
Sit down.
Stand up.
Look at the board.
Turn off your cell phone.
1 Work in pairs.

b Cover the phrases. Look at the pictures and remember the phrases.

YOU SAY

a Match the phrases.

A		B
1 How do you say [image] in English?		Very bad.
2 How do you spell it?		84.
3 Could you repeat that, please?	*1*	A sheep.
4 How do you pronounce it?		See you. Bye.
5 What does *awful* mean?		Yes. S-H-E-E-P.
6 Can I have a (*piece of paper*), please?		That's OK. Sit down.
7 Which page is it?		/ʃip/
8 Sorry I'm late.		You too. See you on Monday.
9 Bye.		S-H-E-E-P.
10 Have a good weekend!		Here you are.

b Cover column **B**. Remember the answers. Then cover column **A**. Remember the phrases.

YOU READ

a Match the instructions and pictures.

	circle		<u>underline</u>		comp<u>lete</u>
	cross out		check	*1*	choose
	copy the <u>rhythm</u>		put an x		
	match		<u>cover the text</u>		

b Cover the instructions. Look at the pictures and remember them.

⬅ p.5

Adjectives

1 Personality adjectives

a Match the adjectives and definitions.

> friendly /ˈfrɛndli/   funny   generous   lazy   shy   ~~talkative~~

	Adjective	Opposite
A person who talks a lot is …	*talkative*	
A person who likes giving presents is …		
A person who never does any work is …		
A person who makes people laugh is …		
A person who is open and nice is …		
A person who is nervous and uncomfortable meeting new people is …		

b Complete the **Opposite** column.

> hardworking   outgoing   quiet /ˈkwaɪət/   serious /ˈsɪriəs/   stingy /ˈstɪndʒi/   unfriendly

c Cover the **Adjective** and **Opposite** columns. Look at the definitions and say the adjective and its opposite.

○ **p.6**

---

2 Opposite adjectives

a Match the words and pictures 1–8.

	Opposite
boring	
crowded /ˈkraʊdəd/	
dangerous /ˈdeɪndʒərəs/	
1 far	*near*
modern	
noisy	
polite /pəˈlaɪt/	
polluted	

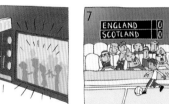

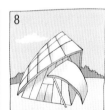

b Match these adjectives with their opposites in **a**.

> clean   empty   exciting / interesting   near   old-fashioned   quiet   rude   safe

c Cover the words and look at the pictures. Remember the adjectives and their opposites.

d Put the adjectives with the correct prefix to make opposites.

> comfortable /ˈkʌmfərtəbl/   happy
> healthy /ˈhɛlθi/   mature /məˈtʃʊr/
> patient /ˈpeɪʃnt/   polite   possible

un *happy*

im

e Test a partner. A say an adjective. B say the opposite.

○ **p.47**

The body

a   Match the words and pictures.

	arm(s)
11	ear(s)
6	eye(s) /aɪ/
	face
	finger(s)
14	hair
	hand(s)
	head /hed/
8	lip(s)
1	mouth /maʊθ/
2	neck
9	nose
	shoulder(s) /ˈʃoʊldər/
	stomach /ˈstʌmək/

	back
	foot (plural *feet*)
	knee(s) /ni/
18	leg(s)

	brain
	heart /hɑrt/
	teeth (singular *tooth*)
	toes /toʊz/
23	tongue /tʌŋ/

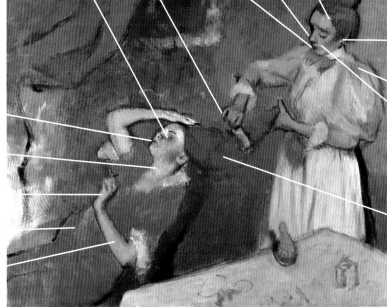

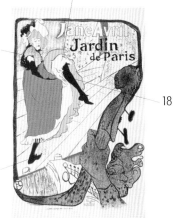

b   Cover the words and test yourself or test a partner.
    Point to a part of the body for your partner to say the word.

c   What part(s) of the body do we use to…?

see _____   hear _____   smell _____   kiss _____   bite _____

touch /tʌtʃ/ _____   think _____   feel _____   kick _____   smile _____

d   Test a partner. Ask *What do you use to see?* etc.

> ⚠ In English we use personal pronouns (*my*, *your*, etc.) with parts of the body, not *the*.
> *Give me your hand.* NOT ~~Give me the hand.~~

⟳ **p.8**

1 Phrases with *go*

a Match the verbs and pictures.

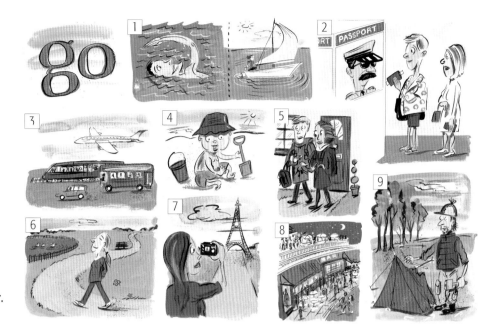

<table>
<tr><td> </td><td>go abroad /əˈbrɔd/</td></tr>
<tr><td>1</td><td>go swimming / sailing</td></tr>
<tr><td> </td><td>go sightseeing</td></tr>
<tr><td> </td><td>go camping</td></tr>
<tr><td> </td><td>go by car / bus / plane / train</td></tr>
<tr><td> </td><td>go to the beach</td></tr>
<tr><td> </td><td>go out at night</td></tr>
<tr><td> </td><td>go away for the weekend</td></tr>
<tr><td> </td><td>go for a walk</td></tr>
</table>

b Cover the phrases and look at the pictures. Test yourself or a partner.

2 Other vacation activities

a Complete the verb phrases.

buy	have	meet	rent	spend	stay	sunbathe /ˈsʌnbeɪð/	take	walk

stay	at a hotel / campsite	_____	on the beach	_____	in the mountains / around the town
_____	photos	_____	a good time	_____	friends
_____	souvenirs	_____	money / time	_____	a car / an apartment

b Test yourself. Cover the verbs. Remember the phrases.

3 The weather

a Match the words and pictures.

<table>
<tr><td> </td><td>sunny</td></tr>
<tr><td> </td><td>windy</td></tr>
<tr><td> </td><td>foggy</td></tr>
<tr><td> </td><td>cloudy /ˈklaʊdi/</td></tr>
<tr><td>1</td><td>rain</td></tr>
<tr><td> </td><td>snow</td></tr>
<tr><td> </td><td>hot</td></tr>
<tr><td> </td><td>cold</td></tr>
<tr><td> </td><td>boiling</td></tr>
<tr><td> </td><td>freezing</td></tr>
</table>

⚠ All these words are adjectives except *rain* and *snow*, which are nouns or verbs.
It's snowing. It snows every year. There's snow on the ground.
It rarely rains. It rained a lot this morning. There was a lot of rain last year.

b Test a partner. Imagine you were on vacation last week. Point to a picture.
  A Say *What was the weather like?*
  B Answer in the simple past.
  It was sunny. / It rained.

🔵 p.16

Prepositions

1 *at / in / on*

Complete the chart with *at*, *in*, or *on*.

PLACE			
Countries and cities *France, Paris* **Rooms** *the kitchen*	**Buildings,** *a store, a museum,* *the library, school* **Closed spaces** *a park, a garden* *a car* *college, school*	**Transportation** *a bike, a bus, train, plane, a ship* (not *car*) **A surface** *the floor, a table, a shelf,* *the balcony, the roof, the wall*	*home, work, the airport, the station,* *a bus stop, a party, the door, the end*

TIME			
Months *February, June* **Seasons** *the winter*	**Years, Centuries** *2008, the 21st century* **Times of day** *the morning,* *the afternoon,* *the evening* (not *night*)	**Dates** *March 1st* **Days** *Tuesday, New Year's Day,* *Valentine's Day* *the weekend, weekends, Monday morning*	**Times** *six o'clock, half past two, 7:45* **Times of day** *night, noon, midnight* *lunchtime*

b Look at the chart for a few minutes. Then test a partner:

A (book open) say a place or time word, e.g., *Singapore, Tuesday*, etc.
B (book closed) say the preposition (*at, in,* or *on*).
Change roles.

⊙ **p.19**

2 Prepositions of movement

Match the prepositions and pictures.

	<u>un</u>der (the railroad)
	a<u>long</u> (the street)
	ar<u>ound</u> (the lake)
	through /θru/ (the tunnel)
	<u>in</u>to (the store)
	a<u>cross</u> (the street)
	over (the bridge)
	up (the steps)
	past (the factory)
	toward /tɔrd/ (the lake)
1	down (the steps)
	out of (the store)

b Cover the prepositions. Where did the
dog go? *It went down the steps…*

⊙ **p.58**

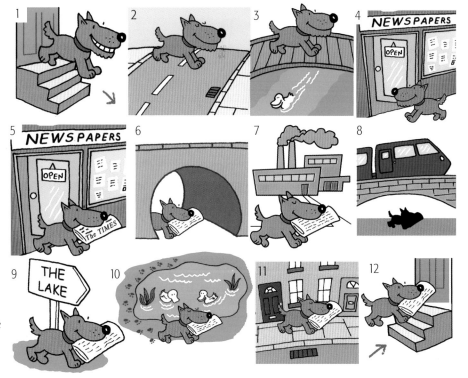

1 Opposite verbs

a Match the verbs and pictures.

		Opposite
	buy (a house)	_____
1	win (a game)	_____
	lend (money to somebody)	_____
	find (your keys)	_____
	push (the door)	_____
	pass (an exam)	_____
	forge<u>t</u> (a name)	_____
	turn on (the TV)	_____
	send (an e-mail)	_____
	miss (a train)	_____
	a<u>rrive</u> (at the station)	_____
	teach (a language)	_____

b Find the opposite verbs below. Write them in the **Opposite** column.

<u>b</u>orrow (from somebody)   catch   fail   <u>g</u>et / re<u>ceive</u>
learn   leave   lose (x2)   pull   re<u>mem</u>ber   sell   turn off

c Cover the verbs and look at the pictures. Remember the verbs and their opposites.   **◑ p.31**

2 Confusing verbs

a Match the verbs and pictures.

wear *clothes*	**carry** *a bag*
win *a prize* *a game*	**earn** *a salary* *money*
know *somebody* *something*	**meet** *somebody for the* *first time*
make *a cake* *lunch, dinner* *a noise*	**do** *homework, housework,* *the dishes, the laundry,* *judo, aerobics, yoga, a job*
hope *that something* *good will happen*	**wait** *for a bus*
watch *TV*	**look at** *a photo*
look *happy*	**look like** *your mother*

◑ p.64

b Cover the words and phrases and look at the pictures.
Test yourself or a partner.

a Match the words and pictures.

Singular clothes

	a dress
1	a top
	a skirt /skərt/
	a shirt
	a belt
	a T-shirt
	a sweater /ˈswɛtər/
	a suit /sut/
	a coat /koʊt/
	a tie /taɪ/
	a scarf
	a warm-up suit
	a jacket
	a hat
	a cap
	a blouse

Plural clothes

	pajamas /pəˈdʒæməz/
	pants
	jeans
	shorts
	shoes /ʃuz/
	boots
	tennis shoes / sneakers
	socks
	tights / pantyhose

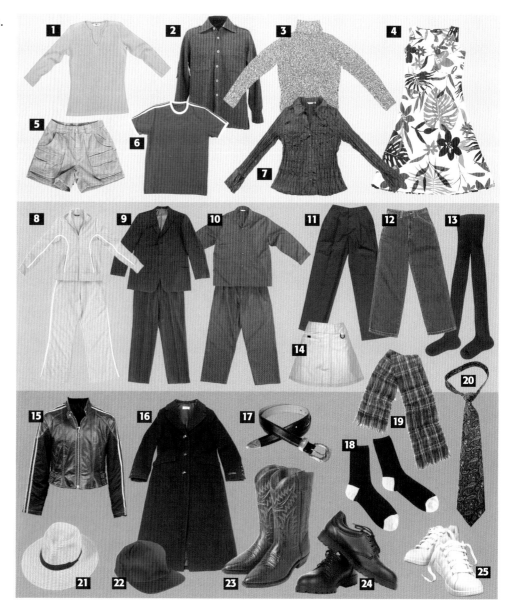

b Cover the words and look at the pictures. Test yourself or a partner.

Verbs used with clothes

a Match the phrases and pictures.

	get dressed
	wear (a black hat)
	take off (her boots)
	try on (a dress)
	put on (her coat)

1  2  3  4  5

b Cover the phrases. What is she doing in each picture?

🔿 **p.40**

Animals

a Match the animals and the pictures.

insects
26 bee
butterfly
fly
mosquito
spider

farm animals
bull
chicken
cow /kau/
goat /goʊt/
horse
pig
sheep

wild animals
bear
camel
crocodile
dolphin
elephant
giraffe
gorilla
kangaroo
lion
mouse (plural *mice*)
rabbit
shark
snake
tiger
whale

birds
duck
eagle
swan /swɑn/

b Cover the words and look at the pictures. Test yourself or a partner.

 p.67

Study Link MultiROM www.oup.com/elt/americanenglishfile/2

151

get

a Match the phrases and the pictures.

get + adjective

	get divorced
1	get angry
	get in shape
	get married
	get lost

get + comparative

	get older
	get worse
	get better

get = buy / obtain

	get a job
	get a ticket
	get a haircut
	get a newspaper

get + preposition (phrasal verbs)

	get along (well) with
	get on (opposite *off*)
	get into (opposite *out of*)
	get up

get = arrive

	get to work
	get home
	get to school

get = receive

	get a paycheck
	get a letter
	get a present
	get an e-mail

b Cover the words and look at the pictures. Test yourself or a partner.

⬅ **p.71**

get

Study Link MultiROM www.oup.com/elt/americanenglishfile/2

a Match the sentences and the pictures.

    We often stay up late on the weekend.

    The game will be over at about 5:30.

    I don't get along with my father.

    I want to find out about hotels in Madrid.

    I should give up chocolate.

    Please put away your clothes.

    Don't throw away that letter!

    Turn down the music! It's very loud.

1   Turn up the TV! I can't hear.

    He looked up the words in a dictionary.

    Could you fill out this form?

    Please pick up that towel.

b Cover the sentences and look at the pictures. Remember the phrasal verbs.

c Look at these other phrasal verbs from Files 1–7. Can you remember what they mean?

get up	turn on (the TV)
come back	turn off (the TV)
go back	put on (clothes)
hurry up	take off (clothes)
go away	try on (clothes)
go out	give back (something you borrowed)
come in	take back (something to a store)
sit down	call back (later)
stand up	pay back (money you borrowed)
run away	write down (the words)

look for (something you lost)
look forward to (a vacation)
look through (the advertisements)

Green = no object. The verb and the particle (*on*, *up*, etc.) are **never separated**.
I get up at 7:30.

Blue = + object. The verb and the particle (*on*, *up*, etc.) are **never separated**.
Look for your keys. NOT ~~Look your keys for~~.

Red = + object. The verb and the particle (*on*, *up*, etc.) **can be separated**.
Turn the TV on. OR *Turn on the TV.*

◐ p.92

Verb forms

A Verbs + infinitive

decide	We decided to go to South America.
forget	Don't forget to turn off all the lights.
*help	He helped her to start the car.
hope	We hope to see you again soon.
learn	I'm learning to drive.
need	I need to go the bank. I don't have any money.
offer	He offered to take me to the airport.
plan	They're planning to get married soon.
pretend	He pretended to be sick, but he wasn't really.
promise	She promised to pay me back.
*remember	Remember to bring your dictionaries tomorrow.
*start	The children started to cry.
*try	I'm trying to find a job, but it's not easy.
want	I want to go home.
would like	I'd like to buy a new car.

○ p.53

B Verbs + -ing

dislike	I dislike flying in bad weather.
enjoy	I enjoy reading in bed.
feel like	I feel like singing.
finish	Have you finished getting dressed?
keep on (=continue)	He keeps on interrupting me.
*hate	I hate getting up early.
*like	I like having lunch in the garden.
*love	I love waking up on a sunny morning.
(don't) mind	I don't mind cooking. It's OK.
practice	I practice playing the piano every day.
spend time	She spends hours talking on the phone.
*start	I started reading this book last week.
*stop	Please stop talking.

○ p.55

⚠ *help* can be used with both the infinitive and base form with no real difference in meaning.
*She helped me **to move**.*
*She helped me **move**.*

start can be used with both the infinitive and verb + *-ing* with no real difference in meaning.
*It started **raining**.*
*It started **to rain**.*
start + verb + *-ing* is more common when we talk about a habit or a longer activity.
*I started **working** here in 2005.*
*When did you start **playing** the piano?*

try and *remember* can also be used with the infinitive and verb + *ing* but the meaning is different.
*Why don't you try **doing** yoga?*
(= experiment with something)
*Do you remember **meeting** him last year?*
(= remember something after it happened)

hate, like, and *love* can be used with the infinitive and verb + *-ing* with no real difference in meaning. The *-ing* form puts a little more emphasis on the action of the verb.
*John hates / likes / loves **watching** TV.*
*John hates / likes / loves **to watch** TV.*

stop can also be used with the infinitive, but the meaning is different.
*I stopped **to get** a newspaper on the way to work.*
(= stop somewhere in order to do something)

C Irregular verbs

Base form	Simple past	Past participle
be	was/were	been
become	became	become
begin	began	begun
bite	bit	bitten
break	broke	broken
bring	brought /brɔt/	brought
build	built /bɪlt/	built
buy	bought /bɔt/	bought
can	could /kʊd/	–
catch	caught /kɔt/	caught
come	came	come
cost	cost	cost
choose	chose	chosen
cut	cut	cut
do	did	done /dʌn/
drink	drank	drunk
drive	drove	driven
eat	ate	eaten
fall	fell	fallen
feel	felt	felt
fight	fought /fɔt/	fought
find	found	found
fit	fit	fit
fly	flew /flu/	flown /floʊn/
forget	forgot	forgotten
get	got	gotten
give	gave	given
go	went	gone
grow	grew /gru/	grown
have	had	had
hear	heard /hərd/	heard
hit	hit	hit
keep	kept	kept
know	knew /nu/	known /noʊn/
leave	left	left
lend	lent	lent
let	let	let
lose	lost	lost

Base form	Simple past	Past participle
make	made	made
mean	meant /mɛnt/	meant
meet	met	met
pay	paid	paid
put	put /pʊt/	put
read	read /rɛd/	read /rɛd/
ring	rang	rung
run	ran	run
say	said /sɛd/	said
see	saw /sɔ/	seen
sell	sold	sold
send	sent	sent
sing	sang	sung
shut	shut	shut
sit	sat	sat
sleep	slept	slept
speak	spoke	spoken
spend	spent	spent
stand	stood /stʊd/	stood
steal	stole	stolen
swim	swam	swum
take	took /tʊk/	taken
teach	taught	taught
tear	tore	torn
tell	told	told
think	thought /θɔt/	thought
throw	threw /θru/	thrown /θroʊn/
understand	understood	understood
wake	woke	woken
wear	wore	worn
win	won /wʌn/	won
write	wrote	written

Vowel sounds

1 tree /tri/
2 fish /fɪʃ/
3 ear /ɪr/
4 cat /kæt/
5 egg /ɛg/
6 chair /tʃɛr/
7 clock /klɑk/
8 saw /sɔ/
9 horse /hɔrs/
10 boot /but/
11 bull /bʊl/
12 tourist /ˈtʊrɪst/
13 up /ʌp/
14 computer /kəmˈpyutər/
15 bird /bərd/
16 owl /aʊl/
17 phone /foʊn/
18 car /kɑr/
19 train /treɪn/
20 boy /bɔɪ/
21 bike /baɪk/

 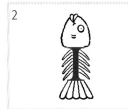 

■ vowels followed by /r/
■ diphthongs

Study Link MultiROM www.oup.com/elt/americanenglishfile/2

	usual spelling	⚠ but also
tree /iː/	ee feel teeth ea teach mean e she we	people machine key niece taxi receive
fish /ɪ/	i thin lips history kiss if since	English women busy decide gym build
ear /ɪr/	eer cheers engineer ere here we're ear near fear	serious
cat /æ/	a hand hat back catch carry match	
egg /ɛ/	e spell lend smell send very red	friendly head sweater any said says
chair /ɛr/	air airport stairs fair hair are square careful	their there wear bear where
clock /ɑ/	o top rock socks college hot box a father	yacht quality
saw /ɔ/	al walk talk aw awful draw augh caught daughter	bought thought abroad August
horse /ɔr/	or boring worn sports airport ore more score oor door floor	four
boot /uː/	oo school choose u* rude use ew new knew	do suit juice shoe lose through
bull /ʊ/	u pull push oo foot book look took	would should woman

	usual spelling	⚠ but also
tourist /ʊr/	A very unusual sound. Europe furious sure plural	
up /ʌ/	u sunny must funny run lucky cut	come does someone enough young touch
computer /ə/	Many different spellings, usually unstressed. nervous arrive polite agree suggest terrible problem	
bird /ɜr/	er person verb ir dirty shirt ur nurse turn er/or painter writer (unstressed) inventor	earn work world worse picture
owl /aʊ/	ou shout around mouth blouse ow crowded down	
phone /oʊ/	o* open hope won't so oa coat goal	snow throw although shoulder
car /ɑr/	ar far arms scarf dark	heart
train /eɪ/	a* face wake ai brain fail ay away pay gray	break steak great eight they
boy /ɔɪ/	oi coin noisy boiling oy toy enjoy	
bike /aɪ/	i* smile bite y shy why igh might sights	buy eyes height

* especially before consonant + e

Consonant sounds

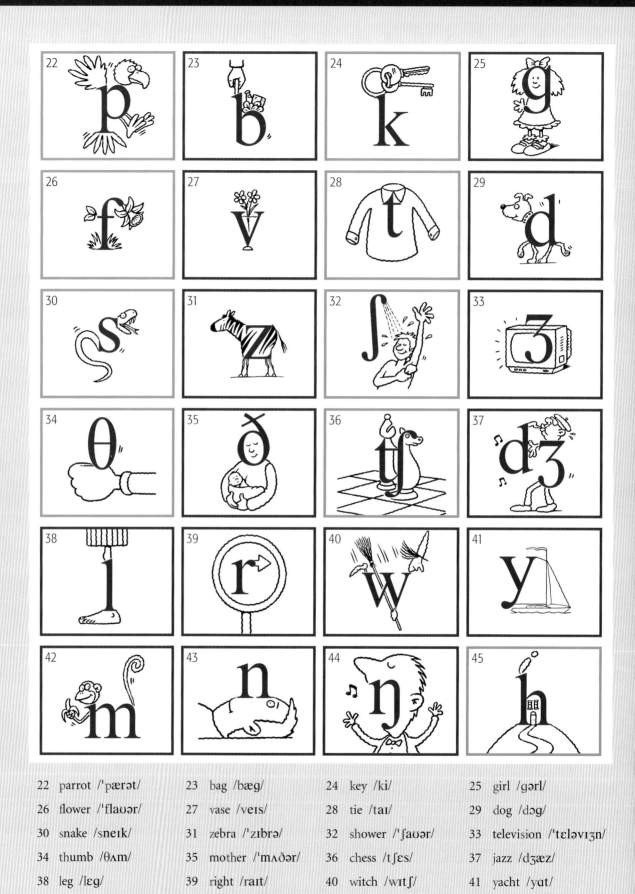

voiced
unvoiced

22 parrot /ˈpærət/	23 bag /bæg/	24 key /ki/	25 girl /gərl/
26 flower /ˈflaʊər/	27 vase /veɪs/	28 tie /taɪ/	29 dog /dɔg/
30 snake /sneɪk/	31 zebra /ˈzɪbrə/	32 shower /ˈʃaʊər/	33 television /ˈtɛləvɪʒn/
34 thumb /θʌm/	35 mother /ˈmʌðər/	36 chess /tʃɛs/	37 jazz /dʒæz/
38 leg /lɛg/	39 right /raɪt/	40 witch /wɪtʃ/	41 yacht /yɑt/
42 monkey /ˈmʌŋki/	43 nose /noʊz/	44 singer /ˈsɪŋər/	45 house /haʊs/

Study Link MultiROM www.oup.com/elt/americanenglishfile/2

	usual spelling		⚠ but also
parrot	**p**	promise possible copy cap	
	pp	opposite appearance	
bag	**b**	belt body probably job cab	
	bb	rabbit robbed	
keys	**c**	camping across	school stomach chemistry mosquito
	k	skirt kind	
	ck	neck kick	
girl	**g**	grow goat forget begin	guest spaghetti
	gg	foggy bigger	
flower	**f**	find afraid safe	enough laugh
	ph	elephant nephew	
	ff	off different	
vase	**v**	video visit love invent over river	of
tie	**t**	try tell start late	walked dressed
	tt	better sitting	
dog	**d**	did dead hard told	loved tired
	dd	address middle	
snake	**s**	stops faster	science answer psychology
	ss	miss message	
	ce/se	place house	
	c	cent city cycle (before **e**, **i**, **y**)	
zebra	**z**	zoo lazy freezing	
	s	reason lose has toes	
shower	**sh**	shut shoes wash finish	sugar sure machine
	ti	patient information (+ vowel)	
television	An unusual sound. Asia decision confusion usually garage		

	usual spelling		⚠ but also
thumb	**th**	thing throw healthy tooth math both	
mother	**th**	weather the sunbathe that clothing either	
chess	**ch**	chicken child beach	question
	tch	catch match	
	t (+ure)	picture future	
jazz	**j**	jacket just June enjoy	generous teenager college
	dge	bridge judge	
leg	**l**	little less plan incredible	
	ll	will silly	
right	**r**	really rest practice train	written wrong
	rr	borrow married	
	re	we're here	
witch	**w**	wet twins worried win	one once question
	wh	why which whale	
yacht	**y**	yet year young yoga	
	before u	useful uniform	
monkey	**m**	mountain modern remember smell	column comb
	mm	summer swimming	
nose	**n**	need nephew none any	knees knock
	nn	funny dinner	
singer	**ng**	tongue fingers along thing bring going	think thank
house	**h**	hit hate ahead perhaps hard	who whose whole

OXFORD
UNIVERSITY PRESS

198 Madison Avenue
New York, NY 10016 USA

Great Clarendon Street, Oxford OX2 6DP

Oxford University Press is a department of the
University of Oxford. It furthers the University's
objective of excellence in research, scholarship, and
education by publishing worldwide in

Oxford New York

Auckland Cape Town Dar es Salaam Hong Kong
Karachi Kuala Lumpur Madrid Melbourne
Mexico City Nairobi New Delhi Shanghai
Taipei Toronto

With offices in

Argentina Austria Brazil Chile Czech Republic
France Greece Guatemala Hungary Italy Japan
Poland Portugal Singapore South Korea Switzerland
Thailand Turkey Ukraine Vietnam

OXFORD and OXFORD ENGLISH are registered
trade marks of Oxford University Press.

© Oxford University Press 2008
Database right Oxford University Press (maker)

Editorial Director: Sally Yagan
Publisher: Laura Pearson
Managing Editor: Anna Teevan
Project Editor: Maria A. Dalsenter
Design Director: Robert Carangelo
Project Leader: Bridget McGoldrick
Manufacturing Manager: Shanta Persaud
Manufacturing Controller: Eve Wong

ISBN: 978 0 19 477432 1

Printed in China

10 9 8 7 6 5 4 3 2 1

Acknowledgments

Design and composition by: Stephen Strong
Cover design by: Jaclyn Smith
The authors would like to thank all the teachers and
students around the world whose feedback has helped us to
shape this series. We would also like to thank: Qarie and
Victoria (Mark and Allie), Dominic and Barbara for the
photos of Rima and Zanzibar, Krysia for *Then he kissed
me* and other ideas, all our friends around the world who
told us "what made them feel good," and Melissa for her
interview. The authors would also like to thank all those at
Oxford University Press (both in Oxford and around the
world), and the design team who have contributed their
skills and ideas to producing this course.

Finally, very special thanks from Clive to María Angeles
and from Christina to Cristina for all their help and
encouragement. Christina would also like to thank her
children Joaquin, Marco, and Krysia for their constant
inspiration.

*The publisher and authors would like to thank the
following for their invaluable feedback on the materials:*
Beatriz Martin; Lester Vaughan; Tom Stutter;
Wendy Armstrong; Javier Santos Asensi; Tim Banks;
Brian Brennan; Susanna Di Gravio; Jane Hudson;
Graham Rumbelow; Krzysztof Wierzba

*The publisher and authors are grateful to those who have
given permission to reproduce the following extracts and
adaptations of copyright material:* p. 18 "A moment in
time" from *Harry Benson: 50 Years in Pictures* © 2001 by
Harry Benson. Published by Harry N. Abrams, Inc.,
New York. All rights reserved; p. 19 "Where are these
lovers now?" Appeared in *Marie Claire* February 1992
© Katie Breen/Marie Claire/IPC Syndication. Reproduced
by permission of IPC Syndication; p. 27 "Alpine climber is
rescued after SOS text to London" by Patrick Barkham,
The Times 7 October 2003. Reproduced by permissions of
NI Syndication; p. 39 "2020: Woman the hunter, man the
house husband" by David Charter, *The Times* 25 April
1998. Reproduced by permissions of NI Syndication;
p. 43 "Spoilt teenagers? You could just evict them" by
Elizabeth Nash, *The Independent* 18 October 1999.
Reproduced by permission; p. 46 "Wish you weren't here"
by Tim Moore, *The Sunday Times* 6 July 2003.
Reproduced by permission of NI Syndication; p. 51
"Hepburn's dress made peasant film star for a day"
by Richard Owen, *The Times* 4 October 2002.
Reproduced by permission of NI Syndication;
p. 63 "Kournikova of chess makes her move" by
Judith O'Reilly, *The Sunday Times* 31 March 2002.
Reproduced by permission of NI Syndication; p. 87
"First accident for 100-year-old motorist" by Gillian
Harris, *The Times* 16 October 2001. Reproduced by
permission of NI Syndication; p. 99 "Haile the Chief"
by Paul Kimmage, *The Sunday Times* 23 February 2003.
Reproduced by permission of NY Syndication;
p. 100 Extracts from "This Life" by Roland White,
The Sunday Times, 16 December 2001, 25 November
2001, 9 September 2001 and 21 November 1999.
Reproduced by permission of NI Syndication;
p. 102 *Then he kissed me* Words and Music by
Phil Spector, Ellie Greenwich and Jeff Barry
© 1963 by EMI Music Publishing. Reproduced by
permission of Hal Leonard.

Although every effort has been made to trace and contact
copyright holders before publication, this has not been
possible in some cases. We apologize for any apparent
infringement of copyright and if notified, the publisher
will be pleased to rectify any errors or omission at the
earliest opportunity.

*The publisher would like to thank the following for their
kind permission to reproduce photographs and other
copyright material:* Action Images p. 59 (Bayern Munich);
Age Fotostock pp. 49 (mariachi/Ken Welsh; Plaza de
Armas/Photographers Choice); Alamy pp. 13
(Photofusion/David Montford), 16 (Stockholm/Robert
Harding Picture Library), 20 (Chris Martin/All Star
Picture), 40 (Zara/Foybles/Reuters/HO), 56
(São Paulo/David R. Frazier Photolibrary, Inc.;
woman/Stockbyte), 58 (tennis/Image State/Lee Atherton;
cycling/Aflo Foto Agency; basketball/Ace Stock;
aerobics/Gai Wyn Williams), 66 (crocodile/Nicholas
Pill/Travelsnaps), 70 (Photofusion Picture Library/
Pete Jones), 82 (pen/Mark Wood), 85
(Madonnina/CuboImages srl/Enzo Signorelli);
Allstar p. 55 (Cinetext/20th Century Fox); Art Institute
of Chicago/Helen Birch Bartlett Memorial Collection
p. 9; Associated Press pp. 21 (Yoko Ono/Paul Baker),
58 (volleyball), 73 (dancing), 79 (Francis Coppola/Kevork
Djansezian), 80 (Mick Jagger); Aurora Photos p. 49 (Plaza
de La Liberacion/Christian Heeb); Harry Benson p. 18;
Mark Boudillon p. 46 (Tim Moore); Bridgeman Art
Library p. 8 (Bridgeman Art Library/Musee Picasso,
Paris); Camera Press pp. 10 (Kate Moss/David Long),
21 (John & Yoko Ono/Tom Hanley); Corbis Images pp. 10 (Bierce),
16 (seafood/Owen Franken), 20 (Nirvana/Henry Diltz;
Spice Girls/Sygma/Touhig Sion; Beyoncé/Reuters),

51 (Reuters), 73 (mountains/Galen Rowe), 79 (Sofia
Coppola/Rufus F. Folkks); El Mundo p. 43, FLPA p. 151
(shark/Mammal Fund/Earthview); Thomas England
pp. 94, 95; Getty Images pp. 4 (family/Taxi/Arthur Tilly;
student/Image Bank), 17 (Robert Harding Picture
Library), 29 (Photo Assignments), 49 (market/Stone),
59 (Manchester United/John Peters), 66 (bear/Darrell
Gulin), 82 (dishwasher and windshield wipers/Image
Bank), 85 (Duomo/Robert Harding Picture Library/Tony
Gervis), 99 (Allsport), 116 (Fiji/Photographers Choice;
Kenya/Taxi), 151 (fly; whale/National Geographic);
PW Henry p. 63; Index Stock p. 151 (snake/Lynn Stone);
Inmagine p. 28 (Creatas); istockphoto.com
p. 150 (sneakers/Emily 2K); Kobal Collection
pp. 76 (Winona Ryder/20th Century Fox),
78 (The Birds/Universal; Kill Bill/A Band
Apart/Miramax/Andrew Cooper); Dominic Latham-
Koenig p. 25; Magnum pp. 109/113 (Eiffel Tower/Marc
Riboud); Museo Botero pp. 108, 112; National Gallery
p. 146 (La Coiffure/Edgar Degas); NPHA p. 151
(mouse/Stephen Dalton; chicken/Ernie James; goat/Kevin
Schafer; mosquito/Harold Palo Jr; horse/Ernie James;
crocodile/Daniel Zupanc; camel/Mike Lane;
butterfly/John Shaw; cow and pig/Andy Rouse;
kangaroo/Martin Harvey; bull/Patrick Fagot; duck;
rabbit); Oxford University Press pp. 4 (windsurfing,
baby), 7, 16, 28 (man), 47, 58 (golf, judo), 67, 90, 106
(jacket/Hemera; bear), 108, 112, 150 (skirt, shirt, belt,
jacket, hat, cap, shorts, shoes, boots), 151 (lion, sheep,
gorilla, eagle, bear, spider, elephant, tiger, swan, giraffe);
Photonica pp. 6 (Lottie Davies), 46 (Eiffel Tower/Steve
Marsel), 61 (tennis/Ko Fujiwara); Private Eye p. 44,
Popperfoto p. 82 (stockings); Punchstock pp. 4 (cafe/Big
Cheese Photo LLC; engineer/MedioImages), 37, 61
(Thai food), 82 (diapers/Photodisc Red/Ryan McVay;
white-out; bulletproof vest/Ingram Publishing;
washing machine/Photodisc Green/Kim Steele),
97 (food/Comstock), 146 (Toulouse-Lautrec/Photodisc
Green); Rapho pp. 19 (Willy Ronis), 109/113
(Leaving for Newfoundland/Willy Ronis); Reuters
p. 40 (Amancio Ortega); Rex Features pp. 20
(Mick Jagger), 58 (baseball, skiing, swimming),
66 (bull), 76 (Rupert Grint and Dennis Bergkamp),
80 (team), 82 (vacuum cleaner), 106 (bee), 151 (dolphin,
bee); Super Stock p. 58 (football/Photographers Choice)

Portrait of Dora Maar 1937 on page 8 is copyright
Succession Picasso/DACS 2005

The painting on page 108 is Pareja Bailando and 112
is Concierto Campestre both by Fernando Botero.

The painting on page 146 (top) is La Coiffure by
Hillaire-Germain-Edgar Degas.

Illustrations by: Paul Dickinson p. 102; Phil Disley
pp. 30, 65, 67, 80, 89, 92 (bottom), 106 (mouth, teeth,
heart), 146, 147; Mark Duffin p. 48; Gary Kaye pp. 42,
68, 69; Freddie Levin pp. 71, 116, 129, 131, 137, 140, 142;
Jan McCafferty pp. 83, 144 (left), 145, 150; Ginna Magee
pp. 88, 92 (top), 106 (dog with newspaper), 144
(complete), 148 (dog with newspaper), 149
(do homework), 152 (bus), 153 (chocolate); Ellis Nadler
pronunciation symbols; Nigel Paige p. 39; Colin
Shelbourn pp. 58, 106 (dog on bridge), 117, 127, 144
(right), 148, 149, 152, 153; Andy J. Smith pp. 52, 53, 64;
Stephen Strong p. 9; Colin Thompson pp. 5, 15, 32, 33,
41, 45, 81, 87, 100, 104, 105, 134, 139; Annabel Wright
pp. 22, 23, 34, 54, 76, 77, 110, 114

Commissioned photography by: Mark Mason pp. 12, 24,
27, 36, 48, 60, 72, 84, 96, 97 (man), 106 (T-shirt), 150
(dress, top, T-shirt, sweater, suit, coat, scarf, warm-up
suit, pajamas, pants, jeans, socks, tights)

Picture research and illustrations commissioned by:
Cathy Blackie, Terry Taylor Studio

Thanks to: Paul Seligson and Carmen Dolz for the
Sounds Chart, pp. 156, 158